Non-State Actors and Terrorism

Applying the Law of State Responsibility and the Due Diligence Principle

Non-State Actors and Terrorism

Applying the Law of State Responsibility and the Due Diligence Principle

Robert P. Barnidge, Jr.

T·M·C·Asser Press
The Hague

Published by T·M·C·ASSER PRESS
P.O. Box 16163, 2500 BD The Hague, The Netherlands
<www.asserpress.nl>

T·M·C·ASSER PRESS' English language books are distributed exclusively by:

Cambridge University Press, The Edinburgh Building, Shaftesbury Road,
Cambridge CB2 2RU, UK,
or
for customers in the USA, Canada and Mexico:
Cambridge University Press, 100 Brook Hill Drive, West Nyack, NY 10994-2133, USA
<www.cambridge.org>

ISBN 978-90-6704-259-8

FOREWORD

Few issues in international law are at once more pressing and momentous than the ones addressed in this study. These questions go to the heart of how responsibility is to be allocated in the international struggle to control terrorism. What must a reasonably diligent State do to ensure that its territory is not used as a base to inflict harm upon another State? How far must a State go in diverting resources from housing, health care, or education to meet such obligations? To what extent is a State required to share counterterrorism information and resources with other States – States that may lack the capacity to combat terrorism without such resources? At what point does absence of *capacity* shade into absence of *will* – and when does an absence of will affect the cooperation obligations of other States? Should unique cultural and historical proclivities be taken into account, or are the relevant due diligence standards uniform, international and universal? What, indeed, *is* international "terrorism"?

Traditional international law scholarship too often seeks to resolve such questions primarily or even exclusively through the application of doctrine. Widely ignored are not only actual State practice, but also the economic, geopolitical and cultural variables that shape that practice. This critical study, in contrast, admirably recognizes the interplay between practice and doctrine, properly construed. It finds, sensibly, that international law imposes a "best efforts" obligation on States – which nonetheless will be carried out, or not carried out, as a function of political will. In doing so the study rejects the mechanical jurisprudence of alternative approaches. For those in search of a framework of bright lines, precise tests and easily-applied rules of *per se* invalidity, this conclusion will not be a happy one. But analytic tidiness is not to be had in this corner of our world. Differing balances must be struck case-to-case in light of changing interests of varying weight. Policy-makers as well as scholars will benefit from this thoughtful explanation of why political intrusion upon the law is inevitable, why due diligence rules must remain indeterminate – and how the struggle to curb terrorism through the rule of law can be waged in the face of continuing juridical uncertainty.

October, 2007 Michael J. GLENNON

ACKNOWLEDGEMENTS

This book draws its inspiration from research that I conducted at the University of Amsterdam and Queen's University Belfast.

Since commencing this research, I have presented aspects of it in Ireland, the United Kingdom, Germany, India, the Netherlands, Italy, and Norway.[1] The comments that I received from colleagues were challenging, always stimulating, and certainly enriched my understanding. I am particularly grateful for the discussions that I had with colleagues at The Hague Academy of International Law's Centre for Studies and Research during the summer of 2006.

In the course of this project, I have become indebted to many people. As a practical matter, this research would not have been possible without the generous financial support of the Overseas Research Students Awards Scheme and Queen's University Belfast. For their feedback on various parts of my research, I would like to acknowledge Professors Riccardo Pisillo Mazzeschi, Colin Harvey, Brice Dickson, Phil Scraton, and Tom Hadden and Drs. Jean Allain, Niaz Shah and Nikolay Kovalev.

Finally, last but not least, I would like to thank my family, my mother and father, George and Chrissy, Patrick, Peter, and John.

Reading, September 2007 Robert P. Barnidge, Jr.

---

[1] The following three sections of this book have appeared, or will shortly appear, as: *The Due Diligence Principle Under International Law*, 8(1) Int'l Cmty. L. Rev. 81 (2006); *Should National Security Trump Human Rights in the Fight Against Terrorism?*, Isr. Y.B.H.R. (forthcoming, 2007); and *Terrorism: Arriving at an Understanding of a Term*, Centre for Studies and Research of The Hague Academy of International Law (forthcoming, 2008).

TABLE OF CONTENTS

ABBREVIATIONS

General

AAPL	Asian Agricultural Products Ltd.
ANC	African National Congress
AU	African Union
BIT	Bilateral Investment Treaty
CE	Council of Europe
CESCR	United Nations Committee on Economic, Social, and Cultural Rights
CIS	Commonwealth of Independent States
CSR	Combinatul Siderugic Resita
CTC	Counter-Terrorism Committee
EU	European Union
IACtHR	Inter-American Court of Human Rights
ICC	International Criminal Court
ICCPR	International Covenant on Civil and Political Rights
ICESCR	International Covenant on Economic, Social, and Cultural Rights
ICJ	International Court of Justice
ICRC	International Committee of the Red Cross
ICSID	International Centre for the Settlement of Investment Disputes
ICTY	International Criminal Tribunal for the former Yugoslavia
IDF	Israel Defense Forces
ILC	International Law Commission
ISG	Iraq Study Group
LTTE	Liberation Tigers of Tamil Eelam

OAS	Organisation of American States
OAU	Organisation of African Unity
OHCHR	Office of the United Nations High Commissioner for Human Rights
OIC	Organisation of the Islamic Conference
PCIJ	Permanent Court of International Justice
SAARC	South Asian Association for Regional Cooperation
SCIRI	Supreme Council for the Islamic Revolution in Iraq
SCO	Shanghai Cooperation Organisation .
STF	Sri Lankan Special Task Force
TRC	Truth and Reconciliation Commission of South Africa
UDF	United Democratic Front
UNHRC	United Nations Human Rights Commission

JOURNALS AND OTHER SOURCES

AFR. SECURITY REV.	African Security Review
AM. J. INT'L L.	American Journal of International Law
AM. U. INT'L L. REV.	American University International Law Review
A.S.I.L. PROC.	American Society of International Law Proceedings
BBC NEWS	British Broadcasting Corporation News
BERKELEY J. INT'L L.	Berkeley Journal of International Law
BRIT. Y.B. INT'L L.	British Yearbook of International Law
CAN. Y.B. INT'L L.	Canadian Yearbook of International Law
CBC NEWS	Canadian Broadcasting Corporation News
CHI. J. INT'L L.	Chicago Journal of International Law
CHIN. J. INT'L L.	Chinese Journal of International Law
CHI. TRIB.	Chicago Tribune
DUKE J. COMP. & INT'L L.	Duke Journal of Comparative and International Law
DUKE L.J.	Duke Law Journal

EUR. ENVTL. L. REV.	European Environmental Law Review
EUR. HUM. RTS. L. REV.	European Human Rights Law Review
EUR. J. INT'L L.	European Journal of International Law
FLETCHER FORUM WORLD AFF.	Fletcher Forum of World Affairs
FOREIGN AFF.	Foreign Affairs
G.A. Res.	General Assembly Resolution
GEO. L.J.	Georgetown Law Journal
GERM. Y.B. INT'L L.	German Yearbook of International Law
HARV. INT'L L.J.	Harvard International Law Journal
HARV. L. REV.	Harvard Law Review
HUM. RTS. Q.	Human Rights Quarterly
I.C.J. STAT.	Statute of the International Court of Justice
I.L.M.	International Legal Materials
I.L.R.	International Law Reports
ILSA J. INT'L & COMP. L.	ILSA Journal of International and Comparative Law
INDIAN J. INT'L L.	Indian Journal of International Law
INT'L AFF.	International Affairs
INT'L CMTY. L. REV.	International Community Law Review
INT'L & COMP. L.Q.	International and Comparative Law Quarterly
INT'L HERALD TRIB.	International Herald Tribune
INT'L L. FORUM DROIT INT'L	International Law FORUM du Droit International
INT'L REV. RED CROSS	International Review of the Red Cross
IR. STUD. INT'L AFF.	Irish Studies in International Affairs
ISR. L. REV.	Israel Law Review
ISR. Y.B. H.R.	Israel Yearbook on Human Rights
J. CONFLICT & SECURITY L.	Journal of Conflict and Security Law
JEWISH WORLD REV.	Jewish World Review
J. INT'L CRIM. JUST.	Journal of International Criminal Justice
LEIDEN J. INT'L L.	Leiden Journal of International Law
MEMRI	Middle East Media Research Institute
MICH. J. INT'L L.	Michigan Journal of International Law
MOD. L. REV.	Modern Law Review

NETH. INT'L L. REV.	Netherlands International Law Review
NOTRE DAME L. REV.	Notre Dame Law Review
N.Y. SUN	New York Sun
N.Y. TIMES	New York Times
N.Y.U. J. INT'L L. & POL.	New York University Journal of International Law and Politics
O.J.	Official Journal of the European Communities
PUB. L.	Public Law
REV. INT'L DROIT PÉNAL	Revue Internationale de Droit Pénal
R.I.A.A.	Reports of International Arbitral Awards
S.C. Res.	Security Council Resolution
SUN. TELEGRAPH	Sunday Telegraph
TERRORISM & POL. VIOLENCE	Terrorism and Political Violence
TRANSNAT'L L. & CONTEMP. PROBS.	Transnational Law and Contemporary Problems
U.N. CHARTER	Charter of the United Nations
U.N. NEWS SERVICE	United Nations News Service
WALL ST. J.	Wall Street Journal
WASH. POST	Washington Post
Y.B. Int'l L. Comm'n	Yearbook of the International Law Commission

Chapter 1
INTRODUCTION

Chapter 1
INTRODUCTION

In *Orientalism,* Edward W. Said asserts that "[t]he idea of beginning, indeed the act of beginning, necessarily involves an act of delimitation by which something is cut out of a great mass of material, separated from the mass, and made to stand for, as well as be, a starting point, a beginning."[1]

Beginnings in legal scholarship require of the author reflection, confidence, and a sense of purpose. Through writing, an author presents a case for something, creates ideas that contribute to knowledge and debate, for good or for ill. "Intellectual representations are the *activity itself,* dependent on a kind of consciousness that is skeptical [sic], engaged, unremittingly devoted to rational investigation and moral judgment; and this puts the individual on record and on the line."[2] Worthwhile scholarship thoughtfully challenges present assumptions and is, or at least can be, perhaps should be, iconoclastic and discomforting to the reader. It expands the marketplace of ideas and is eternally optimistic that the "research consensus"[3] is, indeed, always will be, incomplete and in need of contribution.

This research begins, or situates itself, in a particular context. That context is one in which the Westphalian State, which Weber describes as a "human community that successfully claims for itself the monopoly of the legitimate use of physical violence within a territory with determined bound-

---

[1] Edward W. Said, Orientalism 16 (2003).

[2] Edward W. Said, *Representations of the Intellectual*, in Representations of the Intellectual: The 1993 Reith Lectures 3, 20 (1996). "[W]riting is a deeply personal affair. To write is to wish. The wish to understand the world, to change the world – or perhaps to submit and withdraw. The wish to *be* in the world." David Kennedy, Keynote Address, The TWAIL Conference, Albany, New York (April 2007), *available at* http://www.law.harvard.edu/faculty/dkennedy/speeches/TwailKeynote.htm.

[3] According to Said, "[f]ar from being merely additive or cumulative, the growth of knowledge is a process of selective accumulation, displacement, deletion, rearrangement, and insistence within what has been called a research consensus." Said, Orientalism, *supra* note 1, at 176. *See* Tim May, Social Research: Issues, Methods and Process 197 (3rd ed. 2001); Howard Zinn, A People's History of the United States: 1492-Present 8 (2003).

aries,"[4] has eroded. Falk describes ours as a "post-Westphalian world in which sovereign states are losing control over many tendencies threatening their well-being, including crime, environment, and migration."[5] For former United States Secretary of State Henry Kissinger, the Westphalian paradigm is now in "systemic crisis."[6]

While it would be correct to say that images of the World Trade Center smouldering in ruins in lower Manhattan demonstrated the inherent deficiencies of a framework that could not countenance serious acts of violence by non-State actors, a shift had already been occurring before 11 September 2001.[7] Factors such as the liberalisation of trade, international flows of capital, the growth of civil society, and privatisation contributed, and continue to contribute, to this shift.[8]

The erosion of Westphalia as a convincing model for understanding international affairs and the increasing relevance of non-State actors have important implications for the law of State responsibility.[9] One of the basic principles of this area of the law is that a State cannot be held responsible for the acts of non-State actors.[10] The International Law Commission justi-

---

[4] MAX WEBER, THE PROFESSION OF POLITICS 2 (Simona Draghici ed., 2000). Koskenniemi argues that, "[i]n accordance with the founding myth of the system, the Peace of Westphalia in 1648 lay the basis for an agnostic, procedural international law whose merit consisted in its refraining from imposing any external normative ideal on the international society." Martti Koskenniemi, *What Is International Law For?,* in INTERNATIONAL LAW 89, 90 (Malcolm D. Evans ed., 2003).

[5] Richard Falk, *Human Rights: A Descending Spiral,* in HUMAN RIGHTS IN THE "WAR ON TERROR" 225, 239 (Richard Ashby Wilson ed., 2005).

[6] HENRY KISSINGER, DOES AMERICA NEED A FOREIGN POLICY?: TOWARD A DIPLOMACY FOR THE 21ST CENTURY 21 (2001).

[7] For a discussion of definitions of non-State actors, see Philip Alston, *The "Not-a-Cat" Syndrome: Can the International Human Rights Regime Accommodate Non-State Actors,* in NON-STATE ACTORS AND HUMAN RIGHTS 3, 14-19 (Philip Alston ed., 2005).

[8] *See ibid.* at 17-19.

[9] Becker radically argues that "if non-State terrorist actors can operate as subjects of international law on the international plane then they should also be viewed as capable of operating together with States in overt and covert partnerships without requiring an agency relationship." TAL BECKER, TERRORISM AND THE STATE: RETHINKING THE RULES OF STATE RESPONSIBILITY 279 (2006).

[10] On this, see MALCOLM N. SHAW, INTERNATIONAL LAW 701 (5th ed. 2004); Giuseppe Sperduti, *Responsibility of States for Activities of Private Law Persons,* in 10 ENCYCLOPEDIA OF PUBLIC INTERNATIONAL LAW 373, at 373 (1987); Pierre Dupuy, *International Liability of*

fies this approach "both with a view to limiting responsibility to conduct which engages the State as an organization, and also so as to recognize the autonomy of persons acting on their own account and not at the instigation of a public authority."[11] As the International Court of Justice (ICJ) recently noted in the *Application of the Convention on the Prevention and Punishment of the Crime of Genocide* case, "the fundamental principle governing the law of international responsibility [. . . is that] a State is responsible only for its own conduct, that is to say the conduct of persons acting, on whatever basis, on its behalf."[12]

A State can be held responsible for an internationally wrongful act, however, "where [. . . it] fails to exercise due diligence to prevent the violations or repress them after the event."[13] In many respects, this principle of due diligence approximates the good faith obligation, the latter of which, according to Goodwin-Gill, can be "demonstrated by acts and failures to act which, taken together, render the fulfilment of specific treaty obligations remote or impossible, or which defeat the object and purpose of the treaty."[14]

Cassese asserts that international law imposes a due diligence standard on the territorial State for the unlawful acts of non-State actors not acting as *de facto* State organs.[15] Generally-speaking, according to him, this will be

---

States for Damage Caused by Transfrontier Pollution, in LEGAL ASPECTS OF TRANSFRONTIER POLLUTION 345, 354 (Organisation for Economic Co-operation and Development ed., 1977); SPECIFIC HUMAN RIGHTS ISSUES: NEW PRIORITIES, IN PARTICULAR TERRORISM AND COUNTER-TERRORISM: TERRORISM AND HUMAN RIGHTS: FINAL REPORT OF THE SPECIAL RAPPORTEUR, KALLIOPI K. KOUFA, U.N. ESCOR, at 16, U.N. Doc. E/CN.4/Sub.2/2004/40 (2004); *Mondev International Ltd.* v. *U.S.*, ICSID (Additional Facility) Case No. ARB(AF)/99/2, 40 (2002).

[11] International Law Commission, *Commentaries, Articles on Responsibility of States for Internationally Wrongful Acts,* in JAMES CRAWFORD, THE INTERNATIONAL LAW COMMISSION'S ARTICLES ON STATE RESPONSIBILITY: INTRODUCTION, TEXT AND COMMENTARIES 74, 91 (2003) (2001). Since they are no longer in draft form, reference is made to these articles throughout this research as the *Articles on Responsibility of States for Internationally Wrongful Acts* (*Articles on State Responsibility*).

[12] Application of the Convention on the Prevention and Punishment of the Crime of Genocide (*Bosn. & Herz.* v. *Serb. & Mont.*), 2007 I.C.J., at Para. 406.

[13] HELEN DUFFY, THE "WAR ON TERROR" AND THE FRAMEWORK OF INTERNATIONAL LAW 305 (2005). *See* SPECIFIC HUMAN RIGHTS ISSUES, *supra* note 10, at 17-18.

[14] Guy S. Goodwin-Gill, *State Responsibility and the "Good Faith" Obligation in International Law,* in ISSUES OF STATE RESPONSIBILITY BEFORE INTERNATIONAL JUDICIAL INSTITUTIONS 75, 84 (Malgosia Fitzmaurice & Dan Sarooshi eds., 2004).

[15] *See* ANTONIO CASSESE, INTERNATIONAL LAW 250 (2nd ed. 2005).

breached if the State "omitted to take the necessary measures to prevent attacks on foreigners or foreign assets, or, after perpetration of the unlawful acts, failed to search for and duly punish the authors of those acts, as well as pay compensation to the victims."[16] Shaw argues that the case law in the context of civil wars, insurrections, and mob violence supports a finding that the State is not responsible if it does not act negligently and if it exercises good faith.[17] In cases of localised mob violence and riots, Brownlie notes that "substantial neglect to take reasonable precautionary and preventive action and inattention amounting to official indifference or connivance will create responsibility for damage to foreign public and private property in the area."[18]

It is important to stress that the due diligence inquiry focuses not on the conduct of the non-State actors *per se* but, rather, on the "extent of the obligation of the State to prevent or respond to those acts."[19] Zegveld, writing in the context of armed opposition groups and State responsibility, correctly focuses on the State in this regard, for its "*own* failure to act, the act of armed opposition groups merely constituting the objective condition which gives rise to a breach of the relevant treaty provisions on the part of the state."[20]

This research examines how international law assesses, and on what grounds and through which mechanisms, how a State can bear responsibility for its actions or omissions with regard to its international legal obligations to act with due diligence in confronting non-State actors that engage in terrorism.[21] It excludes from its purview State terrorism and State-spon-

---

[16] *Ibid. See* Jan Arno Hessbruegge, *The Historical Development of the Doctrines of Attribution and Due Diligence in International Law,* 36(2-3) N.Y.U. J. INT'L L. & POL. 265, 268 (2004); LIESBETH ZEGVELD, ACCOUNTABILITY OF ARMED OPPOSITION GROUPS IN INTERNATIONAL LAW 182 (2002).

[17] *See* SHAW, *supra* note 10, at 705 (citing relevant cases). *See also* Rüdiger Wolfrum, *Internationally Wrongful Acts,* in 10 ENCYCLOPEDIA OF PUBLIC INTERNATIONAL LAW 271, 275 (1987).

[18] IAN BROWNLIE, PRINCIPLES OF PUBLIC INTERNATIONAL LAW 437 (6th ed. 2003).

[19] FIRST REPORT ON STATE RESPONSIBILITY BY MR. JAMES CRAWFORD, SPECIAL RAPPORTEUR, U.N. GAOR, Addendum, at 32, U.N. Doc. A/CN.4/490/Add.5 (1998).

[20] ZEGVELD, *supra* note 16, at 181.

[21] On non-State actors and terrorism, see Ruth Wedgwood, *The Multinational Action in Iraq and International Law*, in THE IRAQ CRISIS AND WORLD ORDER: STRUCTURAL, INSTITUTIONAL AND NORMATIVE CHALLENGES 413, 418 (Ramesh Thakur & Waheguru Pal Singh Sidhu eds., 2006).

sored terrorism because these phenomena fall outside the question of due diligence and trigger State responsibility based on, for example, Article 8 of the *Articles on Responsibility of States for Internationally Wrongful Acts.*[22] At the same time, however, this research also recognises that "State failure can take many forms and [that] the legal nuances between different situations can be difficult to gauge."[23] "[T]he power relationship between the State and a terrorist group can differ markedly," Becker asserts, "and the thread connecting the two may be loosely or tightly spun."[24]

Although Condorelli, writing in 1989, was insightful enough to note that "[d]ue diligence is a classic and very important element of general international law, whose usefulness in dealing with terrorism should be emphasized,"[25] scholars have largely neglected and underappreciated this area of the law. There are exceptions to this, of course, but the interface of State responsibility, non-State actors that engage in terrorism, and the due diligence principle requires in-depth investigation, particularly since 11 September.[26] This research makes a unique contribution to knowledge by filling this gap in the literature.

Chapter 2 explores the basic question whether a comprehensive definition of terrorism exists under international law by exploring treaty law, cus-

---

[22] *See* International Law Commission, *Articles on Responsibility of States for Internationally Wrongful Acts,* in JAMES CRAWFORD, THE INTERNATIONAL LAW COMMISSION'S ARTICLES ON STATE RESPONSIBILITY: INTRODUCTION, TEXT AND COMMENTARIES 61, 62, Art. 8 (2003) (2001) (stating that "[t]he conduct of a person or group of persons shall be considered an act of a State under international law if the person or group of persons is in fact acting on the instructions of, or under the direction or control of, that State in carrying out the conduct."). For a recent ICJ discussion of Art. 8, see Application of the Convention on the Prevention and Punishment of the Crime of Genocide, *supra* note 12, at Paras. 396-407. On the distinction between the due diligence principle and cases in which the State endorses private action, see Pierre-Marie Dupuy & Cristina Hoss, Trail Smelter *and Terrorism: International Mechanisms to Combat Transboundary Harm*, in TRANSBOUNDARY HARM IN INTERNATIONAL LAW: LESSONS FROM THE *TRAIL SMELTER* ARBITRATION 225, 238 (Rebecca M. Bratspies & Russell A. Miller eds., 2006).

[23] BECKER, *supra* note 9, at 133. "In practice, if the State has failed to prevent acts of terrorism, it may be hard to determine whether this involves no violation, a violation of the due diligence standard only or amounts to acquiescence in the terrorist activity." *Ibid.* at 132-33.

[24] *Ibid.* at 249.

[25] Luigi Condorelli, *The Imputability to States of Acts of International Terrorism,* 19 ISR. Y.B. H.R. 233, 241 (1989).

[26] This research makes reference to these exceptions as appropriate.

tomary international law, and general principles. Despite this being a difficult issue, an attempt is made by examining treaty law, customary international law, and general principles.[27] Chapter 2 concludes that international law has yet to recognise a comprehensive definition of terrorism without reference to international treaties related to terrorism but that it is still possible to speak of terrorism in a legal sense in certain contexts, such as when a particular regional treaty regime itself recognises a definition of terrorism that binds relevant actors. Throughout, this chapter reveals a general sense of what is meant by terrorism and exposes the persistent cleavages in the debate.

Building on the definitional question of terrorism, Chapter 3 moves to consider the due diligence principle under international law. At a fundamental level, this principle and its operation in practice reveal some of international law's basic assumptions and prejudices about the nature of international responsibility and the proper relationship between State and non-State actors.[28] The due diligence principle is explored by reviewing four distinct eras during the last century, namely early twentieth century arbitral decisions dealing with the duty to protect and apprehend and punish and State action or omission in the context of insurrectional movements,

---

[27] According to Art. 38(1) of the Statute of the ICJ, "The Court, whose function is to decide in accordance with international law such disputes as are submitted to it, shall apply: a. international conventions, whether general or particular, establishing rules expressly recognized by the contesting states; b. international custom, as evidence of a general practice accepted as law; c. the general principles of law recognized by civilized nations; d. subject to the provisions of Article 59, judicial decisions and the teachings of the most highly qualified publicists of the various nations, as subsidiary means for the determination of rules of law." I.C.J. STAT. Art. 38(1). On this article and international law, see ROSALYN HIGGINS, *Sources of International Law: Provenance and Problems*, in PROBLEMS AND PROCESS: INTERNATIONAL LAW AND HOW WE USE IT 17 (1994); Gerald G. Fitzmaurice, *Some Problems Regarding the Formal Sources of International Law,* in SYMBOLAE VERZIJL: PRÉSENTÉES AU PROFESSEUR J. H. W. VERZIJL À L'OCCASION DE SON LXX-IÈME ANNIVERSAIRE 153 (1958). For a critical approach to sources theory and discussion of a distinction between *"norms to be applied by the ICJ"* and *"norms regulating conducts of states,"* see Onuma Yasuaki, *A Transcivilizational Perspective on Global Legal Order in the Twenty-First Century: A Way to Overcome West-Centric and Judiciary-Centric Deficits in International Legal Thoughts,* 8(1) INT'L CMTY. L. REV. 29, 48-52 (2006).

[28] *See* BECKER, *supra* note 9, at 78. According to Becker, "[t]raced through time, the law of State responsibility for private acts represents a historical record of the evolving power relationship between State and non-State actors." *Ibid.* at 361.

activity during the Second World War and during the post-war era, movement during the Cold War, and activity at the end of the Cold War and more recently. This chapter puts the due diligence principle in proper context by also exploring international law's other principles of responsibility.

Chapter 4 demonstrates how the due diligence principle has a particular relevance within the context of States' obligations to confront non-State actors that engage in terrorism. The emphasis in this chapter is on international and regional treaties and United Nations Security Council Resolutions. Many, although not all, of the provisions in these instruments can be understood within a due diligence framework.[29] This chapter makes extensive references to key provisions in these treaties and Resolutions.

The due diligence principle raises numerous theoretical issues, particularly when it operates in the counterterrorism context. Chapter 5 looks at some of these, beginning by suggesting a number of interpretative tools that can provide a degree of clarity. Rather than narrowing the scope for disagreement, however, these tools can themselves actually multiply the parameters for debate *ad nauseam.* Kennedy stresses a similar dynamic in the context of the laws of war when he talks about the "'great conversation' of twentieth-century legitimacy."[30]

This research's final substantive chapter, Chapter 6, examines the relationship between human rights and counterterrorism. One must first determine whether a State's engagement with non-State actors that engage in terrorism on particular facts and circumstances amounts to an armed conflict, thus triggering the application of international humanitarian law, before the role of international human rights law in armed conflict situations can be explored. The second half of Chapter 6 critically engages in the debate by exploring whether human rights observance is necessary to effectively fight terrorism and whether States can effectively fight terrorism while at the same time not violating human rights.[31] It should be stressed

---

[29] It should be stressed, as the ICJ recently did, that "[t]he content of the duty to prevent varies from one instrument to another, according to the wording of the relevant provisions, and depending on the nature of the acts to be prevented." Application of the Convention on the Prevention and Punishment of the Crime of Genocide, *supra* note 12, at Para. 429.

[30] David Kennedy, Of War and Law 160 (2006).

[31] Dunér addresses similar concerns. *See* Bertil Dunér, *Disregard for Security: The Human Rights Movement and 9/11,* 17(1-2) Terrorism & Pol. Violence 89, 91 (2005) (assessing the "question of a *trade-off* between security and human rights [. . .] and [. . .] the *instrumentality* of human rights for security.").

that this chapter's insights are relevant to counterterrorism obligations that operate according to the due diligence principle and also to those that operate according to other principles of responsibility.

As for methodology, this research uses doctrinal analysis. It is important to acknowledge that the documents that this research analyses have been produced within a specific political, social, and economic context[32] and that they are not "simply neutral artefacts from the past."[33] They are products of their environment.

Former Judge of the ICJ Gerald G. Fitzmaurice, writing in 1958, noted that "[m]aterial, historical, indirect sources represent, so to speak, the stuff out of which the law is made. It is they which go to form the *content* of the law."[34] This research embraces a broad, holistic approach to what informs international legal understanding and, in so doing, recognises that particular stakes and interests are advanced in interpreting and pronouncing upon the law.

Ultimately, this research is guided by what Orwell calls an "[h]istorical impulse[, . . . the d]esire to see things as they are, to find out true facts and store them up for the use of posterity [. . . and a p]olitical purpose[, . . . the d]esire to push the world in a certain direction, to alter other people's idea of the kind of society that they should strive after."[35]

---

[32] *See* MAY, *supra* note 3, at 197 (noting the "importance of seeing a document in terms of its potential bias [. . .] History itself and our understanding of it can be informed by a selective reading of documents or those documents themselves may also be selective. Thus, what people decide to record, to leave in or take out, is itself informed by decisions which relate to the social, political and economic environment of which they are a part.").

[33] *Ibid.*

[34] Fitzmaurice, *supra* note 27, at 153 (continuing by stating that "[t]hese are the sources to which the lawgiver goes, so to speak, in order to obtain ideas, or to decide what the law is to consist of.").

[35] GEORGE ORWELL, *Why I Write*, in WHY I WRITE 1, 5 (2004).

Chapter 2
TERRORISM: ARRIVING AT AN UNDERSTANDING OF A TERM

Chapter 2
TERRORISM: ARRIVING AT AN UNDERSTANDING OF A TERM

I. Introduction

Many words, including activists, guerrillas, insurgents, extremists, militants, rebels, radicals, fighters, gunmen, separatists, commandos, captors, and perpetrators, have been used to describe terrorists.[1] The chosen terminology reflects what United Nations Special Rapporteur on the Situation of Human Rights in the Palestinian Territories Occupied Since 1967 John Dugard describes as an "intense conflict in perception."[2] Perhaps no word in the modern discourse raises more conflicting emotions, emotions ranging from hope for radical change to rage and condemnation, than terrorism. Given terrorism's potential to destabilise all aspects of society, political, social, and economic, this should come as little surprise.

This chapter explores the fundamental question of defining terrorism under international law. An attempt is made despite what Chomsky views as the term's propaganda potential.[3] It weighs in on the heady debate whether

---

[1] *See* Daniel Pipes, *They're Terrorists – Not Activists,* N.Y. Sun, 7 September 2004. *See also* H. B. Mishra, Terrorism: Threat to Peace and Harmony 19-21 (1999).

[2] John Dugard, *The Problem of the Definition of Terrorism in International Law,* in September 11, 2001: A Turning Point in International and Domestic Law? 187, 189 (Paul Eden & Thérèse O'Donnell eds., 2005).

[3] *See* Noam Chomsky, *International Terrorism: Image and Reality,* in Western State Terrorism 12, 29 (Alexander George ed., 1991) (stating that the "more normal pattern is for actions undertaken against oppressive regimes and occupying armies to be considered resistance by their perpetrators and terrorism by the rulers, even when they are non-violent."). According to Petman, "[t]he perverse logic at the heart of attempts to define terrorism is well-known: everyone tries to include one's adversaries in the definition while keeping one's allies and one's own (actual or potential) activities outside it." Jarna Petman, *Evil and International Law*, 5(4) Int'l L. Forum Droit Int'l 236, 237 (2003). *See* Alex P. Schmid & Janny de Graaf, Violence As Communication: Insurgent Terrorism and the Western News Media 58 (1982) (commenting that the word terrorism is "generally used so loosely that it has almost become a political slogan to denigrate all kinds of violence used by the 'other side.'"); Abdullahi Ahmed An-Na'im, *Islamic Ambivalence to Political Violence:*

a comprehensive definition of terrorism exists under international law by exploring treaty law, customary international law, and general principles. Ultimately, this chapter concludes that international law has yet to comprehensively define terrorism in a legally obligatory way and without reference to international treaties related to terrorism, but some sense of what is meant by terrorism can be gleaned and is presented. Finally, this chapter addresses the traditional stumbling blocks to finalising a comprehensive treaty on terrorism, namely the questions of State terrorism and the relationship, if any, between freedom fighters and terrorists.[4]

Islamic Law and International Terrorism, 31 GERM. Y.B. INT'L L. 307, 309 (1988) (stating that "the term 'terrorism' in common contemporary usage is generally conceived as applying a strongly negative label on the person(s) identified as 'terrorists' and to their cause.").

[4] *See* A MORE SECURE WORLD: OUR SHARED RESPONSIBILITY: REPORT OF THE SECRETARY-GENERAL'S HIGH-LEVEL PANEL ON THREATS, CHALLENGES, AND CHANGE 51-52 (2004); SPECIFIC HUMAN RIGHTS ISSUES: NEW PRIORITIES, IN PARTICULAR TERRORISM AND COUNTER-TERRORISM: TERRORISM AND HUMAN RIGHTS: FINAL REPORT OF THE SPECIAL RAPPORTEUR, KALLIOPI K. KOUFA, U.N. ESCOR, at 7, U.N. Doc. E/CN.4/Sub.2/2004/40 (2004); Dugard, *supra* note 2, at 197-99; Ben Saul, *Attempts to Define "Terrorism" in International Law,* 52(1) NETH. INT'L L. REV. 57, 76-82 (2005); Surya P. Subedi, *The UN Response to International Terrorism in the Aftermath of the Terrorist Attacks in America and the Problem of the Definition of Terrorism in International Law,* 4(3) INT'L L. FORUM DROIT INT'L 159 (2002); Jörg Friedrichs, *Defining the International Public Enemy: The Political Struggle Behind the Legal Debate on International Terrorism,* 19(1) LEIDEN J. INT'L L. 69, 71-72 (2006). In the legal sense, freedom fighters are those non-State actors who engage in wars of liberation, or those fighting "colonial domination and alien occupation and against racist régimes in the exercise of their right of self-determination, as enshrined in the Charter of the United Nations and the Declaration on Principles of International Law concerning Friendly Relations and Co-operation among States in accordance with the Charter of the United Nations." Protocol Additional to the Geneva Conventions of 12 August 1949, and Relating to the Protection of Victims of International Armed Conflicts, Geneva, 8 June 1977, Art. 1(4). Uibopuu defines this context as when "a non-State community (nation, people), perceiving itself to be distinct from the dominating State (nation, people) and unable to achieve self-determination (independence, statehood) by pacific (democratic, political) means, [. . .] resorts to armed violence to realize that goal and claims a special status under international law (i.e. pursuant to the principles contained in the [. . .] United Nations Charter, and expanded upon in UN resolutions) in order to be treated differently from insurgents and others acting against the State's authority (rebels, rioters, terrorists)." Henn-Jüri Uibopuu, *Wars of National Liberation,* in 4 ENCYCLOPEDIA OF PUBLIC INTERNATIONAL LAW 343, 343 (1982). *See* Math Noortmann, *Non-State Actors in International Law,* in NON-STATE ACTORS IN INTERNATIONAL RELATIONS 59, 67-69 (Bas Arts et al. eds., 2001).

II. A Comprehensive Definition of Terrorism Under International Law?

The question whether a comprehensive definition of terrorism exists under international law is crucial. Without it, discussions would have no legal relevance at international level, the definitional void effectively ensuring that there could not be acts of terrorism at global level as a matter of law. In such a void, terrorism would simply be a "phenomenon which is denounced as shameful and reprehensive by all but understood by none. Its legal value will be instrumental and incantatory, yet inefficient."[5] It would be merely a "word of art meant to brand one's enemies,"[6] a "label used loosely, selectively and invariably pejoratively[, . . .] where the defining elements of terrorism are often confused with value judgements about those accused of it."[7]

Dupuy argues that what he views as the present reality of the "absence of any universally accepted definition of terrorism [. . .] does not necessarily raise a major issue for identifying the rules of international law applicable for combating terrorism, this including the pertinent secondary rules of State Responsibility."[8] Leaving aside for the moment whether "any universally accepted definition of terrorism" exists, that international action against terrorism must ground itself in a definitional framework with respect to each alleged act of terrorism is a necessary starting point and precondition. Definition is necessary because of its "operative legal significance,"[9] as

---

[5] Jean-Marc Sorel, *Some Questions About the Definition of Terrorism and the Fight Against Its Financing,* 14(2) EUR. J. INT'L L. 365, 370 (2003).

[6] Jean Allain, *The Legacy of Lockerbie: Judicial Review of Security Council Actions or the First Manifestation of "Terrorism" as a Threat to International Peace?*, 44(1) INDIAN J. INT'L L. 74, 101 (2004).

[7] HELEN DUFFY, THE "WAR ON TERROR" AND THE FRAMEWORK OF INTERNATIONAL LAW 18 (2005). *See* Colin Warbrick, *The European Response to Terrorism in an Age of Human Rights,* 15(5) EUR. J. INT'L L. 989, 995 (2004) (stating that States use the term to "delegitimize the claims the terrorists make to use violence but also to undermine the political objectives for which they are using force.").

[8] Pierre-Marie Dupuy, *State Sponsors of Terrorism: Issues of International Responsibility,* in ENFORCING INTERNATIONAL LAW NORMS AGAINST TERRORISM 3, 5 (Andrea Bianchi ed., 2004).

[9] Ben Saul, *Definition of "Terrorism" in the UN Security Council: 1985-2004,* 4(1) CHIN. J. INT'L L. 141, 159 (2005).

well as from the standpoint of *nullum crimen sine lege*.[10] Duffy correctly notes that investigation and prosecution on the basis of a crime of terrorism alone would likely violate the precepts of certainty and legality if it were to be concluded that customary international law has not yet sufficiently defined the term.[11]

Of course, any examination of whether a comprehensive definition of terrorism exists under international law must constantly bear in mind the extent to which politics and external influences affect legal understanding and interpretation. While one should not overlook, or underestimate, this political dynamic, however, recourse must be had to the law, politicised though it may be on the subject of terrorism, because of its constructed authority.[12] Bianchi recognises that politics influences the law yet maintains that it is possible, and desirable, to "distinguish the legal dimension from the other components of such a complex social phenomenon as terrorism[, as this] may turn out to be a fairly useful exercise if one is to avoid misplaced expectations."[13]

Methodologically, this chapter proceeds from the perspective that if it can be shown that a comprehensive definition of terrorism exists under international law that generic, pre-set components of the definition should then be rigorously applied to particular facts and circumstances to determine whether a particular act of violence can be legally classified as terrorism. One must attempt to describe the problem and arrive at a workable definition that, as far as possible, "can be applied objectively and dispas-

---

10 *See* Robert Kolb, *The Exercise of Criminal Jurisdiction Over International Terrorists,* in ENFORCING, *supra* note 8, at 227, 227; Louise Arbour, Security Under the Rule of Law, Address of Louise Arbour UN High Commissioner for Human Rights to the Biennial Conference of the International Commission of Jurists (Berlin) (27 August 2004), *available at* http://www.unhchr.ch/huricane/huricane.nsf/view01/3485B28EDDA173F0C1256EFD0035373C?opendocument.

11 *See* DUFFY, *supra* note 7, at 41.

12 According to An-Na'im, "[i]t is not conducive to clarity of thought on the subject to confuse political and sociological considerations regarding the nature of the conflict giving rise to the conduct in question, and/or the psychological processes of motivation of the perpetrators of the act. While all of these perspectives are necessary for understanding terrorism and dealing with it at various levels, a clear definition is imperative from the legal point of view." An-Na'im, *supra* note 3, at 312.

13 Andrea Bianchi, *Enforcing International Law Norms Against Terrorism: Achievements and Prospects,* in ENFORCING, *supra* note 8, at 491, 492.

sionately to all groups engaging in violent actions."[14] Commenting on the quest to comprehensively define terrorism in treaty form in light of discussions at the ninth session of the *ad hoc* Committee on International Terrorism (*ad hoc* Committee) during the spring of 2005, coordinator Carlos Fernando Díaz Paniagua argued that a comprehensive definition must have "legal precision, certainty and fair labelling of the criminal conduct – all of which emanate from the basic human rights obligation to observe due process."[15] Consistency, fidelity to historical context, and clarity are also important considerations.[16] Writing in 2002, former Judge of the Appeals Chamber of the International Criminal Tribunal for the former Yugoslavia (ICTY) Georges Abi-Saab hoped for a comprehensive definition of terrorism under treaty law that would be "exclusively pegged to the acts and the consequences, together with the accompanying intent, regardless of the status or the quality of the actor, as is the case of crimes against humanity and genocide."[17]

It is most helpful for this chapter to proceed by reference to the three sources of law laid out in the International Court of Justice (ICJ)'s Statute.[18] The first two of these sources, treaty law and customary international

---

[14] Kennedy Graham, *The Security Council and Counterterrorism: Global and Regional Approaches to an Elusive Public Good,* 17(1-2) TERRORISM & POL. VIOLENCE 37, 55 (2005). *See* An-Na'im, *supra* note 3, at 314 (stating that, "[a]s a matter of principle, I see no distinction between crime committed by a private person and crime committed by an official of any government.").

[15] REPORT OF THE AD HOC COMMITTEE ESTABLISHED BY GENERAL ASSEMBLY RESOLUTION 51/210 OF 17 DECEMBER 1996: NINTH SESSION (28 MARCH-1 APRIL 2005), U.N. GAOR, Annex II, at 28, U.N. Doc. A/60/37 (2005). Such a treaty, according to Bassiouni, must be, "as much as possible, value-neutral, encompassing all actors, and covering all modalities and techniques of terror-violence." M. Cherif Bassiouni, *Legal Control of International Terrorism: A Policy-Oriented Assessment*, 43(1) HARV. INT'L L.J. 83, 101 (2002).

[16] *See* PAUL WILKINSON, TERRORISM AND THE LIBERAL STATE 57 (2nd ed. 1986). "Nothing is to be gained by ignoring the specifics of violence, be it out of political bias or ignorance. It will certainly not make for a better understanding of the various manifestations of violence, but will only spread confusion. Another frequent source of confusion is the lack of precision in terminology." MISHRA, *supra* note 1, at 19.

[17] Georges Abi-Saab, *The Proper Role of International Law in Combating Terrorism,* 1(1) CHIN. J. INT'L L. 305, 311 (2002).

[18] *See* I.C.J. STAT. Art. 38(1)(a)-(c) (stating that "1. The Court, whose function is to decide in accordance with international law such disputes as are submitted to it, shall apply: a. international conventions, whether general or particular, establishing rules expressly recognized by the contesting states; b. international custom, as evidence of a general practice accepted as law; c. the general principles of law recognized by civilized nations.").

law, should be considered to be, at least in principle, no more legally dominant or persuasive than the third source, general principles.[19] As ICJ Judge Zhengyu Ni noted in his separate opinion in *Military and Paramilitary Activities in and Against Nicaragua*, "the various sources of international law [. . .], in the course of application, usually support, rather than preclude, each other. [. . . I]t would be inconceivable that application of one should exclude that of any other."[20]

A. Treaty Law

One view denies that international law recognises a comprehensive definition of terrorism under either treaty law or customary international law.[21] Relying on the absence of definition at international level during the decades immediately following the United Nations' founding, this school of thought resists definitions that fail to simultaneously address the "historical, economic, social, and political causes underlying resort to terrorism."[22] While not denying the desirability of definition, this perspective stresses the incompleteness of understandings that fail to acknowledge the context in which terrorists operate. Typically, this view sympathises with freedom fighters and makes a fundamental distinction between their actions and the actions of terrorists.

This stance is popular among developing States[23] and has been accepted to some extent by scholars who acknowledge as criminal and terrorist only

---

19 *See* William A. Schabas, An Introduction to the International Criminal Court 72 (2001). *See also* M. Cherif Bassiouni, *A Functional Approach to "General Principles of International Law,"* 11(3) Mich. J. Int'l L. 768, 781-83 (1990).

20 Military and Paramilitary Activities in and Against Nicaragua (*Nicar.* v. *U.S.*), 1986 I.C.J. 14, 207 (Ni, J., separate).

21 *See* Antonio Cassese, *International Criminal Law*, in International Law 721, 750 (Malcolm D. Evans ed., 2003); Yoram Dinstein, *Ius Ad Bellum Aspects of the "War on Terrorism,"* in Terrorism and the Military: International Legal Implications 13, 13-14 (Wybo P. Heere ed., 2003); *International Humanitarian Law and the Challenges of Contemporary Armed Conflicts: Excerpt of the Report Prepared by the International Committee of the Red Cross for the 28th International Conference of the Red Cross and Red Crescent, Geneva, December 2003*, 86(853) Int'l Rev. Red Cross 213, 231 n. 16 (2004).

22 Antonio Cassese, International Criminal Law 120 (2003).

23 For an overview of the British, French, Italian, and (West) German approaches, see Friedrichs, *supra* note 4, at 79-87.

those violent acts that treaties specifically prohibit.[24] According to this position, the prohibition of terrorism operates within the exclusive straight-jacket of particular treaty regimes, and as such, terrorism does not benefit from an autonomous existence under, for example, customary international law.[25] The Office of the United Nations High Commissioner for Human Rights seems to agree with this, as it has asserted that treaties related to terrorism within the context of the United Nations fail to provide a "clear and commonly agreed definition of terrorism [. . . and that it] has yet to be authoritatively defined."[26]

The majority of publicists echo these sentiments and channel discussions of terrorism to the international and region-specific treaty frameworks. Stating that terrorism's definition is "neither new nor settled," Jean notes that it is "'unclear for both jurists and political scientists. No satisfactory definition of terrorism has been given, either by international or by internal law'. The concept is 'legally doubtful.'"[27] Flory asserts that "there is no universally accepted definition of terrorist action in international law"[28] and that the definitions that do exist are accepted by only a small number of States or are fact-specific.[29] Rosalyn Higgins, now President of the ICJ, has argued that the "difficulties of definition are objective and not just subjective [. . . and that t]he technical problems of definition are prodigious."[30] Of terrorism, Meltzer states that "the term is nowhere fully defined as a

---

[24] *See* CASSESE, INTERNATIONAL CRIMINAL LAW, *supra* note 22, at 120. For a criticism of the "significant gaps in the regime of the peacetime anti-terrorism conventions," see Michael P. Scharf, *Defining Terrorism as the Peace Time Equivalent of War Crimes: A Case of Too Much Convergence Between International Humanitarian Law and International Criminal Law?*, 7(2) ILSA J. INT'L & COMP. L. 391, 393 (2001).

[25] *See* CASSESE, INTERNATIONAL CRIMINAL LAW, *supra* note 22, at 120.

[26] OFFICE OF THE UNITED NATIONS HIGH COMMISSIONER FOR HUMAN RIGHTS, DIGEST OF JURISPRUDENCE OF THE UNITED NATIONS AND REGIONAL ORGANIZATIONS ON THE PROTECTION OF HUMAN RIGHTS WHILE COUNTERING TERRORISM 1, U.N. Sales No. HR/PUB/03/1 (2003).

[27] Patrice Jean, *The Jurisprudence of the European Commission and Court of Human Rights with Regard to Terrorism*, in TERRORISM AND INTERNATIONAL LAW 217, 217 (Rosalyn Higgins & Maurice Flory eds., 1997).

[28] Maurice Flory, *International Law: An Instrument to Combat Terrorism*, in TERRORISM AND INTERNATIONAL LAW, *supra* note 27, at 30, 33.

[29] *See ibid.*

[30] Rosalyn Higgins, *The General International Law of Terrorism*, in TERRORISM AND INTERNATIONAL LAW, *supra* note 27, at 13, 14.

legal term [. . . and notes its] legal vagueness,"[31] and Mani asserts that "[c]learly the definition of terrorism itself is fluid and subject to the vagaries of the definers."[32] Finally, Gasser argues that "[n]either experts in international law nor government representatives have yet agreed on a comprehensive and widely acceptable definition."[33]

i. *International Treaties Related to Terrorism*

An examination of the earliest international treaties related to terrorism and several of the region-specific treaties reveals the strong commitment of many States to exclude freedom fighters from being classed as terrorists. Although space constraints preclude this chapter from examining all of the international treaties,[34] it can generally be said that they share in common three characteristics, namely the prohibition of safe haven, the use of municipal criminal law mechanisms for enforcement purposes, and jurisdictional streamlining.[35]

Several of the international treaties clearly accommodate freedom fighters. Consider, for example, the 1963 Convention on Offences and Certain Other Acts Committed on Board Aircraft, which applies to "(a) offences against penal law; (b) acts which, whether or not they are offences, may or do jeopardize the safety of the aircraft or of persons or property therein or

---

[31] David Meltzer, *Al Qa'ida: Terrorists or Irregulars?*, in LAW AFTER GROUND ZERO 71, 71 (John Strawson ed., 2002).

[32] Rama Mani, *The Root Causes of Terrorism and Conflict Prevention,* in TERRORISM AND THE UN: BEFORE AND AFTER SEPTEMBER 11 219, 224 (Jane Boulden & Thomas G. Weiss eds., 2004).

[33] Hans-Peter Gasser, *Acts of Terror, "Terrorism" and International Humanitarian Law,* 84(847) INT'L REV. RED CROSS 547, 552 (2002). *See* Joan Fitzpatrick, *Speaking Law to Power: The War Against Terrorism and Human Rights,* 14(2) EUR. J. INT'L L. 241, 249 (2003).

[34] On these, see Bianchi, *supra* note 13, at 494-95; Kolb, *supra* note 10, at 229-32; Dugard, *supra* note 2, at 189-99; *Prosecutor* v. *Galić* (IT-98-29-T), Trial Chamber I, 2003 I.C.T.Y., at 33, n. 150. On the League of Nations and the 1937 Convention for the Prevention and Punishment of Terrorism, see Ben Saul, *The Legal Response of the League of Nations to Terrorism*, 4(1) J. INT'L CRIM. JUST. 78 (2006); Saul, *Attempts*, *supra* note 4, at 61-66.

[35] *See* C. L. Lim, *The Question of a Generic Definition of Terrorism Under General International Law,* in GLOBAL ANTI-TERRORISM LAW AND POLICY 37, 45-47 (Victor V. Ramraj et al. eds., 2005).

which jeopardize good order and discipline on board."[36] Despite this seemingly unequivocal language, however, a later provision exposes the limited context in which the treaty actually operates. Specifically, it does not apply to, with limited exceptions, "offences against penal laws of a political nature or those based on racial or religious discrimination."[37]

According to the General Assembly Resolution that adopted the 1973 Convention on the Prevention and Punishment of Crimes Against Internationally Protected Persons, Including Diplomatic Agents (Internationally Protected Persons Convention),[38] the provisions of the Internationally Protected Persons Convention "could not in any way prejudice the exercise of the legitimate right to self-determination and independence [. . .] by peoples struggling against colonialism, alien domination, foreign occupation, racial discrimination and *apartheid*."[39] This language should be regarded as the General Assembly's considered interpretive guidance. It reveals an ongoing sympathy with freedom fighters and a reluctance to consider them to be terrorists. It also shows the General Assembly's unwillingness to have the Internationally Protected Persons Convention be used in a way that would undermine freedom fighters' armed struggles.

The General Assembly adopted the 1979 International Convention Against the Taking of Hostages,[40] which prohibits hostage taking, attempted hostage taking, and participation in hostage taking or attempted hostage taking,[41] soon after American diplomats were seized as hostages in Iran.[42] Like earlier treaties, however, it does not unequivocally condemn as terrorist all acts that could conceivably fall under its purview. It excludes, within certain parameters, hostage taking within the context of particular armed

---

[36] Convention on Offences and Certain Other Acts Committed on Board Aircraft, Tokyo, 14 September 1963, Art. 1(1)(a)-(b).

[37] *Ibid.* at Art. 2.

[38] G.A. Res. 3166, U.N. GAOR, Annex, U.N. Doc. A/RES/3166 (1973).

[39] *Ibid.* at 147 (also stating that this right must be exercised "in accordance with the purposes and principles of the Charter of the United Nations and the Declaration on Principles of International Law concerning Friendly Relations and Co-operation among States in accordance with the Charter of the United Nations.").

[40] G.A. Res. 34/146, U.N. GAOR, Annex, U.N. Doc. A/RES/34/146 (1979).

[41] *See ibid.* at Annex, at Art. 1.

[42] On this incident, see Ladan Boroumand & Roya Boroumand, *Terror, Islam, and Democracy*, in UNDERSTANDING THE WAR ON TERROR 134, 145-48 (James F. Hoge, Jr., & Gideon Rose eds., 2005).

conflicts, such as those "in which peoples are fighting against colonial domination and alien occupation and against racist régimes in the exercise of their right of self-determination."[43] This exclusion clause is primarily aimed at bolstering the legitimacy of those who would use hostage taking as a means of struggle, as it ensures that such acts will not be considered acts of terrorism under the treaty.[44]

In 1985, the General Assembly adopted Resolution 40/61.[45] That Resolution "[f]urther recall[s] the existing international conventions relating to various aspects of the problem of international terrorism . . . "[46] By emphasising a treaty framework that includes treaties that, as just described, accommodate freedom fighters in some way and by later in its Preamble "upholding the legitimacy of their struggle,"[47] Resolution 40/61 exposes the General Assembly's continuing view at the time that freedom fighters and terrorists are, and should be, legally distinguished from one another. This remains the case despite the Resolution's unequivocal condemnation of terrorism in Paragraph 1[48] because, according to the General Assembly, the means used by freedom fighters, to the extent that they are excluded by international treaties related to terrorism, do not, and cannot, legally qualify as acts of terrorism.

---

[43] G.A. Res. 34/146, *supra* note 40, at Annex, at Art. 12.

[44] On hostage taking and international efforts to proscribe it, see Saul, *Definition*, *supra* note 9, at 144-45.

[45] G.A. Res. 40/61, U.N. GAOR, U.N. Doc. A/RES/40/61 (1985).

[46] *Ibid.* at Preamble (inclusively listing these as the Convention on Offences and Certain Other Acts Committed on Board Aircraft, Tokyo, 14 September 1963; Convention for the Suppression of Unlawful Seizure of Aircraft, The Hague, 16 December 1970; Convention for the Suppression of Unlawful Acts Against the Safety of Civil Aviation, Montreal, 23 September 1971; Convention on the Prevention and Punishment of Crimes Against Internationally Protected Persons, Including Diplomatic Agents, New York, 14 December 1973; and International Convention Against the Taking of Hostages, New York, 17 December 1979).

[47] *Ibid.* (noting that this struggle must be conducted "in accordance with the purposes and principles of the Charter and of the Declaration on Principles of International Law concerning Friendly Relations and Co-operation among States in accordance with the Charter of the United Nations.").

[48] According to that paragraph, the General Assembly "[u]nequivocally condemns, as criminal, all acts, methods and practices of terrorism wherever and by whomever committed, including those which jeopardize friendly relations among States and their security." *Ibid.* at Para. 1.

ii. *Regional Treaties Related to Terrorism*

Treaties related to terrorism have also been adopted by the major regional organisations.[49] Several of these reveal the commitment of many States to exclude freedom fighters from being classed as terrorists. A number of these do so explicitly. The 1999 Convention of the Organisation of the Islamic Conference (OIC) on Combating International Terrorism (OIC Convention), for example, condemns terrorism and stresses its unjustifiable nature.[50] It sweepingly defines it as

> any act of violence or threat thereof notwithstanding its motives or intentions perpetrated to carry out an individual or collective criminal plan with the aim of terrorizing people or threatening to harm them or imperiling their lives, honour, freedoms, security or rights or exposing the environment or any facility or public or private property to hazards or occupying or seizing them, or endangering a national resource, or international facilities, or threatening the stability, territorial integrity, political unity or sovereignty of independent States.[51]

but explicitly excludes, in a nod to, among others, Palestinian exceptionalism, "[p]eoples' struggle including armed struggle against foreign occupation, aggression, colonialism, and hegemony, aimed at liberation and self-determination in accordance with the principles of international law."[52] The Arab League takes essentially the same position in the 1998 Arab Convention for the Suppression of Terrorism (Arab Convention)[53] in that it excludes "[a]ll

---

[49] *See* EXTRACT FROM THE REPORT OF THE SECRETARY-GENERAL ON MEASURES TO ELIMINATE INTERNATIONAL TERRORISM (DOC. A/58/116), AS UPDATED ON 31 DECEMBER 2003. On these, see FEDERICO ANDREU-GUZMÁN, INTERNATIONAL COMMISSION OF JURISTS, TERRORISM AND HUMAN RIGHTS NO. 2: NEW CHALLENGES AND OLD DANGERS 37-69 (2003); Graham, *supra* note 14, at 49-52; Bianchi, *supra* note 13, at 495; Kolb, *supra* note 10, at 232-33; Dugard, *supra* note 2, at 199-202.

[50] *See* Convention of the OIC on Combating International Terrorism, Ouagadougou, 1 July 1999, Preamble.

[51] *Ibid.* at Art. 1(2).

[52] *Ibid.* at Art. 2(a).

[53] *See* Arab Convention for the Suppression of Terrorism, Cairo, 22 April 1998, Art. 1(2) (defining terrorism as "[a]ny act or threat of violence, whatever its motives or purposes, that occurs in the advancement of an individual or collective criminal agenda and seeking to sow panic among people, causing fear by harming them, or placing their lives, liberty or

cases of struggle by whatever means, including armed struggle, against foreign occupation and aggression for liberation and self-determination, in accordance with the principles of international law."[54] Likewise, the detailed definition of terrorism in the 1999 Organisation of African Unity (OAU) Convention on the Prevention and Combating of Terrorism (OAU Convention)[55] is qualified by its exclusion of the "struggle waged by peoples in accordance with the principles of international law for their liberation or self-determination, including armed struggle against colonialism, occupation, aggression and domination by foreign forces."[56]

Arguably, the sweeping exclusion clauses in these three treaties, reflecting as they do the political and ideological sympathies of the OIC, the Arab League, and the OAU (now the African Union (AU)), almost swallow the rule condemning terrorism, thus meaning that all such "legitimate" forms of violence fall outside the OIC, Arab, and OAU Conventions simply because of the treaties' exculpatory language. However, this oversimplifies the matter. The treaty language clearly requires that such armed struggles, to avoid being considered inclusive of terrorist violence when they otherwise would be, must be conducted, to use language that is identical in this respect in all three of the treaties, "in accordance with the principles of international law." This crucial language requires an assessment based on international legal norms that operate independently of a regional context, be that the context of the OIC, the Arab League, or the AU.[57] Just what bearing the "in accordance with the principles of international law" language will actually have in practice and how widely or narrowly it will be interpreted and with what degree of fidelity to international legal understanding it will be understood remains, however, largely up to the OIC, the Arab League, and the AU.

---

security in danger, or seeking to cause damage to the environment or to public or private installations or property or to occupying or seizing them, or seeking to jeopardize a national resources.").

[54] *Ibid.* at Art. 2(a).

[55] *See* OAU Convention on the Prevention and Combating of Terrorism, Algiers, 14 July 1999, Art. 1(3).

[56] *Ibid.* at Art. 3(1).

[57] Schachter makes a theoretically similar argument with regard to self-determination and armed struggle. *See* Oscar Schachter, *The Lawful Use of Force by a State Against Terrorists in Another Country*, in TERRORISM & POLITICAL VIOLENCE: LIMITS & POSSIBILITIES OF LEGAL CONTROL 243, 244-45 (Henry H. Han ed., 1993).

Other regional organisations do not explicitly exclude freedom fighters in the way that the OIC, the Arab League, and the AU do. Rather, they implicitly make some provision for freedom fighters in their treaties related to terrorism. For example, consider the 2002 Inter-American Convention Against Terrorism (Inter-American Convention).[58] Article 2(1)(a)-(j) of that treaty defines terrorism by reference to certain enumerated international treaties related to terrorism.[59] Several of these referred to treaties themselves, in fact, exclude freedom fighters, meaning that the Inter-American Convention also implicitly makes some distinction between freedom fighters and terrorists.

As a second regional example of an implicit exclusion of freedom fighters, consider the South Asian Association for Regional Cooperation (SAARC). The 2004 Additional Protocol to the SAARC Regional Convention on the Suppression of Terrorism (SAARC Additional Protocol)[60] takes a complicated position on the substantive legal essence of terrorist offences. According to Article 4(1) of the SAARC Additional Protocol, a terrorist offence consists of an offence under one of the international treaties related to terrorism in the Annex to the SAARC Additional Protocol, several treaties themselves of which make some accommodation for freedom fighters,[61] "[a]ny other act intended to cause death or serious bodily injury to a

---

[58] Inter-American Convention Against Terrorism, Bridgetown, 3 June 2002.

[59] *See ibid.* at Art. 2(1)(a)-(j) (exhaustively listing these treaties as the Convention for the Suppression of Unlawful Seizure of Aircraft, The Hague, 16 December 1970; Convention for the Suppression of Unlawful Acts Against the Safety of Civil Aviation, Montreal, 23 September 1971; Convention on the Prevention and Punishment of Crimes Against Internationally Protected Persons, Including Diplomatic Agents, New York, 14 December 1973; International Convention Against the Taking of Hostages, New York, 17 December 1979; Convention on the Physical Protection of Nuclear Material, Vienna, 3 March 1980; Protocol on the Suppression of Unlawful Acts of Violence at Airports Serving International Civil Aviation, Supplementary to the Convention for the Suppression of Unlawful Acts Against the Safety of Civil Aviation, Montreal, 24 February 1988; Convention for the Suppression of Unlawful Acts Against the Safety of Maritime Navigation, Rome, 10 March 1988; Protocol for the Suppression of Unlawful Acts Against the Safety of Fixed Platforms Located on the Continental Shelf, Rome, 10 March 1988; International Convention for the Suppression of Terrorist Bombings, New York, 15 December 1997; and International Convention for the Suppression of the Financing of Terrorism, New York, 9 December 1999).

[60] Additional Protocol to the SAARC Regional Convention on the Suppression of Terrorism, Islamabad, 6 January 2004.

[61] *See ibid.* at Art. 4(1)(a). The Annex exhaustively lists the Convention for the Suppression of Unlawful Seizure of Aircraft, The Hague, 16 December 1970; Convention for

civilian, when the purpose of such act, by its nature or context, is to intimidate a population, or to compel a Government or an international organization to do or to abstain from doing any act,"[62] and offences circumscribed by other treaties which operate according to the extradite or prosecute principle and to which SAARC States are parties.[63]

Although the more recent international treaties related to terrorism do not in a wholesale manner exclude freedom fighters from their purview, it is clear that several of the older ones do. Furthermore, many of the regional treaties explicitly or implicitly exclude freedom fighters in some respect, although it should be noted that the legal instrument in this regard within the framework of the European Union (EU), the EU's Council Framework Decision of 13 June 2002 on Combating Terrorism,[64] does not.[65]

---

the Suppression of Unlawful Acts Against the Safety of Civil Aviation, Montreal, 23 September 1971; Convention on the Prevention and Punishment of Crimes Against Internationally Protected Persons, Including Diplomatic Agents, New York, 14 December 1973; International Convention Against the Taking of Hostages, New York, 17 December 1979; Convention on the Physical Protection of Nuclear Material, Vienna, 3 March 1980; Protocol for the Suppression of Unlawful Acts of Violence at Airports Serving International Civil Aviation, Supplementary to the Convention for the Suppression of Unlawful Acts Against the Safety of Civil Aviation, Montreal, 24 February 1988; Convention for the Suppression of Unlawful Acts Against the Safety of Maritime Navigation, Rome, 10 March 1988; Protocol for the Suppression of Unlawful Acts Against the Safety of Fixed Platforms Located on the Continental Shelf, Rome, 10 March 1988; International Convention for the Suppression of Terrorist Bombings, New York, 15 December 1997; and International Convention for the Suppression of the Financing of Terrorism, New York, 9 December 1999. *See ibid.* at Annex.

62 *Ibid.* at Art. 4(1)(b).

63 *See ibid.* at Art. 4(1)(c).

64 Council Framework Decision of 13 June 2002 on Combating Terrorism, 2002/475/JHA, 2002 O.J. (L 164) 3. On this, see Rudi Troosters, *The European Union Framework Decision of 13th June 2002 on Combating Terrorism*, in EUROPEAN COOPERATION AGAINST TERRORISM: CONFERENCE PROCEEDINGS 67 (2004).

65 This instrument presents what essentially amounts to a three-part definition of terrorism, as "[1.] intentional acts referred to below in points (a) to (i), as defined under national law, [2.] which, given their nature or context, may seriously damage a country or an international organisation [3.] where committed with the aim of: – seriously intimidating a population, or – unduly compelling a Government or international organisation to perform or abstain from performing any act, or – seriously destabilising or destroying the fundamental political, constitutional, economic or social structures of a country or an international organisation." Council Framework Decision, *supra* note 64, at Art. 1, 4. Art. 1(a)-(i) reads "(a) attacks upon a person's life which may cause death; (b) attacks upon the physical integrity of a

The ongoing debate within the context of the *ad hoc* Committee to comprehensively define terrorism in treaty form exposes the main issues that divide States on the definitional question. At the *ad hoc* Committee's eighth session during the summer of 2004, for example, a number of delegations argued that any such treaty should recognise that terrorism can be committed by both State and non-State actors and that the "exercise of the legitimate rights of States, peoples and individuals under international law should be excluded from the scope of the convention to the extent that the exercise of such rights did not target civilians or terrorize them."[66] Because these issues were being discussed, and continue to be discussed, within a treaty-drafting context, a context that, by its very nature, aims to construct an instrument with legally-enforceable rights and obligations, these concerns are both poignant and revealing. Since States make law, furthermore, it is only by resolving their concerns that a viable framework can emerge under treaty law that can sustain a comprehensive definition of terrorism.

B. Customary International Law

Although most scholars are sceptical of the view that customary international law acknowledges a comprehensive definition of terrorism,[67] Cassese argues that a legally sufficient definition of the term exists under this source

person; (c) kidnapping or hostage taking; (d) causing extensive destruction to a Government or public facility, a transport system, an infrastructure facility, including an information system, a fixed platform located on the continental shelf, a public place or private property likely to endanger human life or result in major economic loss; (e) seizure of aircraft, ships or other means of public or goods transport; (f) manufacture, possession, acquisition, transport, supply or use of weapons, explosives or of nuclear, biological or chemical weapons, as well as research into, and development of, biological and chemical weapons; (g) release of dangerous substances, or causing fires, floods or explosions the effect of which is to endanger human life; (h) interfering with or disrupting the supply of water, power or any other fundamental natural resource the effect of which is to endanger human life; (i) threatening to commit any of the acts listed in (a) to (h)." *Ibid.* at Art. 1(a)-(i), 4.

66 REPORT OF THE AD HOC COMMITTEE ESTABLISHED BY GENERAL ASSEMBLY RESOLUTION 51/210 OF 17 DECEMBER 1996: EIGHTH SESSION (28 JUNE-2 JULY 2004), U.N. GAOR, Annex I, at 7, U.N. Doc. A/59/37 (2004).

67 *See* Lim, *supra* note 35, at 60-61; DUFFY, *supra* note 7, at 40-41; Saul, *Definition*, *supra* note 9, at 166.

of law.[68] According to him, such a definition began to evolve in the late-1930s, and while there was general agreement as to the concept, developing States and those States under Soviet influence refused to accept any definition that criminalised the "acts or transactions of national liberation movements or, more generally, 'freedom fighters.'"[69] A shift in international attitudes began in the early-1980s, however, when the Soviet Union was subjected to terrorism in the Middle East for the first time.[70] The collapse of the Soviet Union and the end of liberation struggles in the Third World also contributed to this shift in thinking.[71]

While many commentators have interpreted developing States' refusal to compromise on the definition of terrorism in respect of freedom fighters as evidence of the absence of a comprehensive definition of the term, Cassese disputes this, arguing that "[w]hat indeed was lacking was *agreement on the exception*. The general notion was not in question."[72] This "general notion" was, and continues to be, informed by international treaties related to terrorism, as well as those treaties that operate within a region-specific context.[73]

To support his argument, Cassese contends that the mere existence of treaty provisions that expressly prohibit terrorism but that fail to qualify or

---

[68] *See* Cassese, *International Criminal Law*, *supra* note 21, at 750-52; Antonio Cassese, *Terrorism Is Also Disrupting Some Crucial Legal Categories of International Law,* 12(5) EUR. J. INT'L L. 993, 994 (2001) (noting that "at least trans-national, state-sponsored or state-condoned terrorism amounts to an international crime, and is already contemplated and prohibited by international customary law as a distinct category of such crimes.").

[69] CASSESE, INTERNATIONAL CRIMINAL LAW, *supra* note 22, at 121.

[70] *See* Higgins, *supra* note 30, at 18.

[71] *See* CASSESE, INTERNATIONAL CRIMINAL LAW, *supra* note 22, at 124. *See also* Dugard, *supra* note 2, at 194-95 (describing at page 194 a "radical change of attitude towards international terrorism").

[72] CASSESE, INTERNATIONAL CRIMINAL LAW, *supra* note 22, at 121. According to Cassese, "international rules do cover in sufficiently clear terms at least the most conspicuous and odious manifestations of this phenomenon." *Ibid.* at 130. While not expressly addressing whether a free-standing comprehensive definition of terrorism exists under customary international law, Arbour has asserted that "many of the elements of the crime of terrorism are already established." Arbour, *supra* note 10.

[73] For Saul's response to Cassese on this point, see Ben Saul, *Crimes and Prohibitions of "Terror" and "Terrorism" in Armed Conflict: 1919-2005*, 18(4) HUMANITÄRES VÖLKERRECHT 264, 270-71 (2005).

define the term, such as the Fourth Geneva Convention's Article 33(1),[74] demonstrates that treaty drafters had some independent idea of what was meant by terrorism.[75] According to him, from this "[i]t is warranted to believe that they either deliberately or unwittingly were referring to a general notion underlying treaty provisions and laid down in customary rules."[76]

Conceivably, a similar argument could be made with respect to Security Council Resolution 748, which states that "the suppression of acts of international terrorism, including those in which States are directly or indirectly involved, is essential for the maintenance of international peace and security."[77] The Security Council later in that Resolution ordered Libya to "commit itself definitively to cease all forms of terrorist action and all assistance to terrorist groups and that it must promptly, by concrete actions, demonstrate its renunciation of terrorism."[78] This language, following Cassese's reasoning, arguably also presumes that international law, or at least the Security Council, recognises a pre-existing definition of terrorism under customary international law.[79]

The Annex to General Assembly Resolution 49/60 defines terrorism.[80] According to it:

---

[74] The Fourth Geneva Convention's Art. 33(1) states that "[n]o protected person may be punished for an offence he or she has not personally committed. Collective penalties and likewise all measures of intimidation or of terrorism are prohibited." Convention Relative to the Protection of Civilian Persons in Time of War, Geneva, 12 August 1949, Art. 33(1). On this article, see Saul, *Crimes and Prohibitions*, *supra* note 73, at 268.

[75] *See* CASSESE, INTERNATIONAL CRIMINAL LAW, *supra* note 22, at 121. On terrorism under international humanitarian law, see Jelena Pejic, *Terrorist Acts and Groups: A Role for International Law?*, 75 BRIT. Y.B. INT'L L. 71, 73-76 (2004); Saul, *Crimes and Prohibitions*, *supra* note 73.

[76] CASSESE, INTERNATIONAL CRIMINAL LAW, *supra* note 22, at 121. *See* INTERNATIONAL COMMITTEE OF THE RED CROSS, CUSTOMARY INTERNATIONAL HUMANITARIAN LAW: VOLUME 1: RULES 8-11 (Jean-Marie Henckaerts & Louise Doswald-Beck eds., 2005).

[77] S.C. Res. 748, U.N. SCOR, at Preamble, U.N. Doc. S/RES/748 (1992). For an overview of Security Council definitions of terrorism between 1985 and 2004, see Saul, *Definition*, *supra* note 9.

[78] S.C. Res. 748, *supra* note 77, at 52-53.

[79] *But see* Saul, *Definition*, *supra* note 9, at 148 (asserting in the context of the Security Council that the failure to expressly define terrorism suggests not the existence of a definition but, rather, a determination to decentralise its substantive content).

[80] *See* ANTONIO CASSESE, INTERNATIONAL LAW 259 (2003).

> Criminal acts intended or calculated to provoke a state of terror in the general public, a group of persons or particular persons for political purposes are in any circumstance unjustifiable, whatever the considerations of a political, philosophical, ideological, racial, ethnic, religious or any other nature that may be invoked to justify them.[81]

Cassese argues that this definition reflects the emerging consensus on the definitional question and provides an "acceptable definition."[82] That the General Assembly repeated this definition of terrorism over ten years later in Resolution 60/43[83] would seem to further support Cassese's argument that customary international law recognises a sufficiently-cohesive and sustainable comprehensive definition of terrorism.

According to Cassese's three-part comprehensive definition of terrorism, terrorist acts are those which:

- [. . .] constitute a criminal offence under most national legal systems (for example, assault, murder, kidnapping, hostage-taking, extortion, bombing, torture, arson, etc.);
- [. . . are] aimed at spreading terror (that is, fear and intimidation) by means of violent action or the threat thereof directed against a State, the public, or particular groups of persons; [and]
- [. . . are] politically, religiously, or otherwise ideologically motivated, and not motivated by the pursuit of private ends.[84]

---

81 G.A. Res. 49/60, U.N. GAOR, Annex, at 4, U.N. Doc. A/RES/49/60 (1994).

82 CASSESE, INTERNATIONAL LAW, *supra* note 80, at 259.

83 *See* G.A. Res. 60/43, U.N. GAOR, at 3, U.N. Doc. A/RES/60/43 (2005) (defining terrorism as "criminal acts intended or calculated to provoke a state of terror in the general public, a group of persons or particular persons for political purposes are in any circumstances unjustifiable, whatever the considerations of a political, philosophical, ideological, racial, ethnic, religious or other nature that may be invoked to justify them.").

84 Cassese, *International Criminal Law*, *supra* note 21, at 752. Wilkinson puts forward a similar three-part definition, as do Guillaume, Bassiouni, Laqueur, and Bjørgo. For Wilkinson's definition of political terrorism, see WILKINSON, *supra* note 16, at 51 (defining it as the "systematic use of murder and destruction, and the threat of murder and destruction in order to terrorise individuals, groups, communities or governments into conceding to the terrorists' political demands."). Wilkinson stresses the indiscriminate, unpredictable, and arbitrary nature of terrorism, as well as its refusal to recognise the laws of war. *See ibid.* at 54-55. For the definitions of terrorism by Guillaume, Bassiouni, Laqueur, and Bjørgo, see Gilbert Guillaume, *Terrorism and International Law,* 53(3) INT'L & COMP. L.Q. 537, 540 (2004) (describing it as "any criminal activity involving the use of violence in circumstances

If they are also of a very serious nature or of a large scale, Cassese contends that the acts can be considered international crimes, crimes to which universal jurisdiction attaches.[85]

While Cassese's position that customary international law recognises a comprehensive definition of terrorism is undoubtedly attractive because it seeks to clarify a complex subject, it is not without its limitations. Arguably, its main shortcoming is that it does not rigorously enough assess *opinio juris*.[86] It is too easy to dismiss, as Cassese does, the continuing tendency of many developing States to differentiate between freedom fighters and terrorists as only confusing the issue and contributing to an unfortunate "tendency to hold the view that there still does not exist a generally accepted definition of terrorism."[87] In fact, the freedom fighters versus terrorists debate goes to the heart of the question whether customary

likely to cause bodily harm or a threat to human life, in connection with an enterprise whose aim is to provoke terror."); Bassiouni, *Legal Control*, *supra* note 15, at 84 (referring to it as a "strategy of violence designed to instill terror in a segment of society in order to achieve a power-outcome, propagandize a cause, or inflict harm for vengeful political purposes."); Walter Laqueur, *Left, Right, and Beyond – The Changing Face of Terror,* in UNDERSTANDING, *supra* note 42, at 154, 154 (defining terrorism as "a method – the substate application of violence or the threat of violence to sow panic and bring about political change."); Tore Bjørgo, *Introduction*, in ROOT CAUSES OF TERRORISM: MYTHS, REALITY AND WAYS FORWARD 1, 2 (Tore Bjørgo ed., 2005) (presenting terrorism as a "set of methods or strategies of combat rather than an identifiable ideology or movement, [. . .] that terrorism involves premeditated use of violence against (at least primarily) non-combatants in order to achieve a psychological effect of fear on others than the immediate targets."). Sorel posits a definition of terrorism that resembles the one put forward by Cassese but denies that it exists as a matter of substantive law. *See* Sorel, *supra* note 5, at 371 (stating that, "[a]lthough it is clear that no perfect definition could be given, an attempt might be made along the following lines: International terrorism is an illicit act (irrespective of its perpetrator or its purpose) which creates a disturbance in the public order as defined by the international community, by using serious and indiscriminate violence (in whatever form, whether against people or public or private property) in order to generate an atmosphere of terror with the aim of influencing political action.").

[85] *See* CASSESE, INTERNATIONAL LAW, *supra* note 80, at 259. *But see* Higgins, *supra* note 30, at 24; Saul, *Definition*, *supra* note 9, at 166. It might at least be admitted "that – even in the absence of a general international convention governing all the manifestations of terrorism – some prescribed acts of international terrorism already constitute offences defined by international law." Yoram Dinstein, *Terrorism as an International Crime,* 19 ISR. Y.B. H.R. 55, 72-73 (1989).

[86] For an argument that *opinio juris* is lacking, see Abi-Saab, *supra* note 17, at 310-11.

[87] CASSESE, INTERNATIONAL CRIMINAL LAW, *supra* note 22, at 130.

international law recognises a comprehensive definition of terrorism and cannot be easily dismissed as the mere absence of "*agreement on the exception*."

States' views on this issue expose *opinio juris*, one of the two requirements, of course, of any sustainable customary international law norm, and cannot be easily dismissed.[88] It is true that there are inherent methodological problems with customary international law, namely issues related to its formation and deconstruction,[89] and a troubling "reality of multicausality,"[90] which Glennon refers to as the "epistemological hurdle presented by veiled and crisscrossed causation."[91] As Glennon notes, "how much impact a legal norm actually has in shaping the outcome in any given incident can never be accurately measured."[92] There is much to commend this argument, but exploring recent examples of the enunciated views of diverse States on the freedom fighters versus terrorists debate, in the legally-telling fora in which they have been conveyed and argued, demonstrates the extent of the continuing disjuncture in understanding.

Consider, for example, a 2006 statement on behalf of the Group of African States in the General Assembly that stressed a "clear distinction between terrorism and the legitimate struggle for freedom and independence

---

[88] *See* Nicaragua, *supra* note 20, at 97 (stating that, "[i]n view of this conclusion, the Court has next to consider what are the rules of customary international law applicable to the present dispute. For this purpose, it has to direct its attention to the practice and *opinio juris* of States; as the Court recently observed, 'It is of course axiomatic that the material of customary international law is to be looked for primarily in the actual practice and *opinio juris* of States, even though multilateral conventions may have an important role to play in recording and defining rules deriving from custom, or indeed in developing them.' (*Continental Shelf* (*Libyan Arab Jamahiriya/Malta*), *I.C.J. Reports 1985,* pp. 29-30, Para. 27.)").

[89] *See* Michael Glennon, *Does International Law Matter?*, 2004 A.S.I.L. PROC. 315, 316 n. 4.

[90] *Ibid.* at 315 (continuing by arguing that "[n]either the believers nor the deniers recognize that *multiple factors almost always affect the decisions of policymakers*. In very few situations, probably, is international law wholly determinative of what a state does; but in very few situations, probably, is international law wholly irrelevant.").

[91] Michael J. Glennon, *How International Rules Die*, 93(3) GEO. L.J. 939, 975 (2005).

[92] Glennon, *Does International Law Matter?*, *supra* note 89, at 316. *But see* Thomas M. Franck, *The Power of Legitimacy and the Legitimacy of Power: International Law in an Age of Power Disequilibrium*, 100(1) AM. J. INT'L L. 88 (2006) (cautioning against such an approach).

[. . .] of people under foreign occupation or colonial rule."[93] It also cannot be overlooked that a number of State delegations at the *ad hoc* Committee's ninth session during the spring of 2005 argued that any treaty aiming to comprehensively define terrorism needed to clearly differentiate it from the "legitimate struggle of peoples for self-determination. [. . .] According to that view, the fight against terrorism should not undermine the right to self-determination or lead to violations of human rights."[94] Discussions at the 1998 Rome Conference also revealed a lack of international consensus on terrorism's legal essence, the debate there being so fractious, in fact, that terrorism was excluded as a separate crime before the International Criminal Court (ICC).[95]

As another example of the persistent differentiation between freedom fighters and terrorists by many States, it should be recalled that although

[93] Statement by His Excellency Mr. Crispin Grey-Johnson, Ambassador and Permanent Representative of the Gambia to the United Nations, Chairman of the Group of the African States, Under Agenda Item 100 of the Sixth Committee, "Measures for the Elimination of International Terrorism," New York 1 (12 October 2006) (on file with author). In 1999, Cuba asserted in the same body a "necessary distinction between acts of terrorism and the right of peoples to struggle for their self-determination and against domination or foreign occupation." U.N. GAOR, at 7, U.N. Doc. A/54/PV.76 (1999) (speech by Cuba). For a similar view, see Statement by Mr. Hassan Saleh, Counsellor, at the Sixth Committee, 61st Session of the United Nations General Assembly on Agenda Item 100, "Measures to Eliminate International Terrorism" (12 October 2006) (on file with author). It should be noted that ICJ Judge Hisashi Owada has questioned whether suicide bombings of civilians should be considered acts of terrorism, acts which he has dismissingly described as "so-called terrorist attacks by Palestinian suicide bombers against the Israeli civilian population." Legal Consequences of the Construction of a Wall in the Occupied Palestinian Territory (Advisory Opinion), 2004 I.C.J., at Para. 31 (Owada, J., separate).

[94] REPORT (28 MARCH-1 APRIL 2005), *supra* note 15, at Annex I, at 20. *See* Statement of His Excellency Prof. Ekmeleddin Ihsanoglu, Secretary-General of the Organization of the Islamic Conference, at the High-Level Plenary Meeting of the United Nations General Assembly 2 (16 September 2005), *available at* http://www.un.org/webcast/summit2005/statements16/islamic050916eng.pdf (stressing a need for sensitivity to liberation movements); Saul, *Attempts*, *supra* note 4, at 78 (expressing the similar view of the OIC, the Non-Aligned Movement, and Arab States).

[95] *See* Patrick Robinson, *Jurisdiction* Ratione Materiae: *The Missing Crimes*, in 1 THE ROME STATUTE OF THE INTERNATIONAL CRIMINAL COURT: A COMMENTARY 497, 517-18 (Antonio Cassese et al. eds., 2002). *See also* Saul, *Attempts*, *supra* note 4, at 73-74 (highlighting States' split views on terrorism within the context of the 1998 Rome Statute of the International Criminal Court and the International Criminal Court).

the more recent international treaties related to terrorism do not in a wholesale fashion exclude freedom fighters from their purview several of the older ones do and that many of the regional treaties either explicitly or implicitly exclude freedom fighters in some respect. The Egyptian, Jordanian, and Syrian reservations and declarations to the International Convention for the Suppression of the Financing of Terrorism[96] provide yet further evidence of the fundamental distinction that many States draw between freedom fighters and terrorists.[97]

As the ICJ has stated, albeit in a different context,

> "[a] further confirmation [that Article 2(4) of the United Nations Charter's prohibition on the use of force[98] extends beyond treaty law . . .] may be found in the fact that it is frequently referred to in statements by State representatives as being not only a principle of customary international law but also a fundamental or cardinal principle of such law."[99]

These examples reject any "further confirmation." *Opinio juris* on the definitional question has not crystallised to the extent that Cassese asserts, and this is necessarily fatal to any sustainable comprehensive definition of terrorism under customary international law.

Another shortcoming with Cassese's approach is more methodological than substantive. He arrives at his three-part definition by looking at General Assembly Resolution 49/60. Because customary international law requires an exhaustive and contextualised examination of State practice and *opinio juris*, not simply scrutiny of a General Assembly Resolution, this approach is not without its methodological flaws.

---

[96] Terrorist Financing Convention, *supra* note 59.

[97] *See* Egypt, Reservation and Declaration, Terrorist Financing Convention, *supra* note 59, Ref. No. C.N.176.2005.TREATIES-3, 1 March 2005; Jordan, Declaration, Terrorist Financing Convention, *supra* note 59, Ref. No. C.N.910.2003.TREATIES-32, 28 August 2003; Syrian Arab Republic, Reservation and Declaration, Terrorist Financing Convention, *supra* note 59, Ref. No. C.N.326.2005.TREATIES-6, 24 April 2005.

[98] According to this article, "[a]ll Members shall refrain in their international relations from the threat or use of force against the territorial integrity or political independence of any state, or in any other manner inconsistent with the Purposes of the United Nations." U.N. CHARTER Art. 2, Para. 4.

[99] Nicaragua, *supra* note 20, at 100.

Somewhat related to this, if one were to adopt a comparativist, least common denominator approach to the question whether customary international law supports a comprehensive definition of terrorism by using a Venn diagram and its overlapping circles, each circle of which separately could be said to represent the definition of terrorism contained in, for example, Security Council Resolution 1566,[100] General Assembly Resolution 60/43,[101] *A More Secure World: Our Shared Responsibility: Report of the Secretary-General's High-Level Panel on Threats, Challenges, and Change (High-Level Panel) (A More Secure World)*,[102] the International Convention for the Suppression of Acts of Nuclear Terrorism,[103] and the draft core

---

100 S.C. Res. 1566, U.N. SCOR, at 2, U.N. Doc. S/RES/1566 (2004) (defining terrorism as "criminal acts, including against civilians, committed with the intent to cause death or serious bodily injury, or taking of hostages, with the purpose to provoke a state of terror in the general public or in a group of persons or particular persons, intimidate a population or compel a government or an international organization to do or to abstain from doing any act, which constitute offences within the scope of and as defined in the international conventions and protocols relating to terrorism."). *See* Saul, *Definition*, *supra* note 9, at 164-65.

101 *See* definition *supra* note 83.

102 *See* A MORE SECURE WORLD, *supra* note 4, at 52 (defining terrorism as "any action, in addition to actions already specified by the existing conventions on aspects of terrorism, the Geneva Conventions and Security Council resolution 1566 (2004), that is intended to cause death or serious bodily harm to civilians or non-combatants, when the purpose of such act, by its nature or context, is to intimidate a population, or to compel a Government or an international organization to do or to abstain from doing any act."). A number of delegations at the *ad hoc* Committee's ninth session during the spring of 2005 expressed what they perceived to be this definition's shortcomings. They noted, for example, that it did not suffice as a "technical definition appropriate for a criminal law instrument." REPORT (28 MARCH-1 APRIL 2005), *supra* note 15, at Annex II, at 24. Furthermore, it failed to address related crimes of, for instance, conspiracy and participation. *See ibid.* For a similar definition to that contained in *A More Secure World*, see IN LARGER FREEDOM: TOWARDS DEVELOPMENT, SECURITY AND HUMAN RIGHTS FOR ALL: REPORT OF THE SECRETARY-GENERAL, U.N. GAOR, at 26, U.N. Doc. A/59/2005 (2005).

103 *See* G.A. Res. 59/290, U.N. GAOR, Annex, at 5, Art. 6, U.N. Doc. A/RES/59/290 (2005) (requiring States parties to take necessary steps to "ensure that criminal acts within the scope of this Convention, in particular where they are intended or calculated to provoke a state of terror in the general public or in a group of persons or particular persons, are under no circumstances justifiable by considerations of a political, philosophical, ideological, racial, ethnic, religious or other similar nature and are punished by penalties consistent with their grave nature."). For an account of the concerns expressed at drafting stage, see Saul, *Attempts*, *supra* note 4, at 74-76.

crime as constructed and being debated before the *ad hoc* Committee,[104] a definition would result that would, generally-speaking, resemble the three-part definition that Cassese asserts as being recognised by customary international law.

Undoubtedly, this would, and does, provide a helpful definitional compass, but arriving at customary international law through such a process also cannot be methodologically sustained. Saul makes a similar point in reviewing historical attempts to comprehensively define terrorism in treaty form when he states that, "[w]hile these sources do not carry great weight as evidence of customary law, they illustrate the recurring normative and political disputes surrounding definition and elucidate the basic features of terrorism, as perceived by different actors in the international legal system."[105] It is precisely because of these "recurring normative and political disputes surrounding definition" that customary international law is unable to support a comprehensive definition of terrorism.

C. General Principles

Although treaty law and customary international law do not recognise a comprehensive definition of terrorism, recourse can still be had to a third source of law, namely "general principles of law recognized by civilized nations."[106] Mosler and Oellers-Frahm refer to these as the "corresponding

---

[104] The draft core crime reads: "1. Any person commits an offence within the meaning of the present Convention if that person, by any means, unlawfully and intentionally, causes: (a) Death or serious bodily injury to any person; or (b) Serious damage to public or private property, including a place of public use, a State or government facility, a public transportation system, an infrastructure facility or to the environment; or (c) Damage to property, places, facilities or systems referred to in paragraph 1(b) of the present article resulting or likely to result in major economic loss; when the purpose of the conduct, by its nature or context, is to intimidate a population, or to compel a Government or an international organization to do or to abstain from doing any act." LETTER DATED 3 AUGUST 2005 FROM THE CHAIRMAN OF THE SIXTH COMMITTEE ADDRESSED TO THE PRESIDENT OF THE GENERAL ASSEMBLY, U.N. GAOR, Annex, Appendix II, at 9, Art. 2(1), U.N. Doc. A/59/894 (2005).

[105] Saul, *Attempts*, *supra* note 4, at 58. Commenting on treaties related to terrorism, Friedrichs makes a similar point, noting that, "in the absence of an overarching legal framework[, they . . .] do not agglomerate into a coherent whole." Friedrichs, *supra* note 4, at 71.

[106] I.C.J. STAT. Art. 38(1)(c). On general principles, see Hermann Mosler & Karin Oellers-Frahm, *The International Court of Justice*, in 2 THE CHARTER OF THE UNITED NATIONS: A COMMENTARY 1139, 1159-60 (Bruno Simma et al. eds., 2nd ed. 2002).

rules of the internal legal systems of the world,"[107] and according to Hailbronner and Klein, general principles "originate in concordant national laws, which by way of analogy and comparison become a component of international law. They also include concepts which have developed as principles of form and models of behaviour for new factual conditions in the international legal community."[108] As examples of general principles, Bassiouni refers to good faith, equality, justice, fairness, a preference for treaty interpretation based on plain meaning, and territory as a jurisdictional basis for criminal investigation and prosecution.[109]

The Permanent Court of International Justice (PCIJ)'s and the ICJ's jurisprudence[110] both support a test for recognising a particular general principle as requiring "that the [underlying] rule [. . .] exist in a number of States, but the rule does not have to meet the test of 'universal acceptance,' and no quantitative or numerical test for States having such a 'principle' has ever been established."[111] The wooliness that characterises this discernment of general principles, as well as serious discrepancies regarding the appraisal, identification, application, ranking, content, and enforceability of these rules,[112] makes general principles a particularly frustrating and problematic source of law. In short, there is no methodological consensus.[113] Delmas-Marty, commenting on international criminal tribunals' re-

---

[107] Mosler & Oellers-Frahm, *supra* note 106, at 1160. Bassiouni provides a similar definition, as a "common denominator of certain basic principles embodied in national legal systems which, because of their commonality, rise to an internationally enforceable level." Bassiouni, *A Functional Approach*, *supra* note 19, at 816-17.

[108] Konstanz Hailbronner & Eckart Klein, *The General Assembly: Functions and Powers: Articles 10-12*, in 1 THE CHARTER OF THE UNITED NATIONS: A COMMENTARY 257, 271 (Bruno Simma et al. eds., 2nd ed. 2002). *Cf.* Rome Statute of the International Criminal Court, Rome, 17 July 1998, Art. 21(1)(c) (stating as a source of applicable law "general principles of law derived by the Court from national laws of legal systems of the world including, as appropriate, the national laws of States that would normally exercise jurisdiction over the crime, provided that those principles are not inconsistent with this Statute and with international law and internationally recognized norms and standards."); SCHABAS, *supra* note 19, at 73.

[109] *See* Bassiouni, *A Functional Approach*, *supra* note 19, at 772.

[110] *See ibid.* at 791-99.

[111] *Ibid.* at 788.

[112] *See ibid.* at 816.

[113] *See ibid.* at 809.

course to general principles, highlights this ambiguity and stresses the possible resulting abuse of this source of law to serve pre-determined ends.[114]

The debate whether a comprehensive definition of terrorism exists under international law requires substantive fleshing out and guidance, and since general principles mostly inform procedural, as opposed to substantive, rules,[115] it is more convincing to refer to the core sources of treaty law and customary international law to arrive at substantive, and sustainable, definitional understanding. This is in addition to the methodological concerns already raised, as regards the appraisal, identification, application, ranking, content, and enforceability of general principles. Furthermore, as most scholars regard the usefulness of general principles as being of "fairly limited scope,"[116] it is doubtful that what effectively would be recourse to national laws on the definitional question could produce a convincing result. It is likely that any attempt to define terrorism according to general principles would be regarded, and correctly, as surreptitious and manipulative, as attempting to resort to a source of law for what Bassiouni would regard as merely "self-serving support."[117] For these reasons, one must reject the idea that general principles are a persuasive source for a comprehensive definition of terrorism.

---

[114] *See* Mireille Delmas-Marty, *The ICC and the Interaction of International and National Legal Systems*, in 2 THE ROME STATUTE OF THE INTERNATIONAL CRIMINAL COURT: A COMMENTARY 1915, 1917 (Antonio Cassese et al. eds., 2002).

[115] *See* MALCOLM N. SHAW, INTERNATIONAL LAW 94-99 (5th ed. 2004). *But see* Delmas-Marty, *supra* note 114, at 1917 (arguing that the international criminal tribunals' jurisprudence has arrived at general principles on issues of both substantive criminal law, including the parameters of mitigating circumstances and the essence of criminal participation and rape, and criminal procedure, such as regards plea bargaining and evidentiary rules).

[116] SHAW, *supra* note 115, at 94. Schabas notes that international law has historically relegated general principles to a "rather marginal significance." SCHABAS, *supra* note 19, at 72. "In practice, both the PCIJ and ICJ have been cautious and have often restricted 'General Principles' to a limited role that some would see as a subsidiary function, though nothing in the drafting history of the two courts' Statutes warrants that interpretation. However, one cannot rely on the caution of the courts as evidence that they intended to place 'General Principles' in a subsidiary position to other sources of international law." Bassiouni, *A Functional Approach*, *supra* note 19, at 800.

[117] Bassiouni, *A Functional Approach*, *supra* note 19, at 817 (arguing that, absent methodological agreement, "protagonists for different philosophical propositions will rely on what they consider to be 'General Principles' for self-serving support. This practice does not aid in making the law more certain.").

III. Assessment

Thus, this research ultimately rejects the idea that international law at present comprehensively defines terrorism in a legally obligatory way and without reference to international treaties related to terrorism. Since the United Nations is pushing for a comprehensive definition within the *ad hoc* Committee, this section addresses the traditional stumbling blocks to finalising a comprehensive treaty, namely the questions of State terrorism and the relationship, if any, between freedom fighters and terrorists.

A. State Terrorism

A More Secure World dismissed the argument surrounding State terrorism because, according to it, the "legal and normative framework against State violations is far stronger than in the case of non-State actors."[118] The High-Level Panel cited the Geneva Conventions, the United Nations Charter, and the 1998 Rome Statute of the ICC as forming part of a corpus of laws and norms that regulate States' use of force and conduct during war.[119] It recommended that the preamble to any comprehensive treaty on terrorism should note that a number of instruments, including the Geneva Conventions, regulate the use of force by States against civilians and that such action could, on particular facts and circumstances, constitute crimes against humanity or war crimes[120] and that such a treaty should state that the acts of terrorism prohibited by the international treaties related to terrorism constitute international crimes and that the Geneva Conventions and their Protocols prohibit in times of armed conflict acts of terrorism.[121]

---

[118] A More Secure World, *supra* note 4, at 51.

[119] *See ibid.*

[120] *See ibid.* at 52.

[121] *See ibid. See also* Specific Human Rights Issues, *supra* note 4, at 10-11; Galić, *supra* note 34, at 26-49. A number of delegations at the ninth session of the *ad hoc* Committee during the spring of 2005, however, questioned the sufficiency of the current international legal framework regarding State terrorism. *See* Report (28 March-1 April 2005), *supra* note 15, at Annex I, at 20. It should be noted, furthermore, that the Rome Statute decided against including terrorism as a war crime and does not acknowledge terrorism outside of an armed conflict environment. *See* Saul, *Crimes and Prohibitions*, *supra* note 73, at 271. Dugard, however, describes the Rome Statute as "another multi-lateral convention directed at the suppression of international terrorism." Dugard, *supra* note 2, at 202.

According to a study conducted under the auspices of the International Committee of the Red Cross, customary international law prohibits in armed conflicts of both an international and non-international nature those "[a]cts or threats of violence the primary purpose of which is to spread terror among the civilian population."[122] Ethiopian Emperor Haile Sellassie I's graphic account of Italian mustard gassing of Ethiopia just prior to the Second World War, as a "work of cruelty, carried out with some finesse [. . . that] annihilated people in places far removed from the battlefield and made their country into a desert. The plan was to spread terror and death over the greater part of Ethiopia,"[123] comes to mind as an example of this within the context of armed conflict.

Outside of armed conflict, of course, international humanitarian law does not govern State action. United Nations Special Rapporteur on Human Rights and Terrorism of the Sub-Commission on the Promotion and Protection of Human Rights Kalliopi K. Koufa argues that international human rights law, international criminal law, and municipal law circumscribe acts of terrorism committed by States in non-armed conflict environments.[124] Certainly, Koufa is correct that these areas of law criminalise certain types of State behaviour. It should be stressed, however, that while certain State actions outside of armed conflict may be crimes it oversimplifies the matter to then automatically conclude that these crimes must necessarily be considered crimes of terrorism as a matter of international law.

---

[122] INTERNATIONAL COMMITTEE OF THE RED CROSS, *supra* note 76, at 8 (bold in original).

[123] HAILE SELLASSIE I, MY LIFE AND ETHIOPIA'S PROGRESS: VOLUME ONE 301 (Edward Ullendorff trans., Frontline Dist. Int'l, Inc. 2003). "This most deplorable scheme was eventually accomplished. Man and beast perished completely. The deadly downpour that descended from the aircraft made anyone who touched it fly with torment. Those who drank the water upon which this poisonous rain had settled or ate the food which the poison had touched died in dreadful agony. The people who died as a result of the Italian yperite must be reckoned in many thousands. It was to make known to the civilized world the torment inflicted upon the Ethiopian people that I decided to come to Geneva." *Ibid.* at 301-02.

[124] *See* SPECIFIC HUMAN RIGHTS ISSUES, *supra* note 4, at 10 (asserting that "'terrorism' and 'acts of terrorism' committed in 'peacetime' (i.e. in situations which cannot be classified as armed conflicts) are accommodated (i.e. covered or outlawed) by other legal regimes. These other legal regimes, including, for instance, national legislation, international criminal law and human rights may, of course, also apply or overlap during armed conflict."). "Terrorism can occur during armed conflict or during peacetime (defined as the non-existence of armed conflict)." Scharf, *supra* note 24, at 392.

Further on the State terrorism issue, it should be noted that United Nations bodies have condemned State terrorism and, in so doing, have necessarily acknowledged that States can commit acts of terrorism, even if these same bodies have yet to comprehensively define terrorism in a legally obligatory way and without reference to international treaties related to terrorism. For example, the General Assembly expressly mentioned State terrorism in 1970.[125] It has also denounced "repressive and terrorist acts by colonial, racist and alien régimes in denying peoples their legitimate right to self-determination and independence and other human rights and fundamental freedoms"[126] and recognised State terrorism in a 1984 Resolution that "[*r*]*esolutely condemns* policies and practices of terrorism in relations between States as a method of dealing with other States and peoples."[127] For its part, the Security Council has stated that "the suppression of acts of international terrorism, including those in which States are directly or indirectly involved, is essential for the maintenance of international peace and security."[128] It has also condemned particular States on the basis of terrorist ties.[129]

B. **Freedom Fighters or Terrorists?**

The other traditional stumbling block to finalising a comprehensive treaty on terrorism, the relationship, if any, between freedom fighters and terrorists, requires examination of the relativist view that "one person's terrorism is another person's freedom fighter."[130] In many ways, this view has re-

---

[125] *See* G.A. Res. 2625, U.N. GAOR, Annex, at 123, U.N. Doc. A/RES/2625 (1970) (stating that "[e]very State has the duty to refrain from organizing, instigating, assisting or participating in acts of civil strife or terrorist acts in another State or acquiescing in organized activities within its territory directed towards the commission of such acts, when the acts referred to in the present paragraph involve a threat or use of force.").

[126] G.A. Res. 34/145, U.N. GAOR, at 244, U.N. Doc. A/RES/34/145 (1979).

[127] G.A. Res. 39/159, U.N. GAOR, at 99, U.N. Doc. A/RES/39/159 (1984).

[128] S.C. Res. 748, *supra* note 77, at Preamble.

[129] *See* Bianchi, *supra* note 13, at 498; Saul, *Definition*, *supra* note 9, at 149-51; Allain, *supra* note 6, at 102-08; Bassiouni, *Legal Control*, *supra* note 15, at 96-97.

[130] Mishra rejects this view, arguing that it may be true, but only "to the same extent as it is true to say that both Adolf Hitler and Mother Teresa had many admirers, as if barbarism and humanism were a matter of culinary or sartorial taste." MISHRA, *supra* note 1, at 15. Orwell makes a similar criticism of left-wing intellectuals and Nazism, predicting that "they

sulted from, perhaps understandable, popular frustration to the way in which descriptive language has been used, and abused, by States and their violent opposition. Chomsky refers to this idea in his account of Kosovo and American and British perspectives.[131] According to him, after the United States and the United Kingdom determined that they would attack Serbia, "the 'terrorists' instantly became 'freedom fighters.' After the war, the 'freedom fighters' and their close associates became 'terrorists,' 'thugs,' and 'murderers' as they carried out what from their point of view are similar actions for similar reasons in Macedonia, a U.S. ally."[132]

Although often repeated, the view that "one person's terrorist is another person's freedom fighter" suffers from a number of flaws. Schachter, for example, argues that it misses the point and that, while it "may well be true[, . . .] it does not mean that a person 'fighting for freedom' can not [sic] be a terrorist."[133] He would likely agree that it is too simple to rhetorically ask, as Dugard does, "Are the Israel Defense Forces (IDF) engaged in lawful military action or in state terror? Are the Palestinian militants and suicide bombers terrorists or freedom fighters?"[134] Bassiouni agrees that freedom fighters can employ terrorist means.[135] At a basic level, the insistence that "one person's terrorist is another person's freedom fighter" pre-

---

will proceed to argue that, after all, democracy is 'just the same as' or 'just as bad as' totalitarianism. There is *not much* freedom of speech in England; therefore there is *no more* than exists in Germany. To be on the dole is a horrible experience; therefore it is *no worse* to be in the torture-chambers of the Gestapo. In general, two blacks make a white, half a loaf is the same as no bread." GEORGE ORWELL, *The Lion and the Unicorn*, in WHY I WRITE 11, 89-90 (2004).

131 *See* NOAM CHOMSKY, *Civilizations East and West*, in 9-11 71, 91 (2002). For further on Kosovo and descriptions of the actors, see Saul, *Definition*, *supra* note 9, at 152.

132 CHOMSKY, *Civilizations East and West, supra* note 131, at 91. On the Kosovo Liberation Army and an argument that a "[terrorism] definition would have to be open-ended enough so as to govern *future perceptions* of enemy," see Petman, *supra* note 3, at 238.

133 Schachter, *supra* note 57, at 244.

134 Dugard, *supra* note 2, at 198-99. For a perspective similar to Dugard's in this regard, see Petman, *supra* note 3, at 237-38. On Palestinian suicide bombing, see Tarik Kafala & Martin Asser, *Analysis: Palestinian Suicide Attacks,* BBC NEWS, *available at* http://news.bbc.co.uk/2/hi/middle_east/3256858.stm (last updated 17 April 2006).

135 *See* Bassiouni, *Legal Control*, *supra* note 15, at 97 (stating that, "[w]hile the term 'terrorism' clashed with the legitimacy of such a right to engage in a way of national liberation or to topple dictatorial regimes, it properly described the means employed to those ends.").

sumes that freedom fighters and terrorists fall into exclusive categories without overlap.

A useful starting point on this question is to ask whether the violent non-State actors at issue qualify as freedom fighters. If they do, then they must comply with international humanitarian law.[136] This would clearly not be met if they did not attempt to distinguish between military and civilian targets.[137] As ICJ Judge Pieter Hendrik Kooijmans has noted, "[d]eliberate and indiscriminate attacks against civilians with the intention to kill are the core element of terrorism."[138]

If this understanding of the law is applied to historical examples of freedom fighting, it becomes clear that freedom fighters can act as terrorists, in the sense that they can commit acts of terrorism. The failure of Algerian psychiatrist and scholar of decolonisation Frantz Fanon to distinguish between military and civilian targets, asserting that "[t]he Frenchman in Algeria cannot be neutral or innocent. Every Frenchman in Algeria oppresses, despises, dominates. [. . .] Every Frenchman in Algeria is at the present time an enemy soldier,"[139] for example, is troubling in this respect from a twenty-first century international humanitarian law perspective. An examination of the French Resistance's tactics during the Second World War and the tactics of the National Liberation Front in Algeria and the regimes that

---

136 *See* Dinstein, *Terrorism*, *supra* note 85, at 67-68.

137 Although international law permits freedom fighters to engage in armed struggle, these fighters are not permitted to act *carte blanche*. *See* Subedi, *supra* note 4, at 165; SPECIFIC HUMAN RIGHTS ISSUES, *supra* note 4, at 11-13.

138 Wall, *supra* note 93, at Para. 5 (Kooijmans, J., separate). In addressing the question of freedom fighters, *A More Secure World* noted that "there is nothing in the fact of occupation that justifies the targeting and killing of civilians." A MORE SECURE WORLD, *supra* note 4, at 51. *See* IN LARGER FREEDOM, *supra* note 102, at 26 (stating that "the right to resist occupation must be understood in its true meaning. It cannot include the right to deliberately kill or maim civilians."); UNITING AGAINST TERRORISM: RECOMMENDATIONS FOR A GLOBAL COUNTER-TERRORISM STRATEGY: REPORT OF THE SECRETARY-GENERAL, U.N. GAOR, at 3, U.N. Doc. A/60/825 (2006) (asserting that the right to self-determination, a "fundamental right defined in the Charter of the United Nations[,] does not excuse deliberately killing or maiming civilians and non-combatants."); Wall, *supra* note 93, at Para. 19 (Higgins, J., separate) (arguing that "the protection of civilians remains an intransgressible obligation of humanitarian law, not only for the occupier but equally for those seeking to liberate themselves from occupation.").

139 FRANTZ FANON, TOWARD THE AFRICAN REVOLUTION 91 (Haakon Chevalier trans., Pelican Bks. 1970).

resulted in each case, it has been argued, reveals a symmetry between means and ends.[140] As such, it is unhelpful and erroneous to suggest that "[t]hose groups most likely to be exempt from the 'terrorism' charge are those struggling for national liberation against 'foreign occupation' of their own land"[141] or that "[t]he *cause* is the very thing that separates a freedom fighter from a terrorist."[142] Such groups are no less autonomous or capable of terrorising under international humanitarian law than any other actor, State or non-State.

Consider, as well, the struggle against South African apartheid, an African liberation struggle that was distinct from Fanon's Algeria.[143] The Truth and Reconciliation Commission of South Africa (TRC) recognised the African National Congress (ANC), which the international community acknowledged as a liberation movement engaged in legitimate armed struggle against apartheid,[144] as having been generally compliant with the Geneva law in both word and deed during its struggle.[145] The ANC's waging of war had, however, "in the course of the conflict, contravened the Geneva Protocols and [meant that the ANC] was responsible for the commission of gross human rights violations."[146]

The TRC examined the ANC's actions with regard to attacks carried out by Umkhonto we Sizwe, its military wing, on military and civilian targets,

---

140 *See* Benjamin Netanyahu, *Defining Terrorism,* in TERRORISM: HOW THE WEST CAN WIN 7, 12-13 (Benjamin Netanyahu ed., 1986). *See also ibid.* at 12 (stating that "[i]t is not only that the ends of terrorists do not justify the means they choose. It is that the choice of means indicates what the true ends are."). The cases of Libya, Iran, Cuba, Cambodia, Angola, and Vietnam have been cited in similar vein. *See* Benzion Netanyahu, *Terrorists and Freedom Fighters,* in TERRORISM, *ibid.*, at 25, 28.

141 Graham, *supra* note 14, at 40.

142 Petman, *supra* note 3, at 239.

143 *See* ALAN M. DERSHOWITZ, WHY TERRORISM WORKS: UNDERSTANDING THE THREAT, RESPONDING TO THE CHALLENGE 7 (2002) (noting that the anti-apartheid movement committed acts of terrorism).

144 *See* TRUTH AND RECONCILIATION COMMISSION OF SOUTH AFRICA REPORT 642, *available at* http://www.info.gov.za/otherdocs/2003/trc/rep.pdf (released 21 March 2003).

145 *See ibid.* (recognising the "commitment of the ANC to upholding the Geneva Protocols as well as its comparative restraint in conducting the armed struggle – at least in terms of the manner in which it identified its targets and its leadership's decision to instruct its cadres to abandon the landmine campaign when it became clear that it was resulting in the deaths and injuries of innocent civilians.").

146 *Ibid.*

indiscriminate and unplanned attacks on targets that contravened official ANC policy and that affected civilians, planned armed operations that did not go as planned and that resulted in civilian deaths, and the intentional targeting of alleged traitors[147] and found that they amounted to grave breaches of the Geneva law.[148] The ANC in exile also committed torture on a regular basis and generally failed to extend due process to suspected saboteurs, actions which also contravened the Geneva law.[149]

The actions of the United Democratic Front (UDF), an anti-apartheid organisation, were also critically examined by the TRC. The TRC found that UDF supporters and members of affiliated organisations had violently enforced boycotts and strikes, burned and destroyed homes and property, and committed acts of violence against, to the point of death in some cases, political opponents.[150]

As an example of the politically-motivated violence that these freedom fighters perpetrated, the TRC noted the following:

> Amnesty was also sought for an incident in which a police officer, Mr Benjamin Masinga, was killed by members of UDF affiliated organisations. Masinga was taken from his house, attacked with sticks, stones, bricks and axes rendering him unconscious. He was dragged to a nearby school, was doused with petrol and was then set alight.[151]

Although police officers can be considered legitimate military targets when they engage in hostilities or when there has been an official incorporation

---

[147] *See ibid.* at 650. As examples, the TRC cited the Church Street bombing in 1983 and the 1985 bombing of the Amanzimtoti shopping centre. *See ibid.* at 649.

[148] *See ibid.* at 650-51.

[149] *See ibid.* at 660-61.

[150] *See ibid.* at 655. The TRC stated that "[t]here is no evidence of UDF leadership encouraging killing or the commission of gross human rights violations. It is also clear from the testimony before the Commission that they did not play an active role in the commission of gross human rights violations. However, the general clarion call that they made to make the townships ungovernable and to eliminate those who collaborated led to the commission of gross human rights violations for which the leadership of the UDF must accept responsibility." *Ibid.* at 658.

[151] *Ibid.* at 657. For the decision on amnesty in this case, see Amnesty Committee, Truth and Reconciliation Commission of South Africa, Dec. No. AC/2001/147, *available at* http://www.doj.gov.za/trc/decisions/2001/ac21147.htm (2001).

of them into a State's armed forces,[152] the violent acts against Masinga, being as extreme as they were and because they were so obviously intended to horrify, "so that his death may be known,"[153] arguably amount to terrorism under international humanitarian law.[154]

Like its examination of the ANC, the TRC's examination of the UDF demonstrates that freedom fighters, or those non-State actors whom international law recognises as being able, in principle, to lawfully engage in anti-State violence, can act as terrorists, at least in the sense of being able to commit acts of terrorism as understood by international humanitarian law.

---

152 *See* YORAM DINSTEIN, THE CONDUCT OF HOSTILITIES UNDER THE LAW OF INTERNATIONAL ARMED CONFLICT 95 (2004).

153 Amnesty Committee, *supra* note 151.

154 For a similar argument that acts of terrorism can be committed against combatants, see Saul, *Crimes and Prohibitions*, *supra* note 73, at 271. *See also* TAL BECKER, TERRORISM AND THE STATE: RETHINKING THE RULES OF STATE RESPONSIBILITY 102 (2006); *ibid.* at 102 n. 79. Arguably, the ICTY has also acknowledged, or at least not categorically rejected, this possibility, as it has stated that, "[w]ith respect to the 'acts of violence', these do not include *legitimate attacks against combatants* but only unlawful attacks against civilians." Galić, *supra* note 34, at 49 (emphasis added). Having said that, Falk's assertion that "[i]t is [. . .] misleading if anti-state political violence that is directed at military or government targets is described, as routinely occurs in the mainstream media, as terrorism," Richard Falk, *Human Rights: A Descending Spiral,* in HUMAN RIGHTS IN THE "WAR ON TERROR" 225, 226 (Richard Ashby Wilson ed., 2005), generally holds in situations in which international humanitarian law applies. Outside such contexts, by contrast, it is unclear that "anti-state political violence that is directed at military or government targets" can never be considered terrorism. Certainly, the April 1995 Oklahoma City bombing of the Alfred P. Murrah Federal Building must qualify as terrorism under any reasonable definition of the term. Perhaps even more importantly, the Security Council stated in Resolution 1368 that it "[*u*]*nequivocally condemns* in the strongest terms the horrifying terrorist attacks which took place on 11 September 2001 in New York, Washington, D.C. and Pennsylvania and *regards* such acts, like any act of international terrorism, as a threat to international peace and security." S.C. Res. 1368, U.N. SCOR, at 1, U.N. Doc. S/RES/1368 (2001). 11 September, of course, included an attack on the Pentagon, which Dinstein would describe as a military objective by its very nature, or "Ministries of Defence and any national, regional or local operational or coordination centres of command, control and communication relating to running the war (including computer centres, as well as telephone and telegraph exchanges, for military use)." DINSTEIN, CONDUCT, *supra* note 152, at 89. Given the approach according to which attacks by "illegitimate" freedom fighters on a State's security apparatus can be classified as acts of terrorism, see Colm Campbell, *Extradition to Northern Ireland: Prospects and Problems,* 52(5) MOD. L. REV. 585, 587-88 (1989), there is a need to "convince the international community that a campaign of violence against the established national order is legitimate." Graham, *supra* note 14, at 42.

Assuming that international humanitarian law applies to the use of force by particular non-State actors, those same actors can violate the law in the course of legitimate struggle. "[T]he fact that the liberation movements' cause was just does not mean that they were not required to act justly in the conduct of that war."[155] Even Chomsky, who is highly critical of Israeli policy, has acknowledged that Palestinian suicide bombers act as both freedom fighters and terrorists.[156]

When freedom fighters breach their duties under international humanitarian law on particular facts and circumstances that suggest acts of terrorism, then they should be considered perpetrators of acts of terrorism.[157] Since the hope is that these freedom fighters, once successful, will establish their own State, it arguably also makes sense as a matter of policy to expect them to bear some of the duties of statehood.[158] In fact, this is the position

---

[155] REPORT, *supra* note 144, at 647.

[156] *See Lateline: Bush Criticised for "Confused" Middle East Goals: Noam Chomsky Interviewed by Tony Jones*, 8 April 2002, *available at* http://www.chomsky.info/interviews/20020408.htm (stating that "[t]hey're trying to fight for freedom, but doing it in a totally unacceptable immoral way. Of course they're terrorists and there's been Palestinian terrorism all the way through."). *But see* Noam Chomsky, Amnesty International Annual Lecture, Hosted by Trinity College: "War on Terror" (18 January 2006), *available at* http://www.amnesty.ie/user/content/download/3898/20352/file/chomskylecture06.pdf (establishing separate analytical categories for aggression, terrorism, and resistance that is legitimate). Falk has also described suicide attacks on civilian targets as terrorism. *See* Falk, *supra* note 154, at 227 (stating that, "[a]ssuming the retention of terrorism as a descriptive term, *some* anti-state political violence is properly described as terrorism, as, for instance, suicide bombing of civilian targets.").

[157] *See* Subedi, *supra* note 4, at 163 (conveying the view of many States that a "terrorist activity remained a terrorist activity whether or not it was carried out in the exercise of the right of self determination."). *But see* Conor Gearty, *What is Terror?,* THE TIMES, 9 March 1991 (minimising the acts of terrorism that freedom fighters can commit when he states that "subversive terror is different in kind from the guerrilla-style violence that accompanied the liberation of the formerly colonised world. It does not necessarily embrace the activities of popularly supported groups like the PLO and the ANC, in so far as their actions form part of a carefully controlled struggle against illegal occupation or racist oppression.").

[158] *See* V. S. Mani, *Future Strategies in the War Against Terrorism and Proliferation of Weapons of Mass Destruction: An Indian Perspective,* 44(2) IND. J. INT'L L. 221, 241 (2004) (arguing that "those who cannot respect the human rights of the innocent individuals are obviously incapable of respecting the right of self-determination of peoples they claim to represent."); Eric A. Posner, *Terrorism and the Laws of War*, 5(2) CHI. J. INT'L L. 423, 432 (2005) (arguing that, "[i]f ordinary states can be expected to comply with the laws of war while fighting each other, then quasi-states, terrorist states, rogue states, and state-like terrorist organizations may be expected to do so as well.").

that the International Law Commission effectively takes in the 2001 *Articles on Responsibility of States for Internationally Wrongful Acts*.[159]

As a matter of international law, it is unhelpful to argue that "one person's terrorist is another's person's freedom fighter." Fraught with danger, assertions of this view only protect the interests of those who would rather not admit that freedom fighters can commit acts of terrorism and, in so doing, act as terrorists and those who cannot concede that those who engage in ideologically-attractive campaigns of violence that are not recognised by international law are not freedom fighters but, rather, likely terrorists.[160] As long as international law recognises freedom fighters' right to engage in armed struggle, it would be misleading to refer to them as terrorists, as long as, perhaps, the freedom fighters' terrorist acts do not so predominate as to swallow the *ius in bello*.[161] In a world threatened by terrorism, arguing otherwise may make for interesting polemic, but it obfuscates reality and obscures threats.

Having said all of this as regards freedom fighters and terrorists, one must be careful not to overlook the political dynamic according to which acts of violence associated with particular "root causes" continue to be glossed over, explained away, and selectively covered and condemned. Consider, for example, the 2006 *Report of the Special Rapporteur on the*

---

159 *See* International Law Commission, *Articles on Responsibility of States for Internationally Wrongful Acts*, in JAMES CRAWFORD, THE INTERNATIONAL LAW COMMISSION'S ARTICLES ON STATE RESPONSIBILITY: INTRODUCTION, TEXT AND COMMENTARIES 61, 62, at Art. 10 (2003) (2001) (stating that "1. The conduct of an insurrectional movement which becomes the new government of a State shall be considered an act of that State under international law. 2. The conduct of a movement, insurrectional or other, which succeeds in establishing a new State in part of the territory of a pre-existing State or in a territory under its administration shall be considered an act of the new State under international law. 3. This article is without prejudice to the attribution to a State of any conduct, however related to that of the movement concerned, which is to be considered an act of that State by virtue of articles 4 to 9.").

160 On this latter point, it is legally immaterial that, as Dugard asserts, "many in the Muslim world see Osama Bin Laden and Al Qaeda as freedom fighters, engaged in the task of liberating the Islamic world from a corrupt and decadent West." Dugard, *supra* note 2, at 189.

161 According to Koufa, "[a] group claiming to be using force in defence of self-determination, and whose 'military operations' are predominantly in violation of humanitarian law, could be considered a terrorist group, although an underlying claim of the people in question would not be affected." SPECIFIC HUMAN RIGHTS ISSUES, *supra* note 4, at 13.

Situation of Human Rights in the Palestinian Territories Occupied Since 1967 (*Report*).[162] In that document, Dugard described "F-16s flying low and breaking the sound barrier over Gaza, causing sonic booms that are as loud as the actual bombardments. These sonic booms have caused widespread terror among the population, particularly children. If terrorism has any meaning, then it is surely this."[163] As for the Palestinians' Qassam rockets, they were portrayed as being launched "indiscriminately into Israel, injuring Israeli civilians, damaging civilian infrastructure and causing fear among the civilian population living near the Gaza border."[164] While it was clear to Dugard that the F-16s' sonic booms "caused widespread terror among the population, particularly children. If terrorism has any meaning, then it is surely this," one wonders why the same conclusion as to terrorism could not have been so clearly drawn as regards the Qassam rockets being launched "indiscriminately into Israel, injuring Israeli civilians, damaging civilian architecture and causing fear among the civilian population living near the Gaza border."

Unfortunately, by its cursory analysis and conclusory approach, the *Report* leaves the reader unclear as to the substantive legal difference between causing terror and "merely" causing fear.[165] One might have preferred a more methodical, searching analysis, particularly given the sensitive nature of terrorism and the Israeli/Palestinian conflict, perhaps an analysis that would have seen Dugard carry out a careful assessment according to the international humanitarian law crime of terrorism as articulated in the ICTY's *Galić* decision.[166] However, as Bassiouni has argued, albeit in the context of *jus cogens*, "definition [can] leave[ ] open the differences of values, phi-

---

[162] REPORT OF THE SPECIAL RAPPORTEUR ON THE SITUATION OF HUMAN RIGHTS IN THE PALESTINIAN TERRITORIES OCCUPIED SINCE 1967, U.N. GAOR, U.N. Doc. A/HRC/2/5 (2006).

[163] *Ibid.* at 11.

[164] *Ibid.*

[165] In *Galić*, the ICTY equated "terror" and "extreme fear," see Galić, *supra* note 34, at 49, which equation itself begs the question of the substantive legal difference between "extreme fear" and "fear." On this case, see GUÉNAËL METTRAUX, INTERNATIONAL CRIMES AND THE *AD HOC* TRIBUNALS 127-29 (2006).

[166] Galić, *supra* note 34, at 49 (requiring proof "not only that the Accused accepted the likelihood that terror would result from the illegal acts – or, in other words, that he was aware of the possibility that terror would result – but that that was the result which he specifically intended.")

losophies, goals and strategies of those who claim the existence of the norm in a given situation and its applicability to a given case or controversy."[167]

IV. Conclusion

It is not an overstatement to say that "[d]efining 'terrorism' and identifying a 'terrorist' is perhaps the most complex and highly charged issue of modern times."[168] The fundamental definitional question will be seismically moved along if and when the *ad hoc* Committee completes the comprehensive treaty on terrorism.[169] At present, however, international law has yet to comprehensively define terrorism in a legally obligatory way and without reference to international treaties related to terrorism.[170]

Despite international lawyers' most optimistic of hopes, however, it would be unwise to find too much comfort, as Saul does, in the fact that "much of the argument about [definitional] exceptions is rhetorical or ideological,

---

[167] Bassiouni, *A Functional Approach*, *supra* note 19, at 805. Saul makes a similar point regarding the draft core crime as constructed and being debated before the *ad hoc* Committee. *See* Saul, *Attempts*, *supra* note 4, at 82-83 (arguing that "[t]he principal disadvantage of generic definition is the difficulty and subjectivity of proving motive elements, such as an aim to intimidate or compel, or a political motive."). He raises evidentiary problems related to understanding diverse motives and determining the intent behind particular acts of violence and favours a holistic approach that situates determinations of terrorism within a larger international humanitarian law context. *See* Saul, *Crimes and Prohibitions*, *supra* note 73, at 270-71. Saul finds promising psychiatry and considerations of the "degree of fear that a reasonable person, of ordinary mental firmness of mind, is expected to resist; as well as cultural, age and gender differences affecting the coping capacity of populations." *Ibid.* at 275-76.

[168] Graham, *supra* note 14, at 40.

[169] *But see* Dugard, *supra* note 2, at 202-05.

[170] Although Art. 2(1)(b) of the Terrorist Financing Convention residually defines terrorism in generic form, as "[a]ny other act intended to cause death or serious bodily injury to a civilian, or to any other person not taking an active part in the hostilities in a situation of armed conflict, when the purpose of such act, by its nature or context, is to intimidate a population, or to compel a Government or an international organization to do or to abstain from doing any act," Terrorist Financing Convention, *supra* note 59, at Art. 2(1)(b), treaty law properly understood requires that it be restricted to and interpreted within its unique treaty context. Dinstein argues that this definition "epitomizes the essence of terrorism." Dinstein, *Ius Ad Bellum Aspects*, *supra* note 21, at 14.

not substantive."[171] As a number of delegations expressed at the *ad hoc* Committee's tenth session during the spring of 2006, the extant disagreements are, indeed, inherently rooted in politics.[172] Without political consensus, however, legal understanding and cooperation can be neither sustained nor progressively developed. As Friedrichs argues, "as long as states do not agree on who the international public enemy is, it does not help very much to vest the problem in a legal cloak."[173]

Until political consensus emerges on the issue, the "[l]ack of agreement on a clear and well-known definition [. . . will continue to] undermine[ ] the normative and moral stance against terrorism and [. . .] stain[ ] the United Nations image."[174]

---

[171] Saul, *Attempts*, *supra* note 4, at 83. *See* SPECIFIC HUMAN RIGHTS ISSUES, *supra* note 4, at 7 (echoing Saul in that she describes the argument as involving "issues that have unfortunately become political rather than legal and, thus, continue to stand squarely in the middle of the political controversies impeding agreement on a definition."). According to Friedrichs, "as soon as one looks behind the technicalities of these reputedly legal debates, it becomes clear that the problem is at the centre of a political maelstrom." Friedrichs, *supra* note 4, at 70.

[172] *See* REPORT OF THE AD HOC COMMITTEE ESTABLISHED BY GENERAL ASSEMBLY RESOLUTION 51/210 OF 17 DECEMBER 1996: TENTH SESSION (27 FEBRUARY-3 MARCH 2006), U.N. GAOR, Annex I, at 6, U.N. Doc. A/61/37 (2006). *See also* Petman, *supra* note 3, at 237.

[173] Friedrichs, *supra* note 4, at 70.

[174] A MORE SECURE WORLD, *supra* note 4, at 51.

Chapter 3
THE DUE DILIGENCE PRINCIPLE UNDER INTERNATIONAL LAW

Chapter 3
THE DUE DILIGENCE PRINCIPLE UNDER INTERNATIONAL LAW

I. Introduction

There has been much talk in recent years of the role of non-State actors in an historically State-centric international legal order. Although much progress has been made on the law of State responsibility, particularly thanks to James Crawford's special rapporteurship on the project at the International Law Commission (ILC), there does not yet exist a corresponding comprehensive framework for the international responsibility of non-State actors. This may lead one to conclude that a lacuna exists in the law of responsibility.

This chapter explores the interface of State responsibility, non-State actors, and the due diligence principle. It begins by examining the various principles of responsibility under international law. After doing so, it closely considers the deliberations of the ILC on the topic of State responsibility. In light of these developments, attention is then paid to exactly what has been expected of States with regard to the activities of non-State actors during the last century. This overview focuses on the due diligence principle, a principle which, it is argued, can be restrictively or expansively interpreted, as the particular facts and circumstances require, to hold States responsible for their actions or omissions related to non-State actors.

II. Principles of Responsibility

It should come as little surprise that a legal regime as complex as international law should contain principles of responsibility as varied as they are fundamental.[1] While many of these principles have counterparts in munici-

[1] For the varied types of responsibility in the context of non-State terrorism, see Bertrand G. Ramcharan, *Terrorism and Non-State Organizations,* in Towards World Constitutionalism: Issues in the Legal Ordering of the World Community 681, 691 (Ronald St. John Macdonald & Douglas M. Johnston eds., 2005).

pal law contexts, they assume a unique character and personality at the level of international law.

Pisillo Mazzeschi identifies four main principles of responsibility.[2] First, there is fault-based responsibility.[3] Fault here is defined in subtly varied ways. Fault-based responsibility has historically required a finding of "psychological fault (wilful or negligent conduct) of the organs of the State accused of the wrongful act."[4] This historical formulation examines negligence, or *culpa,* or intent, or *dolus*.[5]

A more nuanced way of defining fault-based responsibility focuses on the underlying rules within a "regime of responsibility for breach of due diligence obligations (considering due diligence as an objective and international standard of behaviour)."[6] Cassese describes fault with reference to intent or recklessness.[7] It is also possible to think of *culpa* to "describe types of blameworthiness based upon reasonable foreseeability, or foresight without desire of consequences (recklessness, *culpa lata*)."[8]

Iwasawa and Nishimura present separate theories based on subjective fault and objective fault.[9] While the former theory "understands fault as an intention or choice on the part of the State in connection with actions or omissions that are involved in a breach of obligation, and this intention or choice is that of the State itself as an entity and not of an individual person operating as a State organ"[10] and while the latter theory understands fault as the "inappropriate or non-diligent nature of the acts judged in light of the

---

[2] *See* Riccardo Pisillo Mazzeschi, *Forms of International Responsibility for Environmental Harm*, in INTERNATIONAL RESPONSIBILITY FOR ENVIRONMENTAL HARM 15, 16-17 (Francesco Francioni & Tullio Scovazzi eds., 1991). *See also* F.V. García Amador, *State Responsibility: Some New Problems,* in 94(2) ACADÉMIE DE DROIT INTERNATIONAL DE LA HAYE: RECUEIL DES COURS 365, 382-92 (1958) (providing a helpful overview of the topic).

[3] *See* Pisillo Mazzeschi, *Forms of International Responsibility for Environmental Harm*, *supra* note 2, at 16.

[4] *Ibid.*

[5] *See* MALCOLM N. SHAW, INTERNATIONAL LAW 698 (5th ed. 2004).

[6] Pisillo Mazzeschi, *Forms of International Responsibility for Environmental Harm*, *supra* note 2, at 16.

[7] *See* ANTONIO CASSESE, INTERNATIONAL LAW 250-51 (2nd ed. 2005).

[8] IAN BROWNLIE, PRINCIPLES OF PUBLIC INTERNATIONAL LAW 425 (6th ed. 2003).

[9] *See* Yuji Iwasawa & Yumi Nishimura, *A Review of Japanese Legal Literature on State Responsibility* 9, *available at* http://www.lcil.cam.ac.uk/Media/ILCSR/rft/JapanRev.rtf (1999).

[10] *Ibid.*

standards that can be set forth *a posteriori* only under particular circumstances of each case,"[11] both theories are rooted in fundamental similarities.[12] Indeed, theories that base themselves on subjective fault and objective fault, such as those that Iwasawa and Nishimura discuss, present subjective fault and objective fault as not the same but, rather, as "two faces of the same coin."[13] The subjective fault theory and the objective fault theory are not so much distinct as they are descriptions of a common phenomenon.

Pisillo Mazzeschi's second and third main principles of responsibility share in common the fact that they are based not on fault but, rather, on an objective assessment of responsibility, or responsibility premised on the "mere breach of an international obligation."[14] Shaw equates the objective principle of responsibility with strict liability: "[o]nce an unlawful act has taken place, which has caused injury and which has been committed by an agent of the state, that state will be responsible in international law to the state suffering the damage irrespective of good or bad faith."[15]

The basic distinction between the two types of objective responsibility identified by Pisillo Mazzeschi is that one form allows for the raising of circumstances precluding wrongfulness as a defence while the other does not.[16] These two principles of objective responsibility could be characterised as relative or absolute responsibility for breach of obligations of result rather than relative or absolute objective responsibility.[17]

---

[11] *Ibid.*

[12] *See ibid.* (asserting these similarities as foreseeability, acknowledgement of obligations, capability of prevention, and means to prevent injuries).

[13] *Ibid.*

[14] Pisillo Mazzeschi, *Forms of International Responsibility for Environmental Harm*, *supra* note 2, at 16.

[15] SHAW, *supra* note 5. For a similar definition of objective responsibility, see TIM HILLIER, SOURCEBOOK ON PUBLIC INTERNATIONAL LAW 338 (1998) (stating that "[p]rovided that the acts complained of can be attributed to the state then it will be liable if those acts constitute a breach of international law regardless of any question of fault or intention.").

[16] *See* Pisillo Mazzeschi, *Forms of International Responsibility for Environmental Harm*, *supra* note 2, at 16. *See also* Riccardo Pisillo Mazzeschi, *The Due Diligence Rule and the Nature of the International Responsibility of States,* 35 GERM. Y.B. INT'L L. 9, 9 (1992) (noting that, "[i]n the regime of objective responsibility, responsibility arises as a sole consequence of conduct contrary to an international obligation, but in the case of objective and relative responsibility the State may be exonerated from responsibility by invoking one of the defenses allowed by international law.").

[17] *See* Pisillo Mazzeschi, *Forms of International Responsibility for Environmental Harm*, *supra* note 2, at 16.

Former Judge of the International Court of Justice (ICJ) Mohammed Bedjaoui characterises Pisillo Mazzeschi's framework of fault-based responsibility and the two types of objective responsibility slightly differently.[18] What Pisillo Mazzeschi describes as fault-based responsibility, Bedjaoui refers to as "'liability for fault' or 'subjective responsibility,'"[19] and what the former states as the two types of objective responsibility, Bedjaoui describes as "'causal liability' or 'objective responsibility.'"[20] Bedjaoui's explanation and further discussion are interesting because they seem to challenge the traditional notion that the main subjective and objective principles of responsibility exist as polar opposites.[21] In large part, this is due to an objectified understanding of fault.[22]

The fourth main principle of responsibility identified by Pisillo Mazzeschi fundamentally differs from his earlier principles of responsibility in that it does not require an unlawful act and because it can be established based solely on a finding of causation to damage.[23] Bedjaoui justifies a framework of responsibility that does not require a wrongful act as inevitably resulting from modern technologies, such as nuclear energy, the use of gaseous and liquid hydrocarbons, and the exploration of space, that States see as necessary yet acknowledge as extremely dangerous.[24]

Having thus described fault-based responsibility, objective responsibility, and liability without a wrongful act, a few observations can be made. Nollkaemper correctly stresses that inquiry into what in the criminal law would be described as the *mens rea* is in the State responsibility context "generally [. . .] either irrelevant or manifests itself in a different, objectified, form in the determination of state responsibility."[25]

---

[18] *See* Mohammed Bedjaoui, *Responsibility of States: Fault and Strict Liability,* in 10 ENCYCLOPEDIA OF PUBLIC INTERNATIONAL LAW 358 (1987).

[19] *Ibid.* at 359.

[20] *Ibid.*

[21] *See ibid.*

[22] *See ibid.*

[23] *See* Pisillo Mazzeschi, *Forms of International Responsibility for Environmental Harm*, *supra* note 2. *See also* Bedjaoui, *supra* note 18, at 360-61. On abuse of rights, see BROWNLIE, PRINCIPLES OF PUBLIC INTERNATIONAL LAW, *supra* note 8, at 429-30.

[24] *See* Bedjaoui, *supra* note 18, at 360 (asserting a "necessity of reconciling the greatest possible freedom of action for States with the justified fear that undisciplined use of technological and industrial power might spell the ruin of mankind.").

[25] André Nollkaemper, *Concurrence Between Individual Responsibility and State Responsibility in International Law,* 52(3) INT'L & COMP. L.Q. 615, 633 (2003).

While acknowledging the existence of four main principles of responsibility, one should recognise that these regimes do not necessarily function in a hermetically sealed manner in relation to each other. In the responsibility discourse, for example, fault's role should not be underestimated, even when the responsibility regime at issue would seem, at first glance, to completely exclude fault.[26] As Former President of the Inter-American Court of Human Rights Antônio Augusto Cançado Trindade states, the subjective element may aggravate a State's responsibility.[27] Goodwin-Gill notes that, particularly under international human rights law, "[c]onduct and result overlap; torture, ill-treatment, arbitrary deprivation of life, and *refoulement*, are all examples of forbidden conduct; but due process and accountability mechanisms are necessary, linked, but still separate bases for determining whether 'protection' is available or effective."[28]

Which responsibility regime applies, whether subjective or objective responsibility or responsibility without a wrongful act, serves particular policy ends and in large part determines the extent to which a party can be held accountable for its actions or omissions.[29] A regime of strict liability, for example, forces States to exert more control over the organs of their State apparatus than under a fault-based responsibility framework.[30] Brownlie asserts that a regime of objective responsibility "provides a better basis for maintaining good standards in international relations and for effectively upholding the principle of reparation."[31] Particular facts and cir-

[26] *See* Iwasawa & Nishimura, *supra* note 9, at 9-10. *See also* Antônio Augusto Cançado Trindade, *Complementarity Between State Responsibility and Individual Responsibility for Grave Violations of Human Rights: The Crime of State Revisited,* in INTERNATIONAL RESPONSIBILITY TODAY 253, 258 (Maurizio Ragazzi ed., 2005) (stating that, "even if one admits the principle of the objective or absolute responsibility of the State, this does not mean that the responsibility based on fault or guilt is entirely dismissed in every and any hypothesis or circumstance.").

[27] *See* Cançado Trindade, *supra* note 26.

[28] Guy S. Goodwin-Gill, *State Responsibility and the "Good Faith" Obligation in International Law,* in ISSUES OF STATE RESPONSIBILITY BEFORE INTERNATIONAL JUDICIAL INSTITUTIONS 75, 78 (Malgosia Fitzmaurice & Dan Sarooshi eds., 2004).

[29] *See* Ian Brownlie, *State Responsibility and the International Court of Justice,* in ISSUES OF STATE RESPONSIBILITY BEFORE INTERNATIONAL JUDICIAL INSTITUTIONS 11, 12 (Malgosia Fitzmaurice & Dan Sarooshi eds., 2004).

[30] *See* SHAW, *supra* note 5, at 700.

[31] BROWNLIE , PRINCIPLES OF PUBLIC INTERNATIONAL LAW, *supra* note 8. On reparation, see Riccardo Pisillo Mazzeschi, *Reparation Claims by Individuals for State Breaches of Humanitarian Law and Human Rights: An Overview,* 1(2) J. INT'L CRIM. JUST. 339 (2003);

cumstances may make it impossible to find a failure of the due diligence principle under a fault-based responsibility regime in some situations but not in others, although special regimes of protection may impose more exacting due diligence obligations than ordinary regimes of protection.[32] Finally, while a fault-based responsibility regime makes more difficult a finding of State responsibility, either of the two objective responsibility regimes identified by Pisillo Mazzeschi makes such a finding considerably easier.[33] This is another way of stating that the international obligation requires more of the party bearing the obligation under the latter responsibility regimes.

Shaw, although recognising a split in the case law and in academia, has noted a tendency favouring strict liability.[34] Brownlie has also advanced evidence of the dominance of the regime of objective responsibility.[35]

Riccardo Pisillo Mazzeschi, *International Obligations to Provide for Reparation Claims?,* in STATE RESPONSIBILITY AND THE INDIVIDUAL: REPARATION IN INSTANCES OF GRAVE VIOLATIONS OF HUMAN RIGHTS 149 (Albrecht Randelzhofer & Christian Tomuschat eds., 1999).

[32] *See* Horst Blomeyer-Bartenstein, *Due Diligence,* in 10 ENCYCLOPEDIA OF PUBLIC INTERNATIONAL LAW 138, 142 (1987) (arguing that "[t]he classic standard of due diligence may thus not suffice, it may require, depending upon the circumstances, a standard more exacting than its own as part of a special régime of protection. In this sense, the régime of absolute liability in the case of damage caused by space objects may be looked upon as 'evidence of the standard of care which the authors of the Convention believed to be reasonable in relation to that particular treaty.'"). *See also* BROWNLIE, PRINCIPLES OF PUBLIC INTERNATIONAL LAW, *supra* note 8, at 423 (asserting that, "in municipal systems of law, the precise mode of applying a *culpa* doctrine, especially in the matter of assigning the burden of proof, may result in a regime of objective responsibility.").

[33] *See* Pisillo Mazzeschi, *The Due Diligence Rule and the Nature of the International Responsibility of States, supra* note 16, at 10. *See also* Gaetano Arangio-Ruiz, *State Fault and the Forms and Degrees of International Responsibility: Questions of Attribution and Relevance,* in LE DROIT INTERNATIONAL AU SERVICE DE LA PAIX, DE LA JUSTICE ET DU DÉVELOPPEMENT 25, 35 (Mélanges Michel Virally ed., 1991) (stating that, "[c]onsidering therefore the far greater difficulty which any determination of intent or motivation presents, as compared with the determination of the so-called 'objective' conduct, attribution of any degree of fault to a State may be frequently more problematic than attribution of 'objective conduct.'").

[34] *See* SHAW, *supra* note 5.

[35] *See* BROWNLIE, PRINCIPLES OF PUBLIC INTERNATIONAL LAW, *supra* note 8, at 423-25. *See also* James Crawford & Simon Olleson, *The Nature and Forms of International Responsibility,* in INTERNATIONAL LAW 445, 459 (Malcolm D. Evans ed., 2003). According to Brownlie, "[a]s a matter of positive law the position is clear. Both the practice of States and the preponderance of the decisions of international tribunals adopt the concept of objective responsibility." Brownlie, *State Responsibility and the International Court of Justice, supra* note 29.

According to Cassese, international courts normally do not concern themselves with subjective questions of intent on the part of State actors.[36]

III. The International Law Commission and State Responsibility

Given the disparate nature of the principles of responsibility under international law, it should not come as a surprise that the law implicates elements of both fault-based responsibility and objective responsibility. Consider the Truth and Reconciliation Commission of South Africa (TRC). The TRC, although unique as a body and operating within a particular context, dealt with the principle of State responsibility in examining the actions and omissions of State and non-State actors under apartheid. According to it, State responsibility for the gross violation of human rights exists according to the following framework: "a It [i.e., the State] is strictly responsible for the acts of its organs or agents or persons acting under its control. b It is responsible for its own failure to prevent or adequately respond to the commission of gross human rights violations."[37] While both of these scenarios trigger State responsibility, the second scenario raises the issue of due diligence.[38]

An examination of the ILC's work provides some insight into the role that the due diligence principle plays within this framework. Since its creation at the end of the Second World War, the ILC has deliberated on varied issues of international law. Created by the General Assembly as part of that body's mandate under the United Nations Charter to "initiate studies and make recommendations for the purpose of [. . .] encouraging the progressive development of international law and its codification,"[39] it had on its agenda since its inception and until recently the issue of State responsibil-

---

[36] *See* CASSESE, *supra* note 7, at 251.

[37] TRUTH AND RECONCILIATION COMMISSION OF SOUTH AFRICA REPORT 602, *available at* http://www.info.gov.za/otherdocs/2003/trc/rep.pdf (released 21 March 2003).

[38] For an explanation of State responsibility and the due diligence principle within the context of small arms used by non-State actors, see Barbara A. Frey, *Small Arms and Light Weapons: The Tools Used to Violate Human Rights*, (3) DISARMAMENT FORUM: HUMAN RIGHTS, HUMAN SECURITY AND DISARMAMENT 37, 41-43 (2004).

[39] U.N. CHARTER Art. 13, Para. 1(a).

ity.[40] The journey of this important agenda item through the ILC, from its initial placement on the agenda to the completion of the 2001 *Articles on Responsibility of States for Internationally Wrongful Acts* (*Articles on State Responsibility*),[41] was, in its ups and downs, much like a roller coaster.

It is clear from the decades' long work of the ILC on the perplexing issue of State responsibility that the nature of the due diligence obligation is a matter to be resolved by the underlying primary rules, not the secondary rules of State responsibility, which Crawford and Olleson refer to as the "framework for the application of these [primary] obligations, whatever they may be."[42] On the difference between the primary and secondary rules of international law, Cassese notes:

> It is now generally acknowledged that a distinction can be made between '*primary rules*' of international law, that is, those customary or treaty rules laying down substantive obligations for States (on State immunities, treatment of foreigners, diplomatic and consular immunities, respect for territorial sovereignty, etc.), and '*secondary rules*', that is, rules establishing (i) on what conditions a breach of a 'primary rule' may be held to have occurred and (ii) the legal consequences of this breach.[43]

Assuming that the primary rules at issue impose a due diligence standard of conduct on the State, then the nature of the rights and interests at issue, as well as a number of other factors, will determine whether the conduct breaches an international obligation.

Under F. V. García Amador's special rapporteurship, the question of State responsibility initially focussed on the traditional concept of diplomatic protection, but a combination of several other agenda items and fundamental disagreement within the ILC on the question of State responsibility pre-

---

[40] *See* James Crawford, *Introduction*, in JAMES CRAWFORD, THE INTERNATIONAL LAW COMMISSION'S ARTICLES ON STATE RESPONSIBILITY: INTRODUCTION, TEXT AND COMMENTARIES 1, 1 (2003). On State responsibility deliberations by the League of Nations and the ILC, see Shabtai Rosenne, *State Responsibility:* Festina Lente, 75 BRIT. Y.B. INT'L L. 363, 363-66 (2004).

[41] International Law Commission, *Articles on Responsibility of States for Internationally Wrongful Acts*, in JAMES CRAWFORD, THE INTERNATIONAL LAW COMMISSION'S ARTICLES ON STATE RESPONSIBILITY: INTRODUCTION, TEXT AND COMMENTARIES 61 (2003) (2001).

[42] James Crawford & Simon Olleson, *The Continuing Debate on a UN Convention on State Responsibility,* 54(4) INT'L & COMP. L.Q. 959, 968 (2005).

[43] CASSESE, *supra* note 7, at 244. *See* HILLIER, *supra* note 15, at 321.

vented any significant progress from being made.[44] It remained for subsequent special rapporteurs to guide the ILC in a more fruitful direction.[45]

Roberto Ago dominated the next phase of the debate. In an inter-sessional subcommittee which he chaired, an ambitious plan was set, one that would broadly apply across international law but that would focus exclusively on the secondary, as opposed to the primary, rules of international law.[46] Thus, Ago's "focus was to be on the framework or matrix of rules of responsibility, identifying whether there has been a breach by a State and what were its consequences."[47] The inter-sessional subcommittee's plan was approved by the ILC, Ago was made special rapporteur, and a prolific period of article drafting began.[48] Ago's special rapporteurship more than made up for what García Amador's special rapporteurship had failed to achieve.[49]

Further progress was made on the question of State responsibility under the subsequent special rapporteurships of Willem Riphagen and Gaetano Arangio-Ruiz.[50] Sufficient progress was made such that 1996 saw the completion of the *Draft Articles on State Responsibility Provisionally Adopted by the International Law Commission on First Reading* (*Draft Articles on State Responsibility Provisionally Adopted on First Reading*).[51]

---

[44] *See* Crawford, *Introduction*, *supra* note 40, at 1-2.

[45] García Amador delivered a comprehensive overview of State responsibility at The Hague Academy of International Law in 1958. His lectures explored international responsibility's legal nature, elements, and subjects, the law of diplomatic protection, including its exercise and the doctrine of exhaustion of local remedies, and the international claim and extent and nature of reparation. *See* García Amador, *supra* note 2.

[46] *See* Crawford, *Introduction*, *supra* note 40, at 2. For a critique of the distinction between the primary and secondary rules of international law, see Daniel Bodansky & John R. Crook, *Introduction and Overview*, 96(4) AM. J. INT'L L. 773, 780-81 (2002). "[T]his distinction," according to Bodansky and Crook, "has proved elusive and in any event is unnecessary. To some degree, classifying an issue as part of the rule of conduct (the primary rule) or as part of the determination of whether that rule has been violated (the secondary rule) is arbitrary." *Ibid.* at 780.

[47] Crawford, *Introduction*, *supra* note 40, at 2.

[48] *See ibid.* at 2-3.

[49] On the separation of the primary and secondary rules, see Blomeyer-Bartenstein, *supra* note 32, at 141-42.

[50] *See* Crawford, *Introduction*, *supra* note 40, at 3-4.

[51] International Law Commission, *Draft Articles on State Responsibility Provisionally Adopted by the International Law Commission on First Reading* (*1996*), in JAMES CRAWFORD,

While not the conclusion of the agenda item, it represented significant progress over several decades.

It is important to examine the *Draft Articles on State Responsibility Provisionally Adopted on First Reading* to arrive at a better understanding of the interface of State responsibility, non-State actors, and the due diligence principle. Article 3, which Gattini describes as its "centrepiece,"[52] is the key article in the *Draft Articles on State Responsibility Provisionally Adopted on First Reading*. It defines an internationally wrongful act of State as occurring when "(a) conduct consisting of an action or omission is attributable to the State under international law; and (b) that conduct constitutes a breach of an international obligation of the State."[53] Attribution and breach are classic requirements of State responsibility under international law,[54] and international case law supports this.[55]

Taking Article 3 as a starting point, it is possible to make a number of observations about the *Draft Articles on State Responsibility Provisionally Adopted on First Reading*. There is no preference expressed *per se* as to whether State responsibility is essentially fault-based or based on intent.[56] According to Crawford, who was special rapporteur at the conclusion of the State responsibility project in 2001, attribution and breach act as the *sine qua non* of an internationally wrongful act of State, "no secondary rule or principle of responsibility imposing any such requirements, over and above those contained in the primary rule."[57] Arangio-Ruiz, writing before the completion of the *Draft Articles on State Responsibility Provisionally Adopted on First Reading*, recognised that fault was not necessarily indis-

---

THE INTERNATIONAL LAW COMMISSION'S ARTICLES ON STATE RESPONSIBILITY: INTRODUCTION, TEXT AND COMMENTARIES 348 app. (2003) (1996).

52 Andrea Gattini, *Smoking/No Smoking: Some Remarks on the Current Place of Fault in the ILC Draft Articles on State Responsibility,* 10(2) EUR. J. INT'L L. 397, 398 (1999).

53 International Law Commission, *Draft Articles on State Responsibility Provisionally Adopted by the International Law Commission on First Reading (1996)*, *supra* note 51, at 348, Art. 3.

54 *See* Rüdiger Wolfrum, *Internationally Wrongful Acts,* in 10 ENCYCLOPEDIA OF PUBLIC INTERNATIONAL LAW 271, 272 (1987).

55 *See* International Law Commission, *Commentaries, Articles on Responsibility of States for Internationally Wrongful Acts*, in JAMES CRAWFORD, THE INTERNATIONAL LAW COMMISSION'S ARTICLES ON STATE RESPONSIBILITY: INTRODUCTION, TEXT AND COMMENTARIES 74, 81 (2003) (2001).

56 *See* Crawford, *Introduction, supra* note 40, at 12.

57 *Ibid.*

pensable, yet questioned the assertion that the "legal consequences of an act which passes that threshold [of unlawfulness] are the same whether or not any fault is present in any degree."[58]

The "essentially neutral position"[59] of the *Draft Articles on State Responsibility Provisionally Adopted on First Reading* on the question of fault ensured that it would not operate under a fixed, rigid regime of responsibility but, rather, that it would have a more comprehensive effect and applicability under international law.[60] Because the secondary rules of State responsibility have nothing to say on the matter, questions of fault must be resolved with reference to the underlying primary rules. Put differently, "[i]f the primary rules require fault (of a particular character) or damage (of a particular kind) then they do; if not, then not."[61] The ILC wisely removed itself from the fray.[62]

As already noted, the ILC completed its decades' long study of State responsibility in 2001 when it adopted the *Articles on State Responsibility*. The *Articles on State Responsibility* were subsequently noted by the General Assembly and have been forwarded to States.[63] Debate among States continues, however, as to what should happen to the *Articles on State Responsibility* in future, with questions arising such as to whether they should be codified and, if so, whether this should take place in the short, medium, or long term, the extent to which they reflect customary international law at present also being raised.[64] Reflecting on the situation in late-2005, Crawford

---

58 Arangio-Ruiz, *supra* note 33, at 25.

59 Crawford, *Introduction, supra* note 40, at 13.

60 *See ibid.* at 13-14 (identifying this as a "more subtle approach, more appropriate to a general set of articles dealing with all international obligations and no longer focusing on the specific field of diplomatic protection. It corresponded to the wider range of possibilities, but it did not go further than that.").

61 James Crawford, *Revising the Draft Articles on State Responsibility,* 10(2) EUR. J. INT'L L. 435, 438 (1999).

62 *See ibid.* (stating that "the long-standing argument about fault might seem to be a false debate; but whether or not this is so, it is not a debate into which the ILC is compelled to enter, at a general level, in relation to this topic.").

63 *See* G.A. Res. 56/83, U.N. GAOR, at Para. 3, U.N. Doc. A/RES/56/83 (2001).

64 *See* Crawford & Olleson, *The Continuing Debate on a UN Convention on State Responsibility, supra* note 42 (exploring this debate). For an overview of developments since 2001, see Rosenne, *supra* note 40, at 366-67. According to an ICSID Tribunal, "[w]hile [. . . they] are not binding, they are widely regarded as a codification of customary international law." *Noble Ventures, Inc. (Noble)* v. *Rom.*, ICSID Case No. ARB/01/11, 69 (2005).

and Olleson argue for "keeping the possibility of a convention open while perpetually postponing a decision on the conclusion of such a convention."[65]

The formulation of an internationally wrongful act of State in what became the 2001 version's central article, Article 2, is very similar to the 1996 equivalent, Article 3, and only differs in minor ways. According to Article 2 in the final version, an internationally wrongful act of State is defined as "conduct consisting of an action or omission [that]: (a) is attributable to the State under international law; and (b) constitutes a breach of an international obligation of the State."[66]

Article 2 of the *Articles on State Responsibility* seems to support the conclusion that the legal consequences arising from active State conduct that satisfies the attribution and breach requirements and omissive State conduct that satisfies the attribution and breach requirements are, or at least should be, the same. The *Commentary* to Article 2 supports this interpretation and, once it can be established that particular facts and circumstances qualify as "conduct consisting of an action or omission" that satisfy the attribution and breach requirements, acknowledges the essentially non-discriminatory position of the law with regard to State action and omission for purposes of finding an internationally wrongful act of State. Specifically, "[c]ases in which the international responsibility of a State has been invoked on the basis of an omission are at least as numerous as those based on positive acts, and no difference in principle exists between the two."[67] Further on this point, State responsibility may be based on a combination of State action and omission.[68]

Although the ICSID Tribunal likely meant to state "not binding as a matter of international treaty law" instead of "not binding," because customary international law is binding, it may have underestimated the degree of progressive development.

[65] Crawford & Olleson, *The Continuing Debate on a UN Convention on State Responsibility*, *supra* note 42, at 971.

[66] International Law Commission, *Articles on Responsibility of States for Internationally Wrongful Acts*, *supra* note 41, at 61, Art. 2.

[67] International Law Commission, *Commentaries, Articles on Responsibility of States for Internationally Wrongful Acts*, *supra* note 55, at 82. *See also* Crawford & Olleson, *The Nature and Forms of International Responsibility*, *supra* note 35 (stating that "[o]f course conduct attributable to a State may consist of both actions and omissions; breach of international obligations by omissions is relatively common.").

[68] *See* International Law Commission, *Commentaries, Articles on Responsibility of States for Internationally Wrongful Acts*, *supra* note 55, at 82.

As with the 1996 version, the *Articles on State Responsibility* dodge the issue when it comes to the underlying nature of responsibility. The *Commentaries* make clear that the final version does not concern itself with subjective, or fault-based, responsibility or objective responsibility.[69] Put differently, "[s]uch standards vary from one context to another for reasons which essentially relate to the object and purpose of the treaty provision or other rule giving rise to the primary obligation."[70] Italian jurist Dionisio Anzilotti, stressing the importance of the underlying primary rule, advanced this view decades earlier.[71] While Rosenne is correct that "the concept of absolute responsibility balanced by circumstances precluding wrongfulness is now firmly implanted in international law,"[72] this absoluteness of responsibility must be understood as such in the sense that once the primary rule at issue imposes responsibility, which can base itself on any of the diverse responsibility regimes, the State is absolutely responsible unless wrongfulness is precluded by consent, self-defence, countermeasures related to an internationally wrongful act, *force majeure*, distress, necessity, and conflict with norms of *jus cogens*.[73]

Despite the silence of the *Articles on State Responsibility* on the underlying regime of responsibility, it is possible to make some general observations. Crawford and Olleson assert that affirmative State action tends to attract objective responsibility, while a State's failure to act, or omission, typically triggers subjective responsibility.[74] This view was also advanced

---

69 *See ibid.* at 81-82.

70 *Ibid.* at 82. *See also* Crawford & Olleson, *The Nature and Forms of International Responsibility, supra* note 35, at 460 (noting that "[e]verything depends on the specific context and on the content and interpretation of the obligation said to have been breached.").

71 *See* García Amador, *supra* note 2, at 385 (stating that "Anzilotti himself, in a later reconsideration of his own original position, suggested that whenever there is a rule providing for State responsibility it is necessary to ascertain whether such rule, tacitly or expressly, makes its imputation dependent on the fault or *dolus* on the part of the organ, or, on the contrary, points only to the existence of a fact objectively contrary to international law. To him, in most cases international law does not make the *animus* of the organ a condition of responsibility.").

72 Rosenne, *supra* note 40, at 368.

73 On these, see International Law Commission, *Articles on Responsibility of States for Internationally Wrongful Acts*, *supra* note 41, at 65-66, Arts. 20-26.

74 *See* Crawford & Olleson, *The Nature and Forms of International Responsibility, supra* note 35, at 460. On a State's omission and due diligence, see Blomeyer-Bartenstein, *supra* note 32, at 140.

decades earlier by García Amador, despite his acknowledgement of a lack of overall clarity on the issue:

> For instance, in cases of omissions relating to acts of private individuals, the subjective element is so closely linked to the wrong imputable to the organ or official that, if it would not exist, no imputation could be made. In this sense, malicious or culpable negligence constitutes by itself the wrongful omission. On the other hand, in cases of positive acts and even of some omissions which originate the direct responsibility of the State, the subjective elements (*culpa* or *dolus*) that might be found behind the conduct of the organ or official play, if any, a very small rôle; that is to say, fall into the background.[75]

As a general rule, then, affirmative State action and a State's failure to act, or omission, tend to attract different principles of responsibility.

IV. State Responsibility, Non-State Actors, and the Due Diligence Principle

Accepting, as one must, that certain primary rules impose a due diligence standard on State conduct, it is useful to examine arbitral decisions, international environmental law,[76] decisions of the ICJ,[77] diplomatic correspon-

---

[75] García Amador, *supra* note 2, at 388 (continuing by noting that "[t]his second submission is made without prejudice to those acts or omissions involving the violation of a rule which, expressly or tacitly, makes responsibility dependent on *culpa* or on any other subjective element. Further submissions, if not made in these general and flexible terms, could fail to reflect actual realities.").

[76] The role played by due diligence within the corporate context with emphasis on environmental factors is not explored in this chapter. On this, however, see Carsten Corino, *Environmental Due Diligence,* 9(4) EUR. ENVTL. L. REV. 120 (2000).

[77] For general overviews of State responsibility and the ICJ, see Brownlie, *State Responsibility and the International Court of Justice, supra* note 29; Rosalyn Higgins, *Issues of State Responsibility Before the International Court of Justice,* in ISSUES OF STATE RESPONSIBILITY BEFORE INTERNATIONAL JUDICIAL INSTITUTIONS 1 (Malgosia Fitzmaurice & Dan Sarooshi eds., 2004). Brownlie argues that, "[w]hilst courts of arbitration may make a contribution, it is the [International] Court [of Justice] which, as a mainstream interpreter of general international law, has produced the most important decisions on State responsibility." Brownlie, *State Responsibility and the International Court of Justice, supra* note 29, at 11.

dence,[78] and other activity during the last century to understand exactly what is expected of States with regard to the activities of non-State actors.[79] That this examination explores disparate areas of the law in different fora does not preclude the drawing of conclusions.[80]

It makes most sense to approach this exercise from the standpoint of *lex posterior derogat priori* because a chronological approach reveals the evolution of these obligations and provides the proper context. To that end, this section examines arbitral decisions in the early twentieth century dealing with the duty to protect and apprehend and punish and State action or omission in the context of insurrectional movements, activity during the Second World War and during the post-war era, movement during the Cold War, and activity at the end of the Cold War and more recently. The due diligence principle having been accepted in theory, it remains to flesh out the contents of this well-established principle of international law.

A. The Beginning of a New Century: Arbitral Decisions in the Early Twentieth Century

It is useful to examine arbitral decisions in the early twentieth century to understand exactly what kind of behaviour international law demands of

---

[78] Fitzmaurice fleshes out the importance of diplomatic correspondence to international law. According to him, "if State practice [. . .] is a source of law, it would be incorrect to regard such things as documents embodying diplomatic representations, notes of protest, etc., as constituting sources of law. They are evidences of it because they demonstrate certain attitudes on the part of States, but it is the State practice so evidenced which is the source of law." Gerald G. Fitzmaurice, *Some Problems Regarding the Formal Sources of International Law,* in SYMBOLAE VERZIJL: PRÉSENTÉES AU PROFESSEUR J.H.W. VERZIJL À L'OCCASION DE SON LXX-IÈME ANNIVERSAIRE 153, 153 (1958).

[79] For a helpful digest prepared by the United Nations Secretariat of international tribunals' decisions relating to various aspects of State responsibility that was compiled in the early 1960s, see DIGEST OF THE DECISIONS OF INTERNATIONAL TRIBUNALS RELATING TO STATE RESPONSIBILITY, PREPARED BY THE SECRETARIAT, U.N. Doc. A/CN.4/169 (1964), in 2 Y.B. Int'l L. Comm'n 132, U.N. Doc. A/CN.4/SER.A/1964/ADD.1 (1964).

[80] *See* Andrea Bianchi, *Enforcing International Law Norms Against Terrorism: Achievements and Prospects,* in ENFORCING INTERNATIONAL LAW NORMS AGAINST TERRORISM 491, 505 (Andrea Bianchi ed., 2004) (arguing that "[t]he availability of numerous multilateral fora in which States may assert their claims and express themselves makes the task of establishing general *opinio juris* less burdensome than in the past and provides evidence of emerging trends in State practice.").

States with regard to the activities of non-State actors. The arbitral decisions relevant for present purposes base themselves in agreed-upon treaty frameworks between States. Classically, the arbitral decisions on this subject deal with the law of diplomatic protection and State action or omission in contexts in which non-State actors inflict harm upon foreign nationals.[81]

i. *The Duty to Protect and Apprehend and Punish*

Although State responsibility will generally not arise when non-State actors commit wrongs against foreign nationals, it will be triggered "if the state can be shown to have connived at or failed to take adequate measures to prevent injuries to foreigners, or if, after the event, the foreign authorities fail to make an adequate attempt to provide justice."[82] Brownlie cites the *Janes*,[83] *Youmans*,[84] and *Massey*[85] claims before the United States/Mexico General Claims Commission established in the early-1920s (General Claims Commission) as representative of the rule that a State must act with due diligence in carrying out its duties to protect and apprehend and punish when non-State actors commit injuries against foreign nationals.[86]

Before proceeding further, it should be stressed that the General Claims Commission's jurisdiction and ability to maneuver were restricted by and necessarily had to operate within the parameters established by the 1923 General Claims Convention signed by the United States and Mexico.[87]

---

[81] On the conduct of insurrectional movements and other movements, see International Law Commission, *Articles on Responsibility of States for Internationally Wrongful Acts*, *supra* note 41, at 62, Art. 10.

[82] HILLIER, *supra* note 15, at 355. For a similar point of view, see G.A. Res. 60/147, U.N. GAOR, Annex, at 5, U.N. Doc. A/RES/60/147 (2005) (stating that, "[i]n cases of gross violations of international human rights law and serious violations of international humanitarian law constituting crimes under international law, States have the duty to investigate and, if there is sufficient evidence, the duty to submit to prosecution the person allegedly responsible for the violations and, if found guilty, the duty to punish her or him.").

[83] Janes (*U.S.* v. *Mex.*), 4 R.I.A.A. 82 (1926).

[84] Youmans (*U.S.* v. *Mex.*), 4 R.I.A.A. 110 (1926).

[85] Massey (*U.S.* v. *Mex.*), 4 R.I.A.A. 155 (1927).

[86] *See* IAN BROWNLIE, SYSTEM OF THE LAW OF NATIONS: STATE RESPONSIBILITY (PART I) 161 (1983). For an overview of the General Claims Commission, see JACOBUS GIJSBERTUS DE BEUS, THE JURISPRUDENCE OF THE GENERAL CLAIMS COMMISSION, UNITED STATES AND MEXICO UNDER THE CONVENTION OF SEPTEMBER 8, 1923 1-9 (1938).

[87] *See* DE BEUS, *supra* note 86, at 10.

According to Article 1 of that treaty, relevant claims were to be decided by a "Commission consisting of three members for decision in accordance with the principles of international law, justice and equity."[88]

The *Janes* claim "may be considered as the prototype of over fourty [sic] claims of its kind presented to the commission, all based on the failure of Mexican authorities, to prosecute, apprehend, condemn or punish effectively the murderers of American citizens killed in Mexico."[89] In that arbitral decision, the General Claims Commission addressed States' obligations under international law to apprehend those who commit wrongs against foreign nationals and provided a theoretical framework for distinguishing between damage caused by non-State actors and damage caused by States.

The foreign national in *Janes*, American Byron Everett Janes, managed a mining company in Mexico, and Pedro Carbajal, a Mexican, had worked for the same company.[90] During the summer of 1918, Carbajal shot Janes twice, killing him.[91] The local police, although informed of the shooting within minutes, delayed for approximately one half hour before searching for Carbajal, who had fled up a canyon.[92] This search ended in failure, as did a similar search the next day.[93] Evidence suggested that Carbajal had hid in a nearby ranch for a week and that he had actually returned to El Tigre, the town of the shooting, twice during the same week.[94] Mexican authorities failed to follow up on a lead that Carbajal was seventy-five miles away from El Tigre until the mining company offered a reward for Carbajal's capture, and when they did finally search for Carbajal, he could not be found.[95]

The General Claims Commission found that "there was clearly such a failure on the part of the Mexican authorities to take prompt and efficient action to apprehend the slayer as to warrant an award of indemnity."[96] Thus, it found that Mexico had breached its obligation to apprehend those who

---

88 *Ibid.*
89 *Ibid.* at 159.
90 *See* Janes, *supra* note 83, at 83-84.
91 *See ibid.* at 84.
92 *See ibid.*
93 *See ibid.*
94 *See ibid.* at 85.
95 *See ibid.*
96 *Ibid.*

commit wrongs against foreign nationals. According to the General Claims Commission, Mexico's responsibility rested on its failure to "take proper steps to apprehend and punish the slayer."[97] The "proper steps" language here is the equivalent of a due diligence obligation. Crawford and Olleson cite *Janes* for the proposition that "[p]urely private acts will not engage the State's responsibility, although the State may in certain circumstances be liable for its failure to prevent those acts, or to take action to punish the individuals responsible."[98]

In *Janes*, the General Claims Commission provided a theoretical framework for distinguishing between damage caused by non-State actors and damage caused by States.[99] One view, which might be termed the "presumed complicity"[100] theory of State responsibility, asserts that a State can be held responsible in cases of serious failure of diligence in apprehension, punishment, or both as a matter of "derivative liability, assuming the character of some kind of complicity with the perpetrator himself and rendering the State responsible for the very consequences of the individual's misdemeanor."[101] The General Claims Commission acknowledged that this view might apply where the State has knowledge of an intended injury and could have prevented it but failed to do so.[102]

The General Claims Commission, however, rejected the "presumed complicity" theory of State responsibility and adopted the view, which might be termed the "nonrepression"[103] theory of State responsibility, which distinguishes between the injury caused by the non-State actor and the injury caused by the State.[104] Unlike the "presumed complicity" theory, the "nonrepression" theory explicitly acknowledges separate injuries and apportions them appropriately between the non-State actor and the State.[105]

---

[97] *Ibid.* at 86.

[98] Crawford & Olleson, *The Nature and Forms of International Responsibility, supra* note 35, at 455.

[99] On this distinction generally, see García Amador, *supra* note 2, at 401-05 (exploring "direct" State responsibility, "vicarious" State responsibility, and "indirect" State responsibility).

[100] Janes, *supra* note 83, at 87.

[101] *Ibid.* at 86.

[102] *See ibid.* at 87.

[103] *Ibid.*

[104] *See ibid.* For a useful visual sketch of this theory of State responsibility, see DE BEUS, *supra* note 86, at 165-66.

[105] *See* Wolfrum, *supra* note 54, at 275 (arguing that the State is "responsible only for the act or omission of its organs where they are guilty of not having done everything within

Applying the "nonrepression" theory of State responsibility to *Janes*, the General Claims Commission concluded that "[t]he damage caused by the culprit is the damage caused to Janes' relatives by Janes' death; the damage caused by the Government's negligence is the damage resulting from the non-punishment of the murderer."[106]

Acknowledging the distinct nature of the injury caused by the non-State actor and by the State when measuring damages forms the basis of the modern rule.[107] According to United Nations Special Rapporteur on the Prevention of Human Rights Violations Committed with Small Arms and Light Weapons Barbara A. Frey, "under a due diligence standard, it is the omission on the part of the state, not the injurious act by the private actor, for which the state may be responsible."[108]

In the *Youmans* claim, the General Claims Commission explored the issue of State responsibility for failure to act with due diligence in the context of a mob uprising against foreign nationals in Mexico. The incident arose out of a labour dispute between American John A. Connelly, Managing Engineer of the San Hilario Tunnel construction project in Mexico, and

---

their power to prevent the injurious act of the private individual or to punish if it has occurred. The State is responsible for having breached not the international obligation with which the individual's act might be in conflict, but the general or special obligation imposed on its organs to provide for protection.").

[106] Janes, *supra* note 83, at 87.

[107] On acknowledging the distinct nature of the injury caused by the non-State actor and by the State, see CASSESE, *supra* note 7, at 250 (stating that, "in the case of violence and other unlawful acts against foreigners, the State is not responsible for the acts of the individuals; it is accountable only if its own 'conduct by omission' may be proved, that is it failed to act in conformity with international legal standards."). *See also* Gilbert Guillaume, *Terrorism and International Law,* 53(3) INT'L & COMP. L.Q. 537, 544 (2004) (asserting that, "[a]ccording to the case law which has thus developed, a careful distinction should be drawn between those acts which are imputable to the individual perpetrators and those acts or omissions for which public authorities are responsible."); Giuseppe Sperduti, *Responsibility of States for Activities of Private Law Persons*, in 10 ENCYCLOPEDIA OF PUBLIC INTERNATIONAL LAW 373, 374 (1987) (noting that, in denial of justice cases, "[t]he State is called upon to answer for an injury that it has itself caused, be this a moral damage which has been inflicted by disregarding the lawful expectation of having the offender punished, or be it an injury arising from a person having been prevented from obtaining from a court a remedy for the damage suffered, as assessable in economic terms.").

[108] Frey, *supra* note 38, at 42. This resembles Reinisch's concept of "vicarious state responsibility for non-state acts." August Reinisch, *The Changing International Legal Framework for Dealing with Non-State Actors,* in NON-STATE ACTORS AND HUMAN RIGHTS 37, 79 (Philip Alston ed., 2005).

local labourer Cayentano Medina.[109] Medina, angered over a dispute that had not been settled to his liking, threw stones at Connelly and threatened him with a machete.[110] Connelly responded by firing a warning shot in Medina's direction and after Medina persisted shot his legs.[111] A mob of approximately one thousand people soon converged on Connelly's house, where Connelly and two other Americans, Henry Youmans and Justin Arnold, found themselves trapped.[112] The local mayor attempted to restore order but could not, and when Mexican soldiers arrived to defuse the situation, they shot at the house and killed Arnold.[113] The soldiers and the mob then proceeded to kill Connelly and Youmans, and "[t]heir bodies were dragged through the streets and left under a pile of stones by the side of the road so mutilated as scarcely to be recognizable."[114] The central issue that the General Claims Commission faced was "the failure of the Mexican Government to exercise due diligence to protect [. . . Youmans] from the fury of the mob at whose hands he was killed, and the failure to take proper steps looking to the apprehension and punishment of the persons implicated in the crime."[115]

In concluding that Mexico bore responsibility, the General Claims Commission found that the State had acted negligently with regard to its duty to protect Connelly, Youmans, and Arnold and that it had violated its obligation to apprehend and punish for failure to make "proper efforts."[116] Mexico's knowledge of the unrest at Connelly's house, combined with the affirmative action that it had taken to protect Connelly, Youmans, and Arnold, namely its unsuccessful attempt by the mayor to restore order and the decision to dispatch Mexican soldiers to the scene, evidenced the State's acknowledgement of a duty to protect.[117] While a State does not bear responsibility for the actions of non-State actors when it acts with due diligence, that Mexico had knowledge and had taken affirmative action, albeit

[109] *See* Youmans, *supra* note 84, at 111.
[110] *See ibid.*
[111] *See ibid.*
[112] *See ibid.*
[113] *See ibid.*
[114] *Ibid.*
[115] *Ibid.* at 114.
[116] *Ibid.* at 112.
[117] On *ultra vires* acts of State and State responsibility, see Noble, *supra* note 64, at 74.

action that was woefully inadequate on the particular facts and circumstances, likely figured into the General Claims Commission's calculus in reaching a finding of State responsibility.

The General Claims Commission in *Youmans* also found that Mexico had breached its duty to apprehend and punish those responsible for killing the three Americans. Once order had been restored, Mexico arrested eighteen people, but some of these were freed on minimal bail.[118] Those who received capital sentences had their sentences reduced.[119] Due to failures in the Mexican criminal justice system, all of those who had received capital sentences and had had them reduced, except for one who had died, fled the jurisdiction, and charges against six others were dropped.[120] Given that a mob of approximately one thousand people had converged on Connelly's house, the inability of Mexico to hold anyone accountable for the killings demonstrated a breach of the State's due diligence obligation to apprehend and punish those who commit criminal offences against foreign nationals.

Less than a year after *Youmans*, the General Claims Commission again addressed the contours of the "rule of international law which requires a government to take proper measures to apprehend and punish nationals who have committed wrongs against aliens."[121] Joaquín R. Saenz, a Mexican, had shot his American boss, William B. Massey, six times, resulting in his death.[122] Mexican authorities jailed Saenz after he had killed Massey and fled for a brief time.[123] However, with the permission of a prison guard, Saenz simply left jail one evening, never to return.[124]

The General Claims Commission found that the United States had successfully made its case for denial of justice.[125] According to it, "[t]here is no proper arrest and there can be no prosecution in the case of a man who is permitted by police authorities to leave prison."[126] The General Claims Commission cited correspondence between American diplomats in early 1904 in language that summarises the legal rule reinforced in *Massey*:

---

118 *See* Youmans, *supra* note 84, at 112.
119 *See ibid.*
120 *See ibid.*
121 Massey, *supra* note 85, at 156.
122 *See ibid.*
123 *See ibid.*
124 *See ibid.* at 160-61.
125 *See ibid.* at 162; *ibid.* at 164.
126 *Ibid.* at 160.

> While a State is not ordinarily responsible for injuries done by private individuals to other private individuals in its territory, it is the duty of the State to diligently prosecute and properly punish such offenders, and for its refusal to do so it may be held answerable in pecuniary damages.[127]

It was for its failure to "diligently prosecute and properly punish" Saenz that the General Claims Commission held Mexico responsible.

Summing up the due diligence principle as it applies in the context of the duty to prevent injury to foreign nationals by non-State actors and the duty to punish those responsible for causing such injury, one can make certain conclusions.[128] The first duty, the duty to prevent injury to foreign nationals by non-State actors, contains two parts, namely the duty to permanently have "a legal and administrative apparatus normally able to guarantee respect for the international norm on prevention"[129] and the duty to employ this State apparatus "with the diligence that the circumstances require."[130] Only the second part of this duty of protection is governed by the due diligence rule.[131] The Inter-American Court of Human Rights' description of the investigation duty, which requires a serious undertaking that is "not [done] as a mere formality preordained to be ineffective [. . . but, rather, with] an objective [. . . that is] assumed by the State as its own legal duty,"[132] applies in this context.

ii. *State Action or Omission in the Context of Insurrectional Movements*

Insurrectional movements fundamentally challenge the viability of regimes and may require that a State dedicate its entire apparatus to maintain its hold on power. Given the seriousness of the situation, international law extends a degree of deference to the State and presumes that it will not be held responsible for its actions with regard to the insurrection.[133] The un-

---

[127] *Ibid.* at 159.

[128] *See* Pisillo Mazzeschi, *The Due Diligence Rule and the Nature of the International Responsibility of States, supra* note 16, at 25-30.

[129] *Ibid.* at 26.

[130] *Ibid.*

[131] *See ibid.* at 27. Becker, however, contests this. *See* TAL BECKER, TERRORISM AND THE STATE: RETHINKING THE RULES OF STATE RESPONSIBILITY 140-46 (2006).

[132] Velásquez Rodríguez, Ser. C, Case No. 4, Inter-Am. Ct. H.R. 1988, Para. 177.

[133] *See* BROWNLIE, PRINCIPLES OF PUBLIC INTERNATIONAL LAW, *supra* note 8, at 437.

derlying idea is that, "even in a regime of objective responsibility, there must exist a normal capacity to act, and a major internal upheaval is tantamount to *force majeure*."[134]

In the 1903 *Sambiaggio* decision,[135] the Italy-Venezuela Mixed Claims Commission (Mixed Claims Commission)[136] addressed the question whether Venezuela bore responsibility for injury inflicted by revolutionaries on Salvatore Sambiaggio, an Italian national living in Venezuela.[137] According to the Mixed Claims Commission, revolutionaries commanded by Colonel Guevara coerced Sambiaggio to give them advances of money and took property from him and caused damage.[138]

Italy, basing its argument on factual considerations, equitable principles, a bilateral treaty with Venezuela and its relevant protocols, general international law principles, relevant arbitral decisions, and special legislation,[139] asserted that Venezuela bore responsibility for Sambiaggio's injury even though Guevara's revolutionaries had been the perpetrators.[140] Venezuela argued that, as a general rule, a State could only be held responsible for the illegal acts of State actors, not for the illegal acts of revolutionaries.[141] However, Venezuela did acknowledge that a State could bear responsibility when, in case of revolution, "it had been negligent in the protection of individuals: but in such case the responsibility would arise from the fact that the government, by its conduct, had laid itself open to the charge of complicity in the injury."[142]

Venezuela wisely noted that a commission such as the one deciding *Sambiaggio* operates within a particular context and on particular facts and circumstances and that it "gives its decision in each case and with especial reference to all its circumstances."[143] Since such commissions generally decide claims within a particular treaty context, claims' usefulness outside

---

134 *Ibid.*

135 Sambiaggio (*Italy* v. *Venez.*), 10 R.I.A.A. 499 (1903).

136 For the historical and legal background, see 9 R.I.A.A. 99-110 (1960); 10 R.I.A.A. 477-84 (1962).

137 *See* Sambiaggio, *supra* note 135, at 512.

138 *See ibid.*

139 *See ibid.* at 501.

140 *See ibid.* at 500-01.

141 *See ibid.* at 507.

142 *Ibid.*

143 *Ibid.* at 508.

the particular treaty regime at issue is often limited to the extent that they accurately reveal the state of international law generally. Thus, *Sambiaggio's* relevance lies in its clarification of international law as it relates to potential State responsibility in the context of revolutionary non-State actors who cause injury to foreign nationals.

In finding that Venezuela did not bear responsibility for Sambiaggio's damage on the basis of the equitable application of the "well-established principles of justice, not permitting sympathy for suffering to bring about a disregard for law,"[144] the Mixed Claims Commission looked at the issue from the "standpoint of abstract rights,"[145] relevant decisions made by commissions and courts, and scholarly commentary.[146] The Mixed Claims Commission noted the general rule of international law that a State can only bear responsibility for the acts of its organs or when the State expressly assumes responsibility.[147] A State cannot be held responsible for the actions of revolutionary non-State actors "unless it clearly appear[s] that the government has failed to use promptly and with appropriate force its constituted authority."[148]

As applied to *Sambiaggio,* the reality that "for six months previous to the taking complained of in the present case a bloody and determined revolution demanding the entire resources of the Government to quell it had been raging throughout the larger part of Venezuela"[149] protected Venezuela from responsibility for Sambiaggio's damage.[150] In its examination of relevant decisions made by commissions and courts, the Mixed Claims Commission cited numerous cases in which States had not been held responsible for damage caused to individuals by revolutionaries.[151] The examined scholarly commentary supported the general rule of States' non-responsibility for damage under such facts and circumstances.[152]

---

[144] *Ibid.* at 524.

[145] *Ibid.* at 512 (stating "[l]et us treat the matter first from the standpoint of abstract right, reserving examination of precedents, the treaties between the two countries, and the question whether there be anything to exempt Venezuela from the operation of such general rule as may be found to exist.").

[146] *See ibid.* at 512-17.

[147] *See ibid.* at 512.

[148] *Ibid.* at 513.

[149] *Ibid.*

[150] *See ibid.*

[151] *See ibid.* at 513-15.

[152] *See ibid.* at 515-17. The Mixed Claims Commission, for example, cited Wharton's Digest of International Law, at Section 223's headnotes, for the principle that "[a] sovereign

The Mixed Claims Commission seemed to have agreed with Venezuela's argument that potential State responsibility in the context of revolutionary non-State actors could only be assessed "in proportion to [. . . the state's] ability to avoid an evil."[153] In such a context, Venezuela contended that a State only needed to afford security and protection "in so far as is permitted by the means at its disposal and according as the circumstances may be verified."[154]

Sambiaggio's main contribution lies in its reaffirmation that the general notion that States "should be held responsible for the acts of revolutionists [. . . is] in derogation of the general principles of international law."[155] While the Mixed Claims Commission clearly deferred to Venezuela because the State had been involved in an intense assault on the revolutionaries at the time that they had inflicted injury on Sambiaggio, it acknowledged, in principle, that Venezuela could have been held responsible had it not acted with due diligence.[156]

B. **The Second World War and the Post-War Dispensation**

One of the most important arbitral decisions within the context of environmental law, *Trail Smelter*,[157] was decided during the middle of the Second World War. It has contributed greatly to international law as relates not only to the law of State responsibility for transboundary harm to the environment, which the ICJ has stated "represents the living space, the quality of life and the very health of human beings, including generations unborn,"[158]

---

is not ordinarily responsible to alien residents for injuries they receive on his territory from belligerent action, or from insurgents whom he could not control or whom the claimant government had recognized as belligerents." *Ibid.* at 515.

[153] *Ibid.* at 509.

[154] *Ibid.* at 510.

[155] *Ibid.* at 521.

[156] *See ibid.* at 524. On the prosecution obligation and the due diligence principle in the context of injury caused by armed opposition groups, see LIESBETH ZEGVELD, ACCOUNTABILITY OF ARMED OPPOSITION GROUPS IN INTERNATIONAL LAW 201-04 (2002).

[157] Trail Smelter Arbitral Tribunal, Decision, Reported on March 11, 1941, to the Government of the United States of America and to the Government of the Dominion of Canada, Under the Convention Signed April 15, 1935, 35 AM. J. INT'L L. 684 (1941).

[158] Legality of the Threat or Use of Nuclear Weapons (Advisory Opinion), 1996 I.C.J. 226, 241.

but also, and perhaps more importantly, to the law of State responsibility for transboundary harm generally.[159]

While the controversy could be succinctly summarised as alleged transboundary environmental harm caused by a non-State actor in Canada to the territory of the United States,[160] it is helpful to provide a bit more detail. As the name of the arbitral decision suggests, the dispute involved a smelter of lead and zinc in Trail, British Columbia.[161] The smelter had significantly expanded, so much so that it had become "one of the best and largest equipped smelting plants on the American continent."[162] With the expansion of the Trail Smelter came increased sulphur dioxide fumes and a higher concentration of them being released into the air.[163] According to the *ad hoc* arbitral Tribunal, these increased levels of released sulphur dioxide caused damage for at least ten years.[164] While it is unnecessary to unduly focus on statistics for present purposes, suffice it to say that the amount of sulphur released from the Trail Smelter was significant, with about 10,000 tons being released monthly in 1930 and a rise from a decade-low 3,250 tons being released monthly in 1939 to 3,875 tons being released monthly in 1940.[165]

---

[159] *See* Luke T. Lee, *The Right to Compensation: Refugees and Countries of Asylum,* 80(3) AM. J. INT'L L. 532, 554 n. 92 (1986) (noting that "[i]t has been pointed out that 'to compare the flow of refugees with the flow of, for example, noxious fumes may appear invidious; the basic issue, however, is the responsibility which derives from the fact of control over territory.' *See* G. GOODWIN-GILL, THE REFUGEE IN INTERNATIONAL LAW 228 n. 49 (1983). Thus, it has been held that the *Trail Smelter* rule extends beyond ecological/ pollution damage to any damage to other states. Garvey, TOWARD A REFORMULATION OF INTERNATIONAL REFUGEE LAW, 26 HARV. INT'L L.J. 483, 495 (1985)."). *But see* Kevin J. Madders, *Trail Smelter Arbitration,* in 2 ENCYCLOPEDIA OF PUBLIC INTERNATIONAL LAW 276, 279-80 (1981) (challenging the precedential value of the case); Pisillo Mazzeschi, *Forms of International Responsibility for Environmental Harm, supra* note 2, at 29 (stating that, "[i]n spite of the fact that it is so well known, the *Trail Smelter* case is not really very significant, since in the compromise between the US and Canada the question of Canada's responsibility had already been resolved affirmatively.").

[160] *See* Trail Smelter, *supra* note 157, at 685.

[161] *See ibid.* at 688.

[162] *Ibid.* at 692.

[163] *See ibid.*

[164] *See ibid.* at 693.

[165] *See ibid.* at 695.

After having determined that the Trail Smelter had caused transboundary environmental damage for a number of years since early 1932,[166] the Tribunal explored whether, pursuant to Article III of the relevant treaty in force, the Trail Smelter should be estopped from causing further transboundary environmental harm in future and, if so, the extent to which it should be so estopped.[167]

The Tribunal began by stating the general rule that "[a] State owes at all times a duty to protect other States against injurious acts by individuals from within its jurisdiction."[168] Neither the United States nor Canada disputed this general rule, although its content and application to particular facts and circumstances were at the core of the dispute, thus exposing difficulties in applying the rule to concrete cases.[169] Indeed, the Tribunal itself noted "the relativity of the rule."[170]

Because the Tribunal faced the reality that international tribunals to date had not reached decisions on facts and circumstances of either transboundary air pollution or transboundary water pollution,[171] it examined by analogy decisions reached by the United States Supreme Court on transboundary air pollution and transboundary water pollution.[172] The Tribunal famously concluded that

> under the principles of international law, as well as of the law of the United States, no State has the right to use or permit the use of its territory in such a manner as to cause injury by fumes in or to the territory of another or the properties or persons therein, when the case is of serious consequence and the injury is established by clear and convincing evidence.[173]

---

[166] *See ibid.* at 696-712.

[167] *See ibid.* at 712.

[168] *Ibid.* at 713.

[169] *See ibid.* at 713-14.

[170] *Ibid.* at 714.

[171] *See ibid.*

[172] *See ibid.* at 714-16.

[173] *Ibid.* at 716. For statements of a similar principle, see Legality of the Threat or Use of Nuclear Weapons, *supra* note 158, at 241-42 (stating that "[t]he existence of the general obligation of States to ensure that activities within their jurisdiction and control respect the environment of other States or of areas beyond national control is now part of the corpus of international law relating to the environment."); Request for an Examination of the Situation in Accordance with Para. 63 of the Court's Judgment of 20 December 1974 in the

As a matter of international law, the Tribunal held Canada responsible for the transboundary environmental harm caused by the Trail Smelter to the territory of the United States.[174] While Cassese may be correct that *Trail Smelter* represents "the first time an international tribunal propounded the principle that a State may not use, or allow its nationals to use, its own territory in such a manner as to cause injury to a neighbouring country,"[175] the issue of States' obligations with regard to non-State actors under the non-interference principle had already enjoyed a long pedigree at the time of the decision.[176]

While often cited, and with good reason, the language of what might be termed the *Trail Smelter* rule begs many questions. To suggest but a few, what is a "case [. . .] of serious consequence"? When can an injury be considered to be "established by clear and convincing evidence"? With reference to which criteria are these determinations to be made? Presumably, individual States make these decisions at first instance, through a balancing of rights and interests, guided by an international law rule of reasonableness.

It is significant that the *Trail Smelter* Tribunal deliberately included the caveat "when the case is of serious consequence and the injury is established by clear and convincing evidence." This highlights the significant nature of the injury at issue and makes clear that the *Trail Smelter* rule excludes *de minimus* injuries.[177] In this context, Koskenniemi stresses that

---

Nuclear Tests (*N.Z.* v. *Fr.*) Case, 1995 I.C.J. 288, 378 (Koroma, J., dissenting) (asserting that, "[u]nder contemporary international law, there is probably a duty not to cause gross or serious damage which can reasonably be avoided, together with a duty not to permit the escape of dangerous substances."); P.W. BIRNIE & A.E. BOYLE, INTERNATIONAL LAW AND THE ENVIRONMENT 265 (2nd ed. 2002) (stating that "[i]f states are responsible for their failure to control soldiers and judges abroad, they may likewise be held responsible for their failure to control transboundary pollution and environmental harm caused by activities within their own territory.").

174 *See* Trail Smelter, *supra* note 157, at 716-17.

175 CASSESE, *supra* note 7, at 484. Cassese notes that "[l]egally the issue was not viewed as different from damage caused to private or public property, for instance by the inadvertent penetration of a foreign State's territory by armed forces." *Ibid.*

176 *See, e.g.,* R.Y. Jennings, *The* Caroline *and McLeod Cases,* 32 AM. J. INT'L L. 82 (1938). On the *Caroline* case, see Bianchi, *supra* note 80, at 506-07.

177 Highlighting the significant nature of the injury contemplated by the *Trail Smelter* rule, the Tribunal made clear to state that the "damage herein referred to and its extent [. . . must be] such as would be recoverable under the decisions of the courts of the United States

transboundary pollution cases raise issues that require the balancing of contrasting liberties.[178]

It is also necessary to understand which of the four main principles of responsibility, subjective and objective responsibility for a wrongful act and liability without a wrongful act, are implicated by the *Trail Smelter* rule. While Pisillo Mazzeschi argues that the rule stands for a form of subjective or objective responsibility for a wrongful act but insists that the rule is confusing as to which exact form of responsibility applies,[179] the established law seems to be that the *Trail Smelter* rule grounds itself in strict liability.[180] Certainly, the rule's plain meaning, with no mention of, for example, an examination into the reasonableness of a State's actions or omissions with regard to transboundary harm to the environment, supports a regime of responsibility based other than on fault.

Even though *Trail Smelter* speaks to a regime of responsibility based other than on fault, it is vitally important in understanding the relationship between the law of State responsibility and transboundary harm. International law frowns on transboundary harm and seeks to construct rules to minimise it or, if possible, to eliminate it altogether.[181] As the ICJ has stated, "[t]he existence of the general obligation of States to ensure that activities within their jurisdiction and control respect the environment of other States

---

in suits between private individuals." Trail Smelter, *supra* note 157, at 717. It is likely that the Tribunal was influenced by the International Joint Commission's definition of "damage" that excluded "'occasional damage that may be caused by SO_2 fumes being carried across the international boundary in air pockets or by reason of unusual atmospheric conditions,' as far, at least, as the duty of the Smelter to reduce the presence of that gas in the air was concerned." *Ibid.* at 713.

[178] *See* Martti Koskenniemi, *The Politics of International Law,* 1(1-2) EUR. J. INT'L L. 4, 19 (1990).

[179] *See* Pisillo Mazzeschi, *Forms of International Responsibility for Environmental Harm*, *supra* note 2, at 29-30.

[180] *See* Thomas W. Merrill, *Golden Rules for Transboundary Pollution*, 46(5) DUKE L.J. 931, 950-51 (1997). *But see* Günther Handl, *State Liability for Accidental Transnational Environmental Damage by Private Persons,* 74(3) AM. J. INT'L L. 525, 537 (1980).

[181] *See* International Law Commission, *Articles on Prevention of Transboundary Harm from Hazardous Activities*, in REPORT OF THE INTERNATIONAL LAW COMMISSION ON THE WORK OF ITS FIFTY-THIRD SESSION 370, 372, Art. 3, U.N. Doc. A/56/10 Supp. No. 10 (2001). Since they are no longer in draft form, reference is made to these articles throughout this research as the *Articles on Prevention of Transboundary Harm from Hazardous Activities* (*Articles on Prevention of Transboundary Harm*).

or of areas beyond national control is now part of the corpus of international law relating to the environment."[182] That the *Trail Smelter* rule supports a regime of responsibility based other than on fault does not detract from this general rule, nor does it make it any less applicable or relevant when the particular facts and circumstances present a regime of responsibility based on fault.[183]

Another case worth exploring during this time period involved a dispute between the United Kingdom and Albania, the *Corfu Channel* case.[184] As background, four British warships, the *Mauritius*, *Saumarez*, *Leander*, and *Volage*, had sailed in October 1946 from Corfu north in the direction of a channel in the North Corfu Strait that had previously been swept for mines.[185] Despite the previous minesweeping operation, a mine near the Bay of Saranda exploded and severely damaged *Saumarez*.[186] A mine subsequently struck *Volage*, which had been ordered to tow *Saumarez,* and severely damaged it.[187]

Putting the incident in context, the ICJ summarised the recent history of minesweeping operations in the North Corfu Channel. The British Navy had swept for mines in the channel during October 1944 and, having found no mines, declared the channel safe for shipping during the next month.[188] Negative results from further minesweeping operations in early 1945 confirmed this declaration of safety.[189] While the ICJ failed to indicate whether any minesweeping operations had been done between 15 May 1946, when

---

[182] Legality of the Threat or Use of Nuclear Weapons, *supra* note 158, at 241-42. According to the ILC, "[p]revention of transboundary harm to the environment, persons and property has been accepted as an important principle in many multilateral treaties concerning protection of the environment, nuclear accidents, space objects, international watercourses, management of hazardous wastes and prevention of marine pollution." International Law Commission, *Commentaries, Articles on Prevention of Transboundary Harm from Hazardous Activities*, in REPORT OF THE INTERNATIONAL LAW COMMISSION ON THE WORK OF ITS FIFTY-THIRD SESSION 377, 379, U.N. Doc. A/56/10 Supp. No. 10 (2001).

[183] Pisillo Mazzeschi identifies the due diligence principle as the crux of international environmental law. *See* Pisillo Mazzeschi, *The Due Diligence Rule and the Nature of the International Responsibility of States, supra* note 16, at 36-41.

[184] Corfu Channel (*U.K.* v. *Alb.*), 1949 I.C.J. 4.

[185] *See ibid.* at 12.

[186] *See ibid.*

[187] *See ibid.* at 12-13.

[188] *See ibid.* at 13.

[189] *See ibid.* at 13-14.

British ships successfully sailed through the channel, and the incident in October 1946, British minesweepers did conduct minesweeping operations in the channel soon after the damage to the *Saumarez* and *Volage* and discovered a number of mines.[190] The ICJ summarised the established facts as follows: "[t]he two ships were mined in Albanian territorial waters in a previously swept and check-swept channel just at the place where a newly laid minefield consisting of moored contact German GY mines was discovered three weeks later."[191]

The ICJ, per the Special Agreement between the two States, addressed whether Albania had incurred international responsibility for the explosions in its waters in October 1946 and the resulting fatalities and damage.[192] It took as its starting point the three possible grounds of responsibility mentioned in the United Kingdom's second submission, namely "that the minefield which caused the explosions was laid between May 15th, 1946, and October 22nd, 1946, by or with the connivance or knowledge of the Albanian Government."[193] The ICJ dealt with each possible ground of responsibility in turn.

First, as to the possible ground of responsibility that the minefield had been laid by the Albanian State, the ICJ noted that the United Kingdom raised this argument only at a superficial level and did not provide evidence to substantiate its position on this point.[194] Further, Albania responded to the argument rather convincingly in stating that, as it did not have a navy, it would have been unable to have laid the minefield.[195] The ICJ easily dismissed this possible ground of responsibility.[196]

The second possible ground of responsibility, that the minefield had been laid with the connivance of the Albanian State, involved an implied theory of collusion between Albania and Yugoslavia, "consisting either of a request by the Albanian Government to the Yugoslav Government for assistance, or of acquiescence by the Albanian authorities in the laying of the mines."[197] Evidence by former Lieutenant-Commander of the Yugoslav

---

190 *See ibid.*
191 *Ibid.* at 15.
192 *See ibid.* at 12. The issue of a compensation obligation was also raised. *See ibid.*
193 *Ibid.* at 15.
194 *See ibid.* at 15-16.
195 *See ibid.* at 15.
196 *See ibid.* at 16.
197 *Ibid.*

Navy Karel Kovacic alleging that he had seen mines being loaded onto two Yugoslav minesweepers in Sibenik that left around 18 October 1946 and returned shortly after 22 October 1946 fell below the standard of "decisive legal proof."[198] The ICJ also rejected British arguments based on circumstantial evidence.[199] As it had done with the first possible ground of responsibility, the ICJ found no merit on the connivance ground of responsibility.[200]

Having rejected the first two possible grounds of responsibility put forward by the United Kingdom, the ICJ assessed whether the mines had been laid with the knowledge of Albania.[201] At the outset, it stated a rule pertaining to State knowledge of unlawful conduct that can be applied in a much wider context: "it cannot be concluded from the mere fact of the control exercised by a State over its territory and waters that that State necessarily knew, or ought to have known, of any unlawful act perpetrated therein, nor yet that it necessarily knew, or should have known, the authors."[202] Knowledge cannot be attributed to a State for all unlawful acts that occur within its territory, and this extends to the unlawful acts of non-State actors. The ICJ noted, however, that the reality of "exclusive territorial control"[203] meant that the complaining State could benefit from a more lenient standard of proof regarding circumstantial evidence and factual inferences.[204] Nonetheless, a finding of knowledge requires that factual inferences leave "*no room* for reasonable doubt."[205] Of course, people may dispute whether certain factual inferences leave "*no room* for reasonable doubt," but like all

---

198 *Ibid.*

199 *See ibid.* at 17.

200 *See ibid.* at 16-17.

201 *See ibid.* at 17-22.

202 *Ibid.* at 18.

203 *Ibid.*

204 *See ibid.* For an application of this principle in the context of counterterrorism and human rights, see HELEN DUFFY, THE "WAR ON TERROR" AND THE FRAMEWORK OF INTERNATIONAL LAW 305 (2005) (asserting that "[l]inked to the foregoing positive obligations is the onus that lies with the state, in certain circumstances, to demonstrate that it has met those obligations, as opposed to the onus resting with the individual to prove the violation. This is particularly so where – as is not infrequently the situation in human rights cases, and all the more so in the shrouded world of counter-terrorism – the facts lie wholly, or in large part, within the exclusive knowledge of the authorities.").

205 Corfu Channel, *supra* note 184, at 18.

courts, the ICJ assesses the evidence and ultimately reaches conclusions based on its mandate.

In assessing whether the mines had been laid with Albania's knowledge, the ICJ examined Albania's attitude prior to and after the incident in October 1946 and explored whether it would have been feasible for it to have observed mine-laying from its coast.[206] As to the first point, the ICJ, noting evidence demonstrating that Albania closely watched the channel, occasionally would employ force in the area, and required permission for foreign vessels to sail through its territorial waters, concluded that the mines must have been laid while Albania had been closely watching the channel.[207] The ICJ, based partly on an experts' report, also found that it was feasible for Albania to have observed mine-laying from its coast and that, given the ICJ's findings as to Albania's attitude prior to and after the incident in October 1946, the mines at issue could not have been laid without Albania's knowledge.[208] Knowledge having been found, the ICJ held Albania internationally responsible for the explosions and the resulting fatalities and damage.[209]

The ICJ assessed Albania's conduct based on fault responsibility, or due diligence.[210] It found that Albania was under a duty to have notified the maritime community about the mines and the danger that they posed, this duty being based on "elementary considerations of humanity, even more exacting in peace than in war; the principle of the freedom of maritime communication; and every State's obligation not to allow knowingly its territory to be used for acts contrary to the rights of other States."[211]

Brownlie's objection, that the ICJ's decision was rooted in objective responsibility and that, "in the light of the subject matter, knowledge was

---

[206] *See ibid.*

[207] *See ibid.* at 18-19.

[208] *See ibid.* at 20-22.

[209] *See ibid.* at 23. The ICJ also found an obligation to compensate. *See ibid.*

[210] *See* Pisillo Mazzeschi, *Forms of International Responsibility for Environmental Harm*, *supra* note 2, at 30. *But see* BROWNLIE, PRINCIPLES OF PUBLIC INTERNATIONAL LAW, *supra* note 8, at 427 (stating that the majority's approach "fails to correspond neatly with either the *culpa* doctrine or the test of objective responsibility."); García Amador, *supra* note 2, at 387-88 (expressing a split of authority on the role that knowledge played in the case); SHAW, *supra* note 5, at 700 (stating that the case "cannot be taken as proof of the acceptance of the fault theory.").

[211] Corfu Channel, *supra* note 184, at 22.

[simply] the prerequisite of the legal duty of the territorial sovereign to give warning of the existence of the mines,"[212] is correct, but only if one bears in mind Nollkaemper's contribution that inquiry into what in the criminal law would be described as the *mens rea* is in the State responsibility context "generally [. . .] either irrelevant or manifests itself in a different, objectified, form in the determination of state responsibility." The ICJ did inquire into Albania's knowledge, and this is crucial. It would not have had to do this had it only been operating within an exclusively objective responsibility regime, a regime which, by definition, does not concern itself with knowledge.

The last element forming the basis of a State's duty of notification in the *Corfu Channel* case, "every State's obligation not to allow knowingly its territory to be used for acts contrary to the rights of other States," has become one of the decision's most lasting contributions to international law, in part because, as a legal rule, it raises so many interesting issues of State responsibility. Dinstein, for example, concludes "from this general principle that a State must not permit its territory to be used as a springboard for operations of armed bands bent on sowing terror in another country."[213] It also raises questions of proving knowledge. For example, how does the more lenient standard of proof regarding circumstantial evidence and factual inferences apply in varied contexts, such as those involving terrorist acts committed by non-State actors? Furthermore, what exactly is meant by a "series of facts linked together and leading logically to a single conclusion,"[214] which triggers the more lenient standard of proof?

C. The Cold War

A review of arbitral decisions, international environmental law, the ICJ's jurisprudence, and diplomatic correspondence during the Cold War also provides a perspective on the interface of State responsibility, non-State actors, and the due diligence principle. *Lake Lanoux*,[215] for example, addressed the relationship between territorial sovereignty and the rights and

212 Brownlie, *State Responsibility and the International Court of Justice, supra* note 29.
213 Yoram Dinstein, *Terrorism as an International Crime,* 19 ISR. Y.B. H.R. 55, 66 (1989).
214 Corfu Channel, *supra* note 184, at 18.
215 Lake Lanoux (*Spain* v. *Fr.*), I.L.R. 100 (1961) (1957).

interests of other States and contributes to an understanding of international law on the subject.

In *Lake Lanoux*, Electricité de France's planned diversion of water from Lake Lanoux was the central fact on the ground in the arbitration between France and Spain.[216] According to the French plan, a dam would be built at Lake Lanoux to more than triple the lake's water capacity, and hydroelectric power would be produced from water diverted from Lake Lanoux to the River Ariège.[217] The diverted water, which had theretofore emptied into the Mediterranean Sea, would then empty into the Atlantic Ocean.[218] To ensure that Spain would not experience a decrease in water flow because of the French plan, the construction of an underground tunnel to transport an amount of water equal to the amount of water diverted would ensure that the River Carol would not experience a net decrease in water.[219] The French plan included safeguards, such as a double set of cocks as a backup mechanism, to ensure that the River Carol would not experience a net decrease in water.[220]

Despite France's contention that the "complete restoration of the volume of water diverted will take place well above the head of the Puigcerda Canal and, *a fortiori*, above the Spanish frontier [. . . and that on] Spanish territory [. . .] neither the course nor the flow of the Carol will suffer the slightest change,"[221] Spain argued that the French plan would violate the 1866 Treaty of Bayonne and its Additional Act, signed by France and Spain, because of its adverse effect on Spanish rights and interests or, alternatively, even if the French plan would not violate the 1866 Treaty of Bayonne and its Additional Act, that Spanish consent to the French plan was required.[222] Thus, Spain argued that the French plan would violate treaty law or, in the alternative, that treaty law required Spanish consent to the French plan. France contended that Spain's position was too rigid and that a dynamic interpretation of treaty law was required to account for modern facts and circumstances and would permit the French plan.[223]

216 *See ibid.* at 107.
217 *See ibid.* at 109.
218 *See ibid.*
219 *See ibid.* at 109-10.
220 *See ibid.* at 110.
221 *Ibid.* at 117.
222 *See ibid.* at 101.
223 *See ibid.* at 114.

The Arbitral Tribunal agreed with France.[224] In doing so, it addressed the relationship between territorial sovereignty and the rights and interests of other States. The Arbitral Tribunal examined restrictions on France's territorial sovereignty in the Additional Act's Article 8.[225] Playing as it does the part of a rebuttable presumption, territorial sovereignty, or the right of a State to do what it will within its territory,[226] "must bend before all international obligations, whatever their origin, but only before such obligations."[227]

The Arbitral Tribunal addressed Spain's argument that treaty law required Spanish consent to the French plan. According to it, another State's consent as a limitation to territorial sovereignty could only be justified based on "clear and convincing evidence."[228] Although the Arbitral Tribunal admitted that cases meeting this standard did exist, they were "exceptional, and international judicial decisions are slow to recognize their existence, especially when they impair the territorial sovereignty of a State, as would be the case in the present matter."[229] Put differently, international law is predisposed against limiting the right of States to do what they will within their territory.[230]

As Lefeber has noted, despite the fact that the principle of territorial sovereignty acts as a rebuttable presumption, a State's exclusive jurisdiction within its territory is limited when the rights of another State are in-

224 *See ibid.* at 142.

225 *See ibid.* at 119-20.

226 *See* Island of Palmas, 2 R.I.A.A. 829, 838 (1928) (defining territorial sovereignty as "[i]ndependence in regard to a portion of the globe[, . . .] the right to exercise therein, to the exclusion of any other State, the functions of a State.").

227 Lake Lanoux, *supra* note 215, at 120.

228 *Ibid.* at 127.

229 *Ibid.*

230 *But see* Legality of the Threat or Use of Nuclear Weapons, *supra* note 158, at 505 (Weeramantry, J., dissenting) (stating that the "principle of good neighbourliness [. . .] is one of the bases of modern international law, which has seen the demise of the principle that sovereign States could pursue their own interests in splendid isolation from each other. A world order in which every sovereign State depends on the same global environment generates a mutual interdependence which can only be implemented by co-operation and good neighbourliness."); IN LARGER FREEDOM: TOWARDS DEVELOPMENT, SECURITY AND HUMAN RIGHTS FOR ALL: REPORT OF THE SECRETARY-GENERAL, U.N. GAOR, at 34, U.N. Doc. A/59/2005 (2005) (asserting that "even harder experience has led us to grapple with the fact that no legal principle – not even sovereignty – should ever be allowed to shield genocide, crimes against humanity and mass human suffering.").

volved.[231] When the interests, something less important than rights, are involved, however, the State whose actions may affect another State "has the right to give preference to the solution contained in its own scheme provided that it takes into consideration in a reasonable manner the interests of the downstream State."[232] While transboundary environmental changes rooted in rights may require the affected State's consent, transboundary environmental changes rooted in interests do not require the affected State's consent but, rather, simply reasonable consideration of its interests.

Although the Arbitral Tribunal spent the greater part of its analysis addressing Spain's argument that the French plan would violate treaty law or, in the alternative, that treaty law required Spanish consent to the French plan, it did engage in a limited discourse that informs an understanding of the due diligence principle, particularly in the context of possible transboundary environmental harm. The French plan, according to the Arbitral Tribunal, did not "entail an abnormal risk in neighbourly relations or in the utilization of the waters,"[233] the safeguards provided were "as satisfactory as possible,"[234] and the risk of the River Carol somehow experiencing a decrease in water could be safely regarded as "only occasional."[235] Pisillo Mazzeschi, commenting, concludes that *Lake Lanoux* stands for a negligence standard of responsibility for transboundary environmental harm, a standard that simply requires a State's taking of "all necessary measures to prevent transboundary damage."[236]

Diplomatic correspondence between States during the Cold War also contributes to an understanding of exactly what international law expects

---

231 *See* RENÉ LEFEBER, TRANSBOUNDARY ENVIRONMENTAL INTERFERENCE AND THE ORIGIN OF STATE LIABILITY 23 (1996).

232 Lake Lanoux, *supra* note 215, at 140. *See* LEFEBER, *supra* note 231, at 24 (noting that "the source state is not free in such cases to disregard a third state's interests altogether.").

233 Lake Lanoux, *supra* note 215, at 123.

234 *Ibid.*

235 *Ibid.*

236 Pisillo Mazzeschi, *Forms of International Responsibility for Environmental Harm*, *supra* note 2, at 30. According to the ICJ, "in the field of environmental protection, vigilance and prevention are required on account of the often irreversible character of damage to the environment and of the limitations inherent in the very mechanism of reparation of this type of damage." Gabčíkovo-Nagymaros (*Hung.* v. *Slovk.*), 1997 I.C.J. 7, 78.

of States with regard to the activities of non-State actors. While one should place diplomatic correspondence in proper context and guard against considering it in isolation, diplomatic correspondence clarifies the rule that States can be held internationally responsible for actions or omissions with respect to non-State actors. By revealing the expectations of States on particular facts and circumstances, it reflects norms of State responsibility. Diplomatic correspondence also exposes the legal views of States, mixed with political considerations, when they face urgent, time-sensitive disputes on the ground and is an example of State practice.[237]

As an example of relevant diplomatic correspondence between States during the Cold War, consider the Soviet Union's lodgement of a protest note with the United States after a Soviet merchant ship filled with sugar was shelled at Caibarien, Cuba, during the night of 26-27 March 1963.[238] Coming in the wake of an attack on a Soviet motorship less than two weeks earlier, the incident constituted, according to the Soviet Union, a "fresh criminal act committed by groups of Cuban counter-revolutionaries who are acting with the approval and under the protection of the American authorities."[239] The Soviet complaint alleged that the United States had supplied anti-Castro Cubans with ships, arms, and "other forms of support"[240] and that these Cubans had acted with the support and knowledge of the United States.[241]

At the heart of the Soviet complaint was the charge that the United States had known of the activities of the "Cuban counter-revolutionary scum"[242] but that it had failed to intervene and had "not taken the necessary measures to prevent similar dangerous provocations."[243] Although the Soviet Union's protest note partly alleged American collusion with the anti-Castro Cubans, it also asserted that the United States had not acted reasonably in control-

---

[237] Dinstein defines State practice as "primarily [. . .] actual conduct (acts of commission or omission), but additionally of declarations and statements (often explaining the conduct of the acting State or challenging the conduct of another State)." YORAM DINSTEIN, THE CONDUCT OF HOSTILITIES UNDER THE LAW OF INTERNATIONAL ARMED CONFLICT 6 (2004).

[238] *See* BROWNLIE, SYSTEM OF THE LAW OF NATIONS: STATE RESPONSIBILITY (PART I), *supra* note 86, at 116.

[239] *Ibid.*

[240] *Ibid.* at 117

[241] *See ibid.*

[242] *Ibid.*

[243] *Ibid.*

ling the anti-Castro Cubans and by failing to take "effective measures"[244] to thwart such "gangster attack[s]."[245] According to the Soviet Union, the United States bore responsibility because its alleged actions and omissions with respect to the anti-Castro Cubans failed to fulfil its international obligations.[246] This protest note demonstrates that an alleged breach of the due diligence obligation can form an integral part of a claim for State responsibility.

China lodged a protest note with Indonesia in December 1965 alleging "serious outrages of persecution of overseas Chinese."[247] The complaint asserted a complex combination of State collusion with non-State actors and failure to control non-State actors that amounted to breaches of Indonesia's international obligations.[248] One incident in the protest note that involved Indonesia's alleged failure to act with due diligence involved Chinese national Oei Tjong Kwi, who after having had his house searched and having been taken into custody and interrogated was later proven innocent by presentation of an unspecified document.[249] Under cover of police escort, "a gang of hooligans, with weapons in their hands, blocked his way, knocked him down, and then poured kerosene on him and burnt him to death."[250] Only a few days later, a "gang of hooligans"[251] abducted another Chinese national and his son during a curfew and murdered them.[252]

While the facts of the Chinese protest note suggest that the perpetrators of both crimes were non-State actors, both incidents reflect the position that a State that enters into a special relationship with an individual, such as by providing a police escort, or that imposes a curfew but, presumably, does not adequately enforce it can be held to a higher standard. That China had apparently informed Indonesia of its concerns on a number of occasions previously, imploring Indonesia to protect Chinese nationals and "urging it

---

244 *Ibid.*

245 *Ibid.*

246 *See ibid.* (maintaining that "[i]t goes without saying that the entire responsibility for the consequences of the Cuban counter-revolutionaries' piratical actions rests wholly with the United States government.").

247 *Ibid.* at 100.

248 *See ibid.* at 100-01.

249 *See ibid.*

250 *Ibid.* at 101.

251 *Ibid.*

252 *See ibid.*

to put a speedy and effective stop to the persecution of Chinese nationals in various parts of Indonesia,"[253] and that Indonesia had failed to provide "any effectual reply"[254] would strengthen the case that Indonesia should have borne some degree of responsibility in the context of the crimes that had been committed against the Chinese nationals.

Another piece of diplomatic correspondence during the Cold War that is worth exploring is a Soviet protest note of 15 April 1971 concerning what the Soviet Union perceived to be the Netherlands' failure to fulfil its international obligations.[255] The incident at issue, an explosion carried out by unknown individuals at the Soviet trade mission in Amsterdam during the night of 14-15 April 1971, caused significant damage to Soviet facilities and injury to staff.[256] The Soviet Union asserted that the explosion directly resulted from the Netherlands' failure to act with due diligence in securing the facility, as the "criminal act [. . .] could only have taken place as the result of failure [. . .] to take effective measures and ensure the security of the trade mission and create normal conditions for its work."[257] According to the protest note, furthermore, the Soviet Union had put the Netherlands on notice about anti-Soviet agitation in the Netherlands against Soviet interests.[258] Evidence of such notice would, from the perspective of States' international obligations for actions or omissions with respect to non-State actors, increase the scrutiny given to a State that would subsequently fail to act with due diligence.

Other relevant diplomatic correspondence between States during the Cold War could be cited at this juncture.[259] The examples above, however, demonstrate that States expect other States to act reasonably and according to their international obligations when non-State actors threaten harm to the complaining State or actually harm it or its nationals abroad.

An additional source during the Cold War that provides perspective on State responsibility, non-State actors, and the due diligence principle involves the ICJ. Islamic revolution and the Ayatollah Khomeini's rise to

253 *Ibid.*
254 *Ibid.*
255 *See ibid.* at 118-19.
256 *See ibid.* at 118.
257 *Ibid.*
258 *See ibid.* at 118-19.
259 For a helpful selection of diplomatic correspondence, see *ibid.* at 90-119.

power in Iran formed the backdrop to the *United States Diplomatic and Consular Staff in Tehran* (*Hostages*) case,[260] another case on the ICJ's docket that assists in understanding exactly what is expected of States with regard to the activities of non-State actors.

On 14 February 1979, an armed crowd seized the United States Embassy in Tehran (Embassy), killing two associates of it, causing serious damage to the facilities, and taking dozens hostage.[261] There is no indication in the ICJ's recitation of facts that the members of the crowd had been in any way associated with Iran.[262] Iranian security forces responded to the unrest by arriving on the scene, expelling the occupiers of the Embassy, and transferring control back to the United States.[263] A letter of early March 1979 from Iranian Prime Minister Mehdi Bazargan to the United States expressed regret at the incident, stated a desire to make reparation, and sought to assure the United States that such an incident would not occur in future.[264] Events several months later, however, would demonstrate the utter inadequacy of Iran's response.

On 22 October 1979, the deposed Shah entered the United States for medical reasons, a turn of events that met with the strong disapproval of Iran and revolutionaries on the ground in Iran.[265] The United States had on a number of occasions received assurances from high level Iranian officials that the Embassy would be protected and that its integrity would be maintained, and in fact, on 1 November 1979, when around 5,000 people protested at the Embassy, Iran maintained order.[266]

The situation drastically changed, however, during the morning of 4 November 1979, when several hundred protesters stormed the Embassy.[267] Amidst the chaos, the ICJ noted, Iranian security forces "are reported to have simply disappeared from the scene; at all events it is established that they made no apparent effort to deter or prevent the demonstrators from

---

[260] United States Diplomatic and Consular Staff in Tehran (Hostages) (*U.S.* v. *Iran*), 1980 I.C.J. 3.

[261] *See ibid.* at 10-11.

[262] *See ibid.*

[263] *See ibid.* at 11.

[264] *See ibid.*

[265] *See ibid.*

[266] *See ibid.* at 11-12.

[267] *See ibid.* at 12.

seizing the Embassy's premises."[268] Hostages were taken, and despite repeated American pleas for assistance, Iran made no attempt to affect the release of the hostages or to restore order.[269] Making matters worse for the United States, its Consulates in Shiraz and Tabriz were overrun, again without any protection from Iran.[270]

The ICJ dealt with what it described as the first phase of events, which covered the "armed attack on the United States Embassy by militants on 4 November 1979, the overrunning of its premises, the seizure of its inmates as hostages, the appropriation of its property and archives and the conduct of the Iranian authorities in the face of those occurrences."[271] Despite the ICJ's conclusion that the protesters who had stormed the premises had acted in a private capacity and, as such, were not State actors and the fact that the protesters' conduct could not, therefore, be attributed to Iran,[272] it found that Iran incurred international responsibility because of its actions or omissions in relation to the incident, "for its own conduct was in conflict with its international obligations."[273] Specifically, the 1961 Vienna Convention on Diplomatic Relations and the 1963 Vienna Convention on Consular Relations, as well as parallel general international law obligations,[274] imposed international legal obligations that Iran did not satisfy.[275] Iran had failed to sufficiently protect the premises or act preventively or during the course of the sieges, despite assurances given to the United States to this effect.[276]

The ICJ succinctly stated the circumstances under which Iran had incurred responsibility. Specifically, Iranian authorities:

---

268 *Ibid.*

269 *See ibid.* at 12-13.

270 *See ibid.* at 13.

271 *Ibid.* at 29. The first phase also included the sieges of the United States Consulates at Shiraz and Tabriz. *See ibid.* at 30.

272 *See ibid.* at 29.

273 *Ibid.* at 30.

274 *See ibid.* at 30-31.

275 *See ibid.* at 32. Note that, "[s]o far as concerns the two private United States nationals seized as hostages by the invading militants, that inaction entailed, albeit incidentally, a breach of its obligations under Article II, paragraph 4, of the 1955 Treaty of Amity, Economic Relations, and Consular Rights which, in addition to the obligations of Iran existing under general international law, requires the parties to ensure 'the most constant protection and security' to each other's nationals in their respective territories." *Ibid.*

276 *See ibid.* at 31-32.

(a) were fully aware of their obligations under the conventions in force to take appropriate steps to protect the premises of the United States Embassy and its diplomatic and consular staff from any attack and from any infringement of their inviolability, and to ensure the security of such other persons as might be present on the said premises;
(b) were fully aware, as a result of the appeals for help made by the United States Embassy, of the urgent need for action on their part;
(c) had the means at their disposal to perform their obligations;
(d) completely failed to comply with these obligations.[277]

Commenting on the *Hostages* decision in the context of the due diligence principle under international law, Dupuy makes an important distinction between obligations of conduct, including obligations of prevention, and obligations of result.[278] According to him, the crucial point is the steps taken by the State in meeting its particular due diligence obligation under international law, such that, on the *Hostages* facts, "if Iran had been willing and able to demonstrate that it had actually taken all appropriate steps to avoid the taking of diplomats as hostages, then it would not have been held responsible by the Court."[279] Put another way, the due diligence obligation requires the State's "*best effort*[*s*]."[280] Without these efforts, or efforts of any kind, the due diligence obligation will be breached, and the State will be responsible.

A final example during the Cold War that touches upon the interface of State responsibility, non-State actors, and the due diligence principle involves a Soviet protest note addressing an incident strikingly similar to that at issue in the *Hostages* case.[281] In late-December 1980, a "large group of

---

[277] *Ibid.* at 32-33. Zegveld refers to "(c) had the means at their disposal to perform their obligations" as the "degree of factual capability." ZEGVELD, *supra* note 156, at 190.

[278] *See* Pierre-Marie Dupuy, *Reviewing the Difficulties of Codification: On Ago's Classification of Obligations of Means and Obligations of Result in Relation to State Responsibility,* 10(2) EUR. J. INT'L L. 371, 379 (1999). *See also* Goodwin-Gill, *supra* note 28, at 77-78; Pisillo Mazzeschi, *The Due Diligence Rule and the Nature of the International Responsibility of States, supra* note 16, at 46-49.

[279] Dupuy, *supra* note 278.

[280] *Ibid.* (stating that "[*w*]*hat counts here is the violation of the best effort obligation, not the end result actually achieved.*"). *See* International Law Commission, *Commentaries, Articles on Prevention of Transboundary Harm, supra* note 182, at 391-92.

[281] *See* BROWNLIE, SYSTEM OF THE LAW OF NATIONS: STATE RESPONSIBILITY (PART I), *supra* note 86, at 119.

rampaging elements, armed with clubs, stones and knives"[282] broke into the Soviet Embassy in Iran, threatened the diplomatic staff, and caused significant damage to the facilities.[283] The charge that Iran had not acted with due diligence in preventing and reacting to the non-State actors who had descended upon the Soviet Embassy was at the heart of the complaint. According to the Soviet Union, Iran had had notice of the impending assault on the Soviet Embassy but had failed to take "measures sufficiently urgent and effective to prevent that attack."[284] Furthermore, according to the Soviets, Iran had been slow to intervene and dispel the "rampaging elements."[285]

D. The End of the Cold War and Recent Developments

Since the end of the Cold War and more recently, the interface of State responsibility, non-State actors, and the due diligence principle has been further clarified and emphasised under international law. In *Asian Agricultural Products Ltd.* (*AAPL*) v. *Sri Lanka*, for example, the International Centre for the Settlement of Investment Disputes (ICSID) heard a claim brought by AAPL against Sri Lanka based on the 1965 ICSID Convention on the Settlement of Investment Disputes Between States and Nationals of Other States and Article 8(1) of a 1980 Bilateral Investment Treaty between the United Kingdom and Sri Lanka.[286] As an ICSID decision, *AAPL* is particularly important.[287] AAPL and Sri Lanka agreed that the Bilateral In-

---

282 *Ibid.*

283 *See ibid.*

284 *Ibid.*

285 *Ibid.*

286 *See Asian Agricultural Products Ltd. (AAPL)* v. *Sri Lanka*, ICSID Case No. ARB/87/3, 30(3) I.L.M. 577, 580-81 (1991). On bilateral investment treaties generally, see SHAW, *supra* note 5, at 747-49. Shaw adopts a cautious approach to bilateral investment treaties and customary international law. *See ibid.* at 750-51.

287 *See* Stephen C. Vasciannie, *Bilateral Investment Treaties and Civil Strife: The AAPL/Sri Lanka Arbitration,* 39(3) NETH. INT'L L. REV. 332, 354 (1992) (promoting a cautious approach to the decision, although admitting that, "[b]ecause the AAPL decision is the first case in which an ICSID tribunal derived its jurisdiction through the consent provision in a bilateral investment treaty, there will probably be a tendency to attach special significance to the decision as a precedent in future cases.").

vestment Treaty acted as the underlying law but disagreed as to how it should be interpreted and applied.[288]

One of AAPL's Sri Lankan investments, a shrimp farming operation, suffered significant damage after a raid by Sri Lankan security forces in pursuit of the Tamil Tigers, a raid described by AAPL as a "murderous overreaction by the STF [i.e., Sri Lankan Special Task Force] which led to [. . .] destruction and civilian deaths."[289] AAPL alleged that the farm's management had cooperated with Sri Lanka in its previous counterterrorism efforts.[290] According to AAPL, the STF unnecessarily destroyed the shrimp crop, burned the office, repair, dormitory, and store facilities, and executed twenty one members of staff during the raid "under circumstances which 'strongly suggest that this incident was a wanton use of force not required by the exigencies of the situation and not planned pursuant to any combat action.'"[291] AAPL also alleged a total investment loss as a result of the operation and claimed compensation.[292] Sri Lanka, however, argued that a cooperative relationship had existed between the Tamil Tigers and the farm's management, that the Tamil Tigers had used the farm in the past, and that the damage caused during the raid had not been inflicted by Sri Lankan forces or, alternatively, had been necessary.[293]

Since *AAPL* operates within a specific treaty regime,[294] its usefulness to international law generally lies in its statement of principles related to States' due diligence obligations that apply outside the particular treaty context at issue. The investment of an alien in a State, even in the absence of a treaty, is entitled to due diligence protection from the State being invested in, the breach of which obligation triggers State responsibility.[295] Furthermore, arbitral decisions and scholarship support the interrelated rules of State responsibility according to which:

(i) A State on whose territory an insurrection occurs is not responsible for loss or damage sustained by foreign investors unless it can be shown

[288] *See* AAPL, *supra* note 286, at 594.
[289] *Ibid.* at 583.
[290] *See ibid.* at 613.
[291] *Ibid.*
[292] *See ibid.* at 581.
[293] *See ibid.* at 585; *ibid.* at 614.
[294] *See ibid.* at 597-98.
[295] *See ibid.* at 608-09.

that the Government of that state failed to provide the standard of protection required, either by treaty, or under general customary law, as the case may be; and

(ii) Failure to provide the standard of protection required entails the state's international responsibility for losses suffered, regardless of whether the damages occurred during an insurgents' offensive act resulting from governmental counter-insurgency activities.[296]

The due diligence standard that applies in such situations, according to the Tribunal, is one that is objective in nature, one which assesses the "required degree of protection and security with regard to what should be legitimately expected to be secured for foreign investors by a reasonably well organized modern State."[297]

The Tribunal found that Sri Lanka had breached its due diligence obligation, therefore triggering its responsibility as a State.[298] Relying on evidence of a cooperative relationship between the farm's management and Sri Lanka over the Tamil Tigers, the Tribunal found that Sri Lanka should have exhausted peaceful measures before resorting to the raid on the farm.[299] According to it, "through said inaction and omission[, Sri Lanka had] violated its due diligence obligation which requires undertaking all possible measures that could be reasonably expected to prevent the eventual occurrence of killings and property destructions."[300] The Tribunal stressed the importance of preventive measures to the due diligence obligation because "such measures fall within the normal exercise of governmental inherent powers – as a public authority – entitled to order undesirable persons out from security sensitive areas."[301] What States do or fail to do to protect innocent people from the dangers posed by non-State actors will heavily factor into assessments of potential State responsibility under the due diligence principle.

Samuel K. B. Asante's dissenting opinion in *AAPL* provides an interesting perspective on States' due diligence obligations during times of insur-

[296] *Ibid.* at 609-10.
[297] *Ibid.* at 612.
[298] *See ibid.* at 615-19.
[299] *See ibid.*
[300] *Ibid.* at 616.
[301] *Ibid.*

rection.[302] Asante stressed that customary international law, as demonstrated by the decisions of international tribunals and publicists, strongly supports the general rule that States do not bear responsibility for loss or damage to foreigners resulting from, among others, insurrections, riots, states of emergency, or armed conflicts.[303] According to Asante, a State's due diligence obligation is "easily discharged in the face of an insurrection or other civil commotion resulting in a temporary loss of control by the host country over the area of insurgency."[304] Asante argued that international law presumes a State's fulfillment of the due diligence obligation in such a situation[305] and questioned the Tribunal's criticism of Sri Lanka's decision to use force, arguing that this "touches on the sovereign prerogatives of a Government fighting for its very life."[306]

While the majority opinion stressed that State responsibility will not be presumed,[307] Asante seems to have confused this general principle with a non-rebuttable presumption, arguing that, "[o]nce it is conceded that the Government had a compelling sovereign duty to undertake a military operation to regain control, the timing and modalities of the security operation must surely fall within its exclusive discretion."[308] Such language seems to undermine the principle of international human rights law according to which certain rights are non-derogable, even during states of emergency and upheaval.[309] Indeed, Asante's "must surely fall" language may actually highlight, although no doubt unintentionally on Asante's part, the aspirational nature of his statement rather than its reflection of the current state of international law. One may concur with Asante that tribunals "should be slow to

---

[302] On due diligence, insurrection, and *force majeure*, see Pisillo Mazzeschi, *The Due Diligence Rule and the Nature of the International Responsibility of States*, *supra* note 16, at 45-46.

[303] *See* AAPL, *supra* note 286, at 646.

[304] *Ibid.* at 647.

[305] *See ibid.*

[306] *Ibid.* at 651. Vasciannie makes a similar theoretical argument. *See* Vasciannie, *supra* note 287, at 353.

[307] *See* AAPL, *supra* note 286, at 606-07.

[308] *Ibid.* at 651-52.

[309] For a more detailed explanation of this human rights principle, see OFFICE OF THE UNITED NATIONS HIGH COMMISSIONER FOR HUMAN RIGHTS GENEVA, DIGEST OF JURISPRUDENCE OF THE UNITED NATIONS AND REGIONAL ORGANIZATIONS ON THE PROTECTION OF HUMAN RIGHTS WHILE COUNTERING TERRORISM 2-3, U.N. Sales No. HR/PUB/03/1 (2003).

second-guess the tactics and strategies of military commanders on the ground,"[310] indeed, that is the essence of the idea that State responsibility will not be presumed, but it is unfortunate that his dissent could be construed, rightly or wrongly, as justifying a "blank check" to States when battling insurgencies. International law no longer accepts that "the Crown can do no wrong."

ICSID also dealt with the due diligence principle more recently, in *Noble Ventures, Inc.* (*Noble*) v. *Romania*.[311] That arbitral decision involved Noble, an American corporation, and Romania and Romania's role in a privatised formerly State-run steel company, Combinatul Siderugic Resita (CSR), that Noble had come to acquire.[312] Noble raised issues that mostly involved the 1992 United States-Romania Bilateral Investment Treaty (BIT).[313]

The most interesting claim that Noble raised in relation to the due diligence principle involved its contention that "from January 2001 onwards demonstrations and protests by CSR's employees occurred frequently and on a large scale and that they were accompanied by unlawful acts for which the Respondent is responsible by reason of its failure to provide full protection and security as provided for under the BIT."[314] Noble argued that Romania had known about the direct action and that the company had complained to the State about it but that Romania had simply inflamed the situation.[315] Furthermore, according to Noble, Romania, in a factual situation generally similar to that in the *Hostages* case, through its "local police refused to exercise adequate measures to protect Noble Ventures and CSR in Resita from unlawful activity on its premises."[316] Because of this, Noble complained that its managers had been unlawfully imprisoned and sometimes beaten by the strikers, that its industrial capital had been damaged, and that its facilities had been occupied and looted.[317] Noble asserted an objective complaint, that Romania had breached its obligation to "*provide*

310 AAPL, *supra* note 286, at 652.

311 Noble, *supra* note 64.

312 *See ibid.* at 9-11.

313 *See ibid.* at 11-16.

314 *Ibid.* at 103. According to Art. II(2)(a), "[*i*]*nvestment shall at all times be accorded fair and equitable treatment, shall enjoy full protection and security and shall in no case be accorded treatment less than that required by international law.*" *Ibid.* at 47.

315 *See ibid.* at 13-14.

316 *Ibid.* at 14.

317 *See ibid.*

the reasonable measures of protection which a well-administered government would be expected to exercise under similar circumstances."[318] By contrast, Romania argued that it had satisfied its obligation, grounded in the due diligence principle, to Noble.[319]

In rejecting Noble's argument,[320] the Tribunal clearly understood the BIT provision, the "*full protection and security*" obligation, as being no more demanding than the due diligence standard under the law of diplomatic protection.[321] It analogised to the ICJ's judgment in *Elettronica Sicula S.p.A.*[322] and noted that, in such situations, "violations of protection standards are not easily to be established."[323] In this sense, *Noble* demonstrates the difficulties that courts and tribunals face in dealing with the due diligence principle.

Another important development since the end of the Cold War and more recently has been the ILC's completion in 2001 of the *Articles on Prevention of Transboundary Harm from Hazardous Activities* (*Articles on Prevention of Transboundary Harm*).[324] According to Article 1, the *Articles on Prevention of Transboundary Harm* are only applicable to "activities not prohibited by international law which involve a risk of causing significant transboundary harm through their physical consequences."[325] While it is true, as Article 1 and its *Commentary* make clear, that the *Articles on Prevention of Transboundary Harm* must be read within the context of international liability without a wrongful act and not in the context of State responsibility,[326] the ILC's description of the due diligence principle can be analogised to international law generally when the operative rule at issue imposes a due diligence obligation.

Article 3 of the *Articles on Prevention of Transboundary Harm* requires that States of origin take "all appropriate measures to prevent significant

---

318 *Ibid.* at 104.

319 *See ibid.* at 104-05.

320 *See ibid.* at 106.

321 *See ibid.* at 105.

322 Elettronica Sicula S.p.A. (*U.S.* v. *Italy*), 1989 I.C.J. 15.

323 Noble, *supra* note 64, at 106.

324 International Law Commission, *Articles on Prevention of Transboundary Harm, supra* note 181.

325 *Ibid.* at 371, Art. 1.

326 *See* International Law Commission, *Commentaries*, *Articles on Prevention of Transboundary Harm, supra* note 182, at 382.

transboundary harm or at any event to minimize the risk thereof."[327] While it is not possible to describe the "all appropriate measures" duty with much more precision than general rules of this nature permit, the *Commentaries* do provide some guidance. While States of origin only have to bear the risk of foreseeable consequences, they do have to take an active stance in identifying activities that, while not presently foreseeable, may evolve into foreseeable risks.[328]

As the *Commentaries* make clear, the prevention or minimisation duty is a due diligence duty.[329] While States of origin are expected to prevent "significant transboundary harm," if such harm does occur, they must take "best possible efforts"[330] at minimisation. To phrase the due diligence obligation within the context of the *Articles on Prevention of Transboundary Harm* a different way, the due diligence rule requires "reasonable efforts by a State to inform itself of factual and legal components that relate foreseeably to a contemplated procedure and to take appropriate measures in timely fashion, to address them."[331] This general due diligence language will necessarily be assessed within a particular context, and what is required is, in the context of the prevention of transboundary harm from hazardous activities, conduct that is "generally considered to be appropriate and proportional to the degree of risk of transboundary harm in the particular instance."[332]

The *Articles on Prevention of Transboundary Harm* impose upon States due diligence obligations in the context of "significant transboundary harm." While general principles can be, and should be, sketched in the abstract,

---

327 International Law Commission, *Articles on Prevention of Transboundary Harm, supra* note 181. With Art. 4, Art. 3 describes in full the due diligence obligation. *See* International Law Commission, *Commentaries, Articles on Prevention of Transboundary Harm, supra* note 182, at 390. Art. 4 states that concerned States should "cooperate in good faith and, as necessary, seek the assistance of one or more competent international organizations in preventing significant transboundary harm or at any event in minimizing the risk thereof." International Law Commission, *Articles on Prevention of Transboundary Harm, supra* note 181, at 372, Art. 4.

328 *See* International Law Commission, *Commentaries, Articles on Prevention of Transboundary Harm, supra* note 182, at 391.

329 *See ibid.* The ILC describes the "obligation of due diligence [. . . as] the core basis of the provisions intended to prevent significant transboundary harm, or at any event to minimize the risk thereof." *Ibid.* at 411.

330 *Ibid.* at 392.

331 *Ibid.* at 393. This involves policy formulation and implementation. *See ibid.*

332 *Ibid.* at 394.

here, as elsewhere, assessment under the due diligence rule is necessarily specific to particular facts and circumstances. The due diligence obligation can be simply stated, yet its complexity and rigour cannot be overstated: "the degree of care in question is that expected of a good Government."[333] In this sense, to suggest, as Duffy does, that "[t]here is no single, agreed-upon definition of 'due diligence'"[334] misleads because the due diligence principle's definition, as a flexible reasonableness standard adaptable to particular facts and circumstances, provides the underlying legal framework. It amounts to "due, or merited, care."[335]

In assessing the question of transboundary harm to the environment that States must guard against, Article 2 of the *Articles on Prevention of Transboundary Harm* defines "risk of causing significant transboundary harm" by reference to "risks taking the form of a high probability of causing significant transboundary harm and a low probability of causing disastrous transboundary harm."[336] An assessment of "risk of causing significant transboundary harm" necessarily must balance probability and magnitude, or risk and harm.[337] Like the due diligence principle generally, the question of "risk of causing significant transboundary harm" is flexible and adaptable to particular facts and circumstances and operates along a continuum, in the case of "risk of causing significant transboundary harm," along a "spectrum of relationships between 'risk' and 'harm', all of which would reach the level of 'significant.'"[338]

The objective nature of the determination to be made must be constantly kept in mind when assessing the question of transboundary harm to the environment against which States must guard. The cases are necessarily

---

333 *Ibid.* at 395.

334 DUFFY, *supra* note 204, at 57 n. 55.

335 Corino, *supra* note 76, at 120.

336 International Law Commission, *Articles on Prevention of Transboundary Harm, supra* note 181, at 371, Art. 2. Such probability-based language is common in international environmental law generally. European Directive 2004/35/CE, for example, defines the concept of "'imminent threat of damage' [. . . as] a sufficient likelihood that environmental damage will occur in the near future." Directive 2004/35/CE of the European Parliament and of the Council of 21 April 2004 on Environmental Liability with Regard to the Prevention and Remedying of Environmental Damage, Art. 2(9), 2004 O.J. (L 143) 56, 60.

337 *See* International Law Commission, *Commentaries, Articles on Prevention of Transboundary Harm, supra* note 182, at 387.

338 *Ibid.*

specific to particular facts and circumstances and must balance a number of concerns, such as property, human health, and the environment in other States, while at the same time the ill effects must be "susceptible of being measured by factual and objective standards."[339] In that the *Articles on Prevention of Transboundary Harm* clearly assess risk objectively, with reference to an "appreciation of possible harm resulting from an activity which a properly informed observer had or ought to have had,"[340] the assessment of risk is similar to the assessment of foreseeable risk of harm under the American tort law of negligence.[341] The foreseeability of the risk of harm is rooted in reasonableness.[342]

Another example since the end of the Cold War and more recently of the interface of State responsibility, non-State actors, and the due diligence principle in the context of international environmental law is European Directive 2004/35/CE.[343] That Directive addresses itself to "establish[ing] a framework of environmental liability based on the 'polluter-pays' principle, to prevent and remedy environmental damage."[344] To that end, it details preventive and remedial measures that must be taken, preferably by the operator, in the context of environmental damage and the imminent threat thereof.[345] Article 7(2) states that the competent authority determines which measures must be taken in remedial situations.[346] In doing so with respect

---

339 *Ibid.* at 388.

340 *Ibid.* at 385.

341 On Anglo-American law in this regard, see H.L.A. HART, THE CONCEPT OF LAW 132-33 (2nd ed. 1994).

342 *See* BIRNIE & BOYLE, *supra* note 173, at 115 (stating that, "[c]learly, a state cannot be required to regulate activities of which it is not and could not reasonably have been aware; equally clearly the same is true of activities which the state did not know, and could not reasonably have known, to be potentially harmful.").

343 Directive 2004/35/CE, *supra* note 336.

344 *Ibid.* at Art. 1, 59. "According to the 'polluter-pays' principle, an operator causing environmental damage or creating an imminent threat of such damage should, in principle, bear the cost of the necessary preventive or remedial measures. In cases where a competent authority acts, itself or through a third party, in the place of an operator, that authority should ensure that the cost incurred by it is recovered from the operator. It is also appropriate that the operators should ultimately bear the cost of assessing environmental damage and, as the case may be, assessing an imminent threat of such damage occurring." *Ibid.* at Preamble, Para. 18, 57-58.

345 *See ibid.* at Arts. 5-6, 61-62.

346 *See ibid.* at Arts. 7(2), 62.

to damage to protected species, water, or natural habitats, Annex II notes that "[t]he reasonable remedial options should be evaluated, using best available technologies,"[347] with regard being had to such factors as cost, effectiveness, prophylactic potential, and sensitivity to local concerns.[348] The question of due diligence arises in this context because what a competent authority may regard as a reasonable remedial option may, in fact, be patently unreasonable on the particular facts and circumstances. The State cannot expect to shield itself when it acts, to use words already quoted from the *Commentaries* to the *Articles on Prevention of Transboundary Harm*, contrary to the "the degree of care [. . .] expected of a good Government."

Within the context of international human rights law, Chinkin notes that the due diligence principle has undermined the public *versus* private divide that had hitherto strictly separated those activities for which the State, respectively, could and could not be held responsible.[349] As the Inter-American Court of Human Rights noted in 1988:

> [a]n illegal act which violates human rights and which is initially not directly imputable to a State (for example, because it is the act of a private person or because the person responsible has not been identified) can lead to international responsibility of the State, not because of the act itself, but because of the lack of due diligence to prevent the violation or to respond to it as required by the [American] Convention [on Human Rights].[350]

---

347 *Ibid.* at Annex II, Paras. 1.3.1, 68.

348 *See ibid.*

349 *See* Christine Chinkin, *A Critique of the Public/Private Dimension,* 10(2) EUR. J. INT'L L. 387 (1999). *See also* Jan Arno Hessbruegge, *The Historical Development of the Doctrines of Attribution and Due Diligence in International Law,* 36(2-3) N.Y.U. J. INT'L L. & POL. 265, 275 (2004).

350 Velásquez Rodríguez, *supra* note 132, at Para. 172. Chinkin discusses this case at Chinkin, *supra* note 349, at 394. For further on this point, see Luigi Condorelli, *The Imputability to States of Acts of International Terrorism,* 19 ISR. Y.B. H.R. 233, 241-42 (1989); Olivier de Schutter, *The Accountability of Multinationals for Human Rights Violations in European Law,* in NON-STATE ACTORS AND HUMAN RIGHTS 227, 233-35 (Philip Alston ed., 2005); DUFFY, *supra* note 204, at 301-03; Frey, *supra* note 38; Reinisch, *supra* note 108, at 78-82; Colin Warbrick, *The European Response to Terrorism in an Age of Human Rights,* 15(5) EUR. J. INT'L L. 989, 1006 (2004).

The Northern Ireland Human Rights Commission has also made a similar point.[351] In realising human rights, States' procedural obligations are particularly crucial.[352]

A further example of the due diligence principle is provided by the General Assembly's adoption of the *Basic Principles and Guidelines on the Right to a Remedy and Reparation for Victims of Gross Violations of International Human Rights Law and Serious Violations of International Humanitarian Law* in Resolution 60/147.[353] Regarding international human rights law and international humanitarian law, Resolution 60/147 recognises States' obligations to act with due diligence. States must, for example, "[t]ake appropriate legislative and administrative and other appropriate measures to prevent violations,"[354] "[i]nvestigate violations effectively, promptly, thoroughly and impartially and, where appropriate, take action against those allegedly responsible in accordance with domestic and international law,"[355] "[p]rovide those who claim to be victims of a human rights or humanitarian law violation with equal and effective access to justice, as described below, irrespective of who may ultimately be the bearer of responsibility for the violation,"[356] and "[p]rovide effective remedies to victims, including reparation, as described below."[357]

Like the due diligence principle generally under international law, the question whether a State has complied with the obligations spelled out in

---

[351] *See* MARK KELLY, NORTHERN IRELAND HUMAN RIGHTS COMMISSION, A PRACTICAL GUIDE TO THE EUROPEAN CONVENTION ON HUMAN RIGHTS: THE RIGHT TO LIFE 14-15 (2005) (maintaining that the "European Court of Human Rights takes the view that Article 2 of the ECHR not only prohibits unlawful killing by agents of the State, but also places States under a 'positive obligation' to take preventive operational measures to protect persons whose lives are threatened, even if those threats are from another private person, rather than an agent of the state.").

[352] *See* Jan Klabbers, *Straddling Law and Politics: Judicial Review in International Law,* in TOWARDS WORLD CONSTITUTIONALISM: ISSUES IN THE LEGAL ORDERING OF THE WORLD COMMUNITY 809, 828 (Ronald St. John Macdonald & Douglas M. Johnston eds., 2005). Klabbers tends toward the view that "the substantive core of rights can only come to life by being surrounded by procedural notions, or perhaps consists exclusively of bundles of procedural rights." *Ibid.*

[353] G.A. Res. 60/147, *supra* note 82.

[354] *Ibid.* at Annex, 4.

[355] *Ibid.*

[356] *Ibid.* at Annex, 5.

[357] *Ibid.*

General Assembly Resolution 60/147 will trigger an assessment on the basis of a reasonableness standard. It is important to note that the "equal and effective access to justice" obligation applies "irrespective of who may ultimately be the bearer of responsibility for the violation."[358] This language suggests that a State's obligation in this respect is no less demanding if non-State actors inflict injury.

A final example since the end of the Cold War and more recently of the interface of State responsibility, non-State actors, and the due diligence principle can be found in the ICJ's 2005 decision in *Armed Activities on the Territory of the Congo*.[359] In that contentious case, the ICJ held that Uganda bore the obligations in Ituri region in the Democratic Republic of the Congo of an occupying power,[360] one of which was the duty to "take appropriate measures to prevent the looting, plundering and exploitation of natural resources in the occupied territory to cover private persons in this district and not only members of Ugandan military forces."[361] The ICJ referred to this elsewhere as a "duty of vigilance."[362] Demonstrating that the due diligence obligation under international law also extends to occupying powers in situations when natural resources are exploited, the ICJ found Uganda responsible as a State.[363]

Finally, it should be noted that the *Hostages* due diligence test continues to demonstrate its relevance as a legal framework within which to assess State action and omission. As applied to destruction caused by rioters to the Danish and Norwegian embassies in Damascus in early-February 2006, for example, it informs whether Syria bears responsibility as a State for an internationally wrongful act.[364]

---

358 *Ibid.*

359 Armed Activities on the Territory of the Congo (*Congo* v. *Uganda*), 2005 I.C.J.

360 *See ibid.* at Para. 178.

361 *Ibid.* at Para. 248.

362 *Ibid.* at Para. 247.

363 *See ibid.* at Para. 250.

364 On this incident, see *Uproar at Syrian Cartoon Protests*, BBC NEWS, 5 February 2006, *available at* http://news.bbc.co.uk/go/pr/fr/-/1/hi/world/middle_east/4682388.stm. For a similar example, see *China Rejects Japan's Demand for Apology,* CBC NEWS, 17 April 2005, *available at* http://www.cbc.ca/storyview/MSN/world/national/2005/04/17/china-japan050417.html.

V. Conclusion

In conclusion, international law recognises a number of principles of responsibility. One of these, the due diligence principle, applies across diverse areas of international law, and international legal developments during the last century support this. Condorelli accurately refers to the due diligence principle, as this chapter has demonstrated, as a "basic principle of international law."[365]

The due diligence principle is especially important under international law because it can be applied to varied facts and circumstances. In an age of modern terrorism, for example, it can be used to hold States responsible for their actions or omissions when dealing with terrorism committed by non-State actors.[366] How, whether, and with what breadth the due diligence principle is applied, however, remains one of political will.

---

365 Condorelli, *supra* note 350, at 240.

366 *See* Robert P. Barnidge, Jr., *States' Due Diligence Obligations with Regard to International Non-State Terrorist Organizations Post-11 September 2001: The Heavy Burden That States Must Bear*, 16 Ir. Stud. Int'l Aff. 103, 103-25 (2005); Condorelli, *supra* note 350, at 241.

Chapter 4
THE DUE DILIGENCE OBLIGATION OF STATES IN THE CONTEXT OF NON-STATE ACTORS THAT ENGAGE IN TERRORISM

Chapter 4
THE DUE DILIGENCE OBLIGATION OF STATES IN THE CONTEXT OF NON-STATE ACTORS THAT ENGAGE IN TERRORISM

I. Introduction

As the previous chapter has shown, international legal developments during the last century support the existence of a due diligence principle under international law. Although this standard exists generally, this chapter focuses on how it operates with specific regard to non-State actors that engage in terrorism. Many of the most important international legal rules that impose obligations on States in this regard operate within a due diligence framework.

Although some argue that the prevention and combating of terrorism are obligations imposed upon States by general international law[1] and that "even mere tolerance of activities carried out in [. . . a State's] own territory by individuals against the security of foreign States may amount to a breach of international law, if it can be proved that the State has been negligent in failing to prevent or punish such conduct,"[2] such statements of legal principle alone do not suffice for purposes of this chapter. Rather, this chapter focuses on treaty law and Security Council Resolutions and shows how many of their provisions operate within a due diligence framework. It avoids methodically listing and describing all international and regional instruments that oblige States to confront non-State actors that engage in terrorism.[3]

---

[1] *See* Pierre-Marie Dupuy, *State Sponsors of Terrorism: Issues of International Responsibility*, in Enforcing International Law Norms Against Terrorism 3, 11 (Andrea Bianchi ed., 2004). *See also* Pierre-Marie Dupuy & Cristina Hoss, Trail Smelter *and Terrorism: International Mechanisms to Combat Transboundary Harm*, in Transboundary Harm in International Law: Lessons from the *Trail Smelter* Arbitration 225, 235 (Rebecca M. Bratspies & Russell A. Miller eds., 2006).

[2] Andrea Bianchi, *Enforcing International Law Norms Against Terrorism: Achievements and Prospects*, in Enforcing, *supra* note 1, at 491, 497.

[3] There are a number of excellent resources for further exploration of the legal landscape. The United Nations' own dedicated website, *UN Action to Counter Terrorism, avail-*

II. Identifying the Due Diligence Principle in International Legal Rules

Reference to the insights developed in the previous chapter on the due diligence principle under international law provides some assistance as to how international legal rules operate within a specifically due diligence framework. At the most basic level, one can recall the four regimes of responsibility that Pisillo Mazzeschi identifies, namely fault-based responsibility, objective responsibility that allows for the raising of circumstances precluding wrongfulness, objective responsibility that does not allow for such a defence, and liability without a wrongful act.[4] A fault-based responsibility regime triggers an assessment of the relevant international legal rule under the due diligence principle.

International legal developments during the last century provide clues with regard to determining when a fault-based responsibility regime, and a corresponding due diligence assessment, applies. Language plays an important role in this regard. A State's failure to, as the United States/Mexico General Claims Commission put it, "take proper steps to apprehend and punish the slayer"[5] involves the due diligence principle. "[E]very State's obligation not to allow knowingly its territory to be used for acts contrary to the rights of other States,"[6] albeit bearing in mind Nollkaemper's assertion that examining what would be considered the *mens rea* for purposes of individual responsibility is generally in the State responsibility context "either irrelevant or manifests itself in a different, objectified, form,"[7] involves

---

able at http://www.un.org/terrorism/ (last visited 12 April 2007), is one of these. In early-2005, then Chairman of the Security Council's Counter-Terrorism Committee Andrey Denisov put together in helpful form actions related to terrorism taken by international, regional, and subregional organisations and specialised United Nations agencies, funds, and programmes. *See* Letter Dated 3 February 2005 from the Chairman of the Security Council Committee Established Pursuant to Resolution 1373 (2001) Concerning Counter-Terrorism Addressed to the President of the Security Council, U.N. SCOR, U.N. Doc. S/2005/87 (2005). Also helpful is 1-2 International Terrorism: A Compilation of U.N. Documents (1972-2001) (M. Cherif Bassiouni ed., 2002).

[4] *See* Riccardo Pisillo Mazzeschi, *Forms of International Responsibility for Environmental Harm,* in International Responsibility for Environmental Harm 15, 16-17 (Francesco Francioni & Tullio Scovazzi eds., 1991).

[5] Janes (*U.S.* v. *Mex.*), 4 R.I.A.A. 82, 86 (1926).

[6] Corfu Channel (*U.K.* v. *Alb.*), 1949 I.C.J. 4, 22.

[7] André Nollkaemper, *Concurrence Between Individual Responsibility and State Responsibility in International Law,* 52(3) Int'l & Comp. L.Q. 615, 633 (2003).

a due diligence assessment based on knowledge. Likewise, the *Lake Lanoux* Arbitral Tribunal referred to the adequacy of safeguards against harm as having to be "as satisfactory as possible."[8] In late 2005, the ICJ recognised in its *Armed Activities on the Territory of the Congo* (*Congo*) decision that the international legal duty to "take appropriate measures to prevent the looting, plundering and exploitation of natural resources in the occupied territory [. . .] cover[ed] private persons in this district and not only members of Ugandan military forces."[9] It is the "take proper steps," "allow knowingly," "as satisfactory as possible," and "appropriate measures" language in these examples that highlights a due diligence assessment.

While these examples are not exhaustive of the linguistic permutations that international law recognises as requiring an assessment under the due diligence principle, they are helpful as a frame of reference. With this as perspective, this chapter now turns to the international legal rules that operate within a due diligence framework and that oblige States to act or abstain from acting in certain ways with regard to non-State actors that engage in terrorism.

III. The Due Diligence Obligation of States in the Context of Non-State Actors that Engage in Terrorism

International law, reflecting as it predominantly does the concerns of States, does not operate in a vacuum. Historical context carefully understood allows one to situate legal developments within a particular moment and anticipate, and appreciate, changes in future. Whether it be the creation of the Convention on the Prevention and Punishment of the Crime of Genocide[10] on the heels of the Holocaust or any of a number of other legal developments, involving both treaty law and customary international law, a contex-

---

[8] Lake Lanoux (*Spain* v. *Fr.*), I.L.R. 100, 123 (1961) (1957). According to Dupuy and Hoss, the "primary obligations imposed on states to prevent terrorism arise out of the same general principle as the obligation of prevention in environmental law – the principle of *sic utere laedas*." Dupuy & Hoss, *supra* note 1, at 231.

[9] Armed Activities on the Territory of the Congo (*Congo* v. *Uganda*), 2005 I.C.J., at Para. 248.

[10] G.A. Res. 260, U.N. GAOR, Annex, Convention on the Prevention and Punishment of the Crime of Genocide (1948).

tual approach provides valuable insights and assists in understanding the law. The development of international and regional treaties related to terrorism, continuing to the present, and Security Council Resolutions over the last decade reflects the fundamental and serious concerns of States about disturbing acts of violence taking a variety of forms.[11]

A. **Treaty Law**

i. *International Treaties Related to Terrorism*

Some of the first international treaties related to terrorism reflect the international community's increasing revulsion at violence perpetrated against civilian aircraft and civilian aviation. The first of these, the Convention on Offences and Certain Other Acts Committed on Board Aircraft, criminalises "acts which [. . .] may or do jeopardize the safety of the aircraft or of persons or property therein or which jeopardize good order and discipline onboard."[12] It operates on the principle of extradite or prosecute[13] and imposes a due diligence obligation on States parties. Specifically,

> When a person on board has unlawfully committed by force or threat thereof an act of interference, seizure, or other wrongful exercise of control of an aircraft in flight or when such an act is about to be committed, Contracting States shall take all appropriate measures to restore control of the aircraft to its lawful commander or to preserve his control of the aircraft.[14]

Once "all appropriate measures" have been identified on particular facts and circumstances, assessing the measures taken by a State party will determine whether a breach of the due diligence obligation can be sustained.

A second aviation-related treaty, the Convention for the Suppression of Unlawful Seizure of Aircraft (Unlawful Seizure Convention), covers aircraft hijackings, whether successfully completed or merely attempted, and

---

[11] On the generally reactive nature of treaty law's development on terrorism, see Jörg Friedrichs, *Defining the International Public Enemy: The Political Struggle Behind the Legal Debate on International Terrorism*, 19(1) LEIDEN J. INT'L L. 69, 71 (2006).

[12] Convention on Offences and Certain Other Acts Committed on Board Aircraft, Tokyo, 14 September 1963, Art. 1(1)(b).

[13] *See ibid.* at Art. 13(2).

[14] *Ibid.* at Art. 11(1).

related acts of accomplices.[15] Article 4 requires States parties to establish their jurisdiction "as may be necessary."[16] The due diligence principle also arises under the treaty when an aircraft hijacking has happened or is about to happen, as States parties are required to "take all appropriate measures to restore control of the aircraft to its lawful commander or to preserve his control of the aircraft."[17]

Like the Unlawful Seizure Convention, the Convention for the Suppression of Unlawful Acts Against the Safety of Civil Aviation imposes upon States parties requirements to establish jurisdiction "as may be necessary."[18] Obligations of prevention operate according to the due diligence principle, States parties being required to, "in accordance with international and national law, endeavour to take all practicable measure[s] for the purpose of preventing the offences mentioned in Article 1."[19] Likewise, information dissemination must be carried out "as promptly as possible."[20]

---

[15] *See* Convention for the Suppression of Unlawful Seizure of Aircraft, The Hague, 16 December 1970, Art. 1.

[16] *Ibid.* at Art. 4(1)-(2).

[17] *Ibid.* at Art. 9(1).

[18] Convention for the Suppression of Unlawful Acts Against the Safety of Civil Aviation, Montreal, 23 September 1971, Art. 5(1)-(2). The Protocol for the Suppression of Unlawful Acts of Violence at Airports Serving International Civil Aviation, which supplements the Convention for the Suppression of Unlawful Acts Against the Safety of Civil Aviation, criminalises unlawful and intentional acts involving violence at civilian airports. *See* Protocol for the Suppression of Unlawful Acts of Violence at Airports Serving International Civil Aviation, Supplementary to the Convention for the Suppression of Unlawful Acts Against the Safety of Civil Aviation, Montreal, 24 February 1988, Art. 2.

[19] Civil Aviation Convention, *supra* note 18, at Art. 10(1). According to Art. 1, "1. Any person commits an offence if he unlawfully and intentionally: (a) performs an act of violence against a person on board an aircraft in flight if that act is likely to endanger the safety of that aircraft; or (b) destroys an aircraft in service or causes damage to such an aircraft which renders it incapable of flight or which is likely to endanger its safety in flight; or (c) places or causes to be placed on an aircraft in service, by any means whatsoever, a device or substance which is likely to destroy that aircraft, or to cause damage to it which renders it incapable of flight, or to cause damage to it which is likely to endanger its safety in flight; or (d) destroys or damages air navigation facilities or interferes with their operation, if any such act is likely to endanger the safety of aircraft in flight; or (e) communicates information which he knows to be false, thereby endangering the safety of an aircraft in flight. 2. Any person also commits an offence if he: (a) attempts to commit any of the offences mentioned in paragraph 1 of this Article; or (b) is an accomplice of a person who commits or attempts to commit any such offence." *Ibid.* at Art. 1.

[20] *Ibid.* at Art. 13. On this international treaty related to terrorism and Lockerbie, see Jean Allain, *The Legacy of Lockerbie: Judicial Review of Security Council Actions or the*

Outside the context of terrorist violence against civilian aircraft and civilian aviation, the particular interests of "internationally protected persons" are protected from threats and more severe forms of targeting by political dissidents. Article 2 of the Convention on the Prevention and Punishment of Crimes Against Internationally Protected Persons, Including Diplomatic Agents, criminalises the intentional "murder, kidnapping or other attack upon the person or liberty of an internationally protected person,"[21] "violent attack upon the official premises, the private accommodation or the means of transport of an internationally protected person likely to endanger his person or liberty,"[22] and threats, attempts, and accomplice participation.[23] To ensure that States parties take active steps at prevention, they are required to, among others, take "all practicable measures to prevent preparations in their respective territories for the commission of those crimes within or outside their territories."[24] Whether it can be said that a State party has breached its obligation in this regard requires inquiring into the particular facts and circumstances of the case and asking whether the State party could reasonably have been expected to have taken other "practicable measures" than, in fact, it did.

Terrorism, of course, has not limited itself in its manifestations to civilian aircraft, civilian aviation, and internationally protected persons, and international treaties reflect this. Hostage taking, for example, has played, and continues to play, a prominent role. Article 1 of the International Convention Against the Taking of Hostages (Hostage Taking Convention) defines the key offence of hostage taking and related offences of attempt and accomplice participation.[25] The Hostage Taking Convention very much operates according to the due diligence principle. When a hostage is held on a State party's territory, for example, that State must "take all measures it considers appropriate to ease the situation of the hostage."[26] As to prevention, States parties must, among others, take "all practicable measures

First Manifestation of "Terrorism" as a Threat to International Peace?, 44(1) INDIAN J. INT'L L. 74, 75-78 (2004).

[21] G.A. Res. 3166, U.N. GAOR, Annex, Art. 2(1)(a) (1973). For the definition of "internationally protected person," see *ibid.* at Art. 1(1).

[22] *Ibid.* at Art. 2(1)(b).

[23] *See ibid.* at Art. 2(1)(c)-(e).

[24] *Ibid.* at Art. 4(a).

[25] *See* G.A. Res. 34/146, U.N. GAOR, Annex, International Convention Against the Taking of Hostages, Art. 1 (1979).

[26] *Ibid.* at Art. 3(1).

to prevent preparations in their respective territories for the commission of those offences within or outside their territories."[27] The Hostage Taking Convention also imposes upon States parties establishment of jurisdiction obligations that operate according to the due diligence principle.[28]

Because the successful completion of acts of terrorism requires skill, coordination, and ingenuity, as well as access to physical hardware, international treaty law has developed to restrict and eliminate access to certain types of material conducive to terrorist violence. The Convention on the Physical Protection of Nuclear Material and Nuclear Facilities, for example, applies to "nuclear material used for peaceful purposes in use, storage and transport and to nuclear facilities used for peaceful purposes, provided, however, that articles 3 and 4 and paragraph 4 of article 5 of this Convention shall only apply to such nuclear material while in international nuclear transport."[29] The treaty requires the establishment, implementation, and maintenance of "an appropriate physical protection regime applicable to nuclear material and nuclear facilities under its jurisdiction."[30] To satisfy this obligation, the detailed Fundamental Principles of Physical Protection of Nuclear Material and Nuclear Facilities must be applied "insofar as is reasonable and practicable."[31] The treaty creates a number of offences based on intent, including the commission of "an act without lawful authority which constitutes the receipt, possession, use, transfer, alteration, disposal or dispersal of nuclear material and which causes or is likely to cause death or serious injury to any person or substantial damage to property or to the environment."[32] Furthermore, it imposes upon States parties a number of due diligence obligations in addition to those already noted, in particular as regards cases of credible threats of or actual robbery, theft, or other unlawful taking[33] and credible threats of or actual sabotage.[34]

---

27 *Ibid.* at Art. 4(a).

28 *See ibid.* at Art. 5.

29 Amendment to the Convention on the Physical Protection of Nuclear Material, Vienna, 8 July 2005, Art. 2(1). The Convention on the Physical Protection of Nuclear Material and Nuclear Facilities amends the Convention on the Physical Protection of Nuclear Material, Vienna, 26 October 1979, and is referred to in these footnotes as Amendment to the Convention on the Physical Protection of Nuclear Material, Vienna, 8 July 2005.

30 *Ibid.* at Art. 2A(1).

31 *Ibid.* at Art. 2A(3).

32 *Ibid.* at Art. 7(1)(a).

33 *See ibid.* at Art. 5(2).

34 *See ibid.* at Art. 5(3).

The Convention for the Suppression of Unlawful Acts Against the Safety of Maritime Navigation, another important international treaty related to terrorism, was signed in Rome in 1988 under the auspices of the International Maritime Organisation.[35] Although not applicable to customs, police, and military ships and inactive ships,[36] it contains a detailed list of intentional and unlawful violent acts against ships, as well as related offences, such as attempt, abetting, and threatening to commit such offences.[37] Essentially, it ensures that violent acts against noted ships can be legally classified as terrorism. States parties are required to act with due diligence in carrying out their obligations under the treaty. An establishment of jurisdiction duty, for example, requires them to "take such measures as may be necessary."[38] Penalties must be "appropriate[, . . .] which take into account the grave nature of those offences,"[39] and prevention obligations require the "taking [of] all practicable measures"[40] and coordinating "as appropriate."[41]

The Convention on the Marking of Plastic Explosives for the Purpose of Detection responds to the threat posed by unmarked plastic explosives.[42] It obliges each State party to "take the necessary and effective measures to

---

[35] *See* Convention for the Suppression of Unlawful Acts Against the Safety of Maritime Navigation, Rome, 10 March 1988. The Protocol for the Suppression of Unlawful Acts Against the Safety of Fixed Platforms Located on the Continental Shelf was signed in Rome on the same day and essentially extends the Maritime Convention's application "mutatis mutandis to the offences set forth in article 2 of this Protocol where such offences are committed on board or against fixed platforms located on the continental shelf." Protocol for the Suppression of Unlawful Acts Against the Safety of Fixed Platforms Located on the Continental Shelf, Rome, 10 March 1988, Art. 1(1). A "fixed platform" is defined as "an artificial island, installation or structure permanently attached to the sea-bed for the purpose of exploration or exploitation of resources or for other economic purposes." *Ibid.* at Art. 1(3).

[36] *See* Maritime Convention, *supra* note 35, at Art. 2(1).

[37] *See ibid.* at Art. 3.

[38] *Ibid.* at Art. 6(1).

[39] *Ibid.* at Art. 5.

[40] *Ibid.* at Art. 13(1)(a).

[41] *Ibid.* at Art. 13(1)(b).

[42] *See* Convention on the Marking of Plastic Explosives for the Purpose of Detection, Montreal, 1 March 1991. The treaty defines "explosives" as "explosive products, commonly known as 'plastic explosives', including explosives in flexible or elastic sheet form, as described in the Technical Annex to this Convention." *Ibid.* at Art. 1(1). For background, see Ben Saul, *Definition of "Terrorism" in the UN Security Council: 1985-2004,* 4(1) CHIN. J. INT'L L. 141, 146 (2005).

prohibit and prevent the manufacture in its territory of unmarked explosives"[43] and "take the necessary and effective measures to prohibit and prevent the movement into or out of its territory of unmarked explosives."[44] These measures operate within a due diligence framework and require the identification of "necessary and effective measures" that a State party could reasonably be expected to take on particular facts and circumstances. Another crucial treaty provision, Article 4, also imposes obligations that operate according to the due diligence principle.[45]

The turn of the millennium saw increased efforts to tackle terrorism at the level of international treaty law. The International Convention for the Suppression of Terrorist Bombings (Terrorist Bombing Convention) prohibits the actions of anyone who "unlawfully and intentionally delivers, places, discharges or detonates an explosive or other lethal device in, into or against a place of public use, a State or government facility, a public transportation system or an infrastructure facility" when he or she does so intending to cause serious bodily harm or death or significant destruction that is likely to result in or actually does result in extensive economic damage.[46] The Terrorist Bombing Convention imposes due diligence obligations upon States parties with regard to such matters as the investigation of facts[47] and the prevention of terrorist bombings.[48] As to the investigation of facts, for example, particular facts and circumstances may require that "the State Party concerned [. . .] take such measures as may be necessary under its domestic law to investigate the facts contained in the information."[49]

The International Convention for the Suppression of the Financing of Terrorism is also important, not only because it aims to suppress the financing of terrorism but also because it residually defines terrorism.[50] Article

---

43 Plastic Explosives Convention, *supra* note 42, at Art. 2.

44 *Ibid.* at Art. 3(1).

45 *See ibid.* at Art. 4.

46 *See* G.A. Res. 52/164, U.N. GAOR, Annex, International Convention for the Suppression of Terrorist Bombings, Art. 2(1), U.N. Doc. A/RES/52/164 (1998). Lesser offences are also criminalised. *See ibid.* at Art. 2(2)-(3).

47 *See ibid.* at Art. 7(1).

48 *See ibid.* at Art. 15.

49 *Ibid.* at Art. 7(1).

50 *See* G.A. Res. 54/109, U.N. GAOR, Annex, Art. 2(1), U.N. Doc. A/RES/54/109 (2000) (residually defining terrorism as "[a]ny [. . .] act intended to cause death or serious bodily

2(1) creates an offence of the wilful and unlawful provision or collection of funds when done with the intent that they be used or with the knowledge that they be used to further an offence under one of the annexed international treaties related to terrorism or an act that qualifies under the residual definition of terrorism.[51] States parties must take action with regard to corporate liability,[52] sweepingly act against the financing of terrorism,[53] and create an environment that stresses terrorism's unjustifiable nature.[54] As to the creation of an environment that stresses terrorism's unjustifiable nature, Article 6 states that "[e]ach State Party shall adopt such measures as may be necessary, including, where appropriate, domestic legislation, to ensure that criminal acts within the scope of this Convention are under no circumstances justifiable by considerations of a political, philosophical, ideological, racial, ethnic, religious or other similar nature."[55] This obligation, based on "such measures as may be necessary, including, where appropriate, domestic legislation," requires an assessment according to the due diligence principle.

The most recent international treaty related to terrorism, the Russian-inspired International Convention for the Suppression of Acts of Nuclear Terrorism (Nuclear Terrorism Convention),[56] was the first such treaty to be adopted prophylactically.[57] As Pakistan noted in the General Assembly upon the treaty's adoption, nuclear terrorism represents "obviously an unacceptable threat: the ultimate nightmare scenario."[58] The treaty, which was opened for signature in September 2005, criminalises a host of offences related to

---

injury to a civilian, or to any other person not taking an active part in the hostilities in a situation of armed conflict, when the purpose of such act, by its nature or context, is to intimidate a population, or to compel a Government or an international organization to do or to abstain from doing any act."). According to Dinstein, this definition "epitomizes the essence of terrorism." Yoram Dinstein, *Ius Ad Bellum Aspects of the "War on Terrorism,"* in TERRORISM AND THE MILITARY: INTERNATIONAL LEGAL IMPLICATIONS 13, 14 (Wybo P. Heere ed., 2003).

[51] *See* Terrorist Financing Convention, *supra* note 50, at Art. 2(1). Art. 2(4)-(5) creates lesser offences.

[52] *See ibid.* at Art. 5.

[53] *See ibid.* at Art. 8.

[54] *See ibid.* at Art. 6.

[55] *Ibid.*

[56] International Convention for the Suppression of Acts of Nuclear Terrorism, New York, 14 September 2005.

[57] *See* U.N. GAOR, at 8, U.N. Doc. A/59/PV.91 (2005) (speech by Russia).

[58] *Ibid.* at 12 (speech by Pakistan). On nuclear terrorism, see SAMUEL P. HUNTINGTON, THE CLASH OF CIVILIZATIONS AND THE REMAKING OF WORLD ORDER 187-88 (2002). For the

nuclear terrorism.[59] Two examples of provisions in the Nuclear Terrorism Convention that operate according to the due diligence principle are articles dealing with the harmonisation of municipal criminal laws "as may be necessary"[60] and cooperation between States parties.[61]

ii. *Regional Treaties Related to Terrorism*

According to the Security Council, action at regional level is indispensable to the defeat of terrorism.[62] This section explores how the due diligence principle operates within the context of regional treaties related to terrorism, with particular emphasis on the Organisation of the Islamic Conference (OIC), the League of Arab States (Arab League), the African Union (AU), successor organisation of the Organisation of African Unity (OAU), the Organisation of American States (OAS), the South Asian Association for Regional Cooperation (SAARC), the Commonwealth of Independent States (CIS), and the Shanghai Cooperation Organisation (SCO). The most relevant instrument within the context of the European Union (EU) is also examined.

At the outset, it should be stressed that while many of the obligations imposed upon States parties in the regional context operate within the framework of the due diligence principle, these duties only exist within each particular treaty context to the extent that the underlying instrument classifies particular acts of violence as terrorism. While this may seem obvious, such an understanding is foundational and should not be overlooked. States that do not consider particular acts of violence to be terrorism might still be obliged to act in certain ways toward those non-State actors that engage in violence, but they would be required to do so because of international legal norms that exist and apply to them outside of, and above, the purely regional context.[63]

---

framework in place at United Nations level to deny terrorists access to conventional and unconventional weapons, see UNITING AGAINST TERRORISM: RECOMMENDATIONS FOR A GLOBAL COUNTER-TERRORISM STRATEGY: REPORT OF THE SECRETARY-GENERAL, U.N. GAOR, at 9-12, U.N. Doc. A/60/825 (2006).

[59] *See* Nuclear Terrorism Convention, *supra* note 56, at Art. 2.

[60] *Ibid.* at Art. 5.

[61] *See ibid.* at Art. 7.

[62] *See* S.C. Res. 1456, U.N. SCOR, Annex, at 2, U.N. Doc. S/RES/1456 (2003).

[63] On regionalism versus universalism, see FRAGMENTATION OF INTERNATIONAL LAW: DIFFICULTIES ARISING FROM THE DIVERSIFICATION AND EXPANSION OF INTERNATIONAL LAW:

Because of significant overlap in the membership and agenda of the OIC and the Arab League, the Convention of the OIC on Combating International Terrorism (OIC Convention) and the Arab Convention for the Suppression of Terrorism (Arab Convention) closely resemble one another, both formally and substantively, and contain a number of due diligence provisions. As to measures to counter terrorism, both treaties require that criminal justice workers be afforded "effective protection,"[64] that witnesses and informational sources be given "effective protection,"[65] that terrorist victims be extended "necessary assistance,"[66] and that States parties ensure that there is between the State apparatus and the public "effective cooperation."[67] The OIC and Arab Conventions also require that States parties provide in investigation and prosecution, respectively, "every possible assistance as may be necessary"[68] and "all possible and necessary assistance."[69] A due diligence standard governs the safeguarding of evidence under both treaties,[70] as well as the protection of experts and witnesses.[71] The most demanding provision in both treaties states, according to the terms of the provision in the Arab Convention, that States parties:

> shall endeavour [. . . t]o prevent the use of their territories as a base for planning, organizing, executing, attempting or taking part in terrorist crime in any manner whatsoever. This includes the prevention of terrorists; [sic] infiltration into, or residence in their territories either as individuals or groups, re-

---

REPORT OF THE STUDY GROUP OF THE INTERNATIONAL LAW COMMISSION, FINALIZED BY MARTTI KOSKENNIEMI, U.N. GAOR, at 102-14, U.N. Doc. A/CN.4/L.682 (2006).

64 Convention of the OIC on Combating International Terrorism, Ouagadougou, 1 July 1999, Art. 3(II)(B)(2); Arab Convention for the Suppression of Terrorism, Cairo, 22 April 1998, Art. 3(II)(2).

65 OIC Convention, *supra* note 64, at Art. 3(II)(B)(3); Arab Convention, *supra* note 64, at Art. 3(II)(3).

66 OIC Convention, *supra* note 64, at Art. 3(II)(B)(4); Arab Convention, *supra* note 64, at Art. 3(II)(4).

67 OIC Convention, *supra* note 64, at Art. 3(II)(B)(5); Arab Convention, *supra* note 64, at Art. 3(II)(5).

68 OIC Convention, *supra* note 64, at Art. 14.

69 Arab Convention, *supra* note 64, at Art. 13.

70 *See* OIC Convention, *supra* note 64, at Art. 21; Arab Convention, *supra* note 64, at Art. 21.

71 *See* OIC Convention, *supra* note 64, at Art. 37; Arab Convention, *supra* note 64, at Art. 37.

> ceiving or giving refuge to them, training, arming, financing, or providing any facilitation to them.[72]

As has been mentioned in an earlier chapter, the OAU Convention on the Prevention and Combating of Terrorism (OAU Convention), like the OIC and Arab Conventions, contains an exclusion clause for freedom fighters. Once particular facts and circumstances satisfy the OAU Convention's rather broad definition of terrorism, however, obligations ensue for States parties as a matter of treaty law.[73] For example, they must punish terrorist offences under their criminal law "by appropriate penalties that take into account the grave nature of such offences."[74] States parties must also "take all necessary measures to prevent the establishment of terrorist support networks in any form whatsoever."[75] Other due diligence obligations arise under the OAU Convention, such as the duty of "effective co-operation,"[76] the requirement that the State party "take such measures as may be necessary to establish its jurisdiction over the acts set forth in Article 1,"[77] and the onus on it to "take the appropriate measures under its national law so as to ensure that person's presence for the purpose of prosecution."[78]

In the Americas, the most important OAS treaty related to terrorism is the Inter-American Convention Against Terrorism (Inter-American Convention). Unsurprisingly, many of its provisions operate according to the due diligence principle. As to the prevention, punishment, and elimination of terrorism, for example, States parties must take "necessary measures."[79] As relates to the identification, seizure, and freezing of terrorist assets, States parties must, in accordance with municipal law, "take such measures as

---

[72] Arab Convention, *supra* note 64, at Art. 3(I)(1). Art. 3(II)(A)(1) of the OIC Convention contains the corresponding provision in the OIC context.

[73] On the AU and counterterrorism since 11 September, see Kathryn Sturman, *The AU Plan on Terrorism: Joining the Global War or Leading an African Battle?*, 11(4) AFR. SECURITY REV. 103 (2002).

[74] OAU Convention on the Prevention and Combating of Terrorism, Algiers, 14 July 1999, Art. 2(a). The OAU Convention has since been amended by the Protocol to the OAU Convention on the Prevention and Combating of Terrorism, Addis Ababa, 8 July 2004.

[75] *Ibid.* at Art. 4(2)(f).

[76] *Ibid.* at Art. 4(2)(i).

[77] *Ibid.* at Art. 6(4).

[78] *Ibid.* at Art. 7(2).

[79] Inter-American Convention Against Terrorism, Bridgetown, 3 June 2002, Art. 1.

may be necessary."[80] The danger of cross-border flows of terrorists requires States parties to, "consistent with their respective domestic legal and administrative regimes, [. . .] promote cooperation and the exchange of information."[81] Determining whether a State party has violated the "promote cooperation and the exchange of information" obligation requires assessing how a reasonable State party could have been expected to have acted under the particular facts and circumstances, although some action will always be required. To ensure that refugee and asylum law are not abused by potentially terrorist applicants, States parties under the Inter-American Convention must act with due diligence, by "tak[ing] appropriate measures, consistent with the relevant provisions of national and international law."[82]

On the Asian subcontinent, the most important coordinating regional body is the SAARC. A core treaty in that context, the SAARC Regional Convention on Suppression of Terrorism, sets out the modalities related to the extradite or prosecute principle in Article 4.[83] Each State party is obliged to, "upon receiving a request for extradition from another Contracting State, take appropriate measures, subject to its national laws, so as to ensure his presence for purposes of extradition or prosecution,"[84] share in relation to mutual legal assistance "all evidence at their disposal necessary for the proceedings,"[85] and cooperate in a preventive manner "as may be appropriate."[86] These obligations of "take appropriate measures," "necessary for the proceedings," and "as may be appropriate" require an assessment according to the due diligence principle. Account should be taken of particular facts and circumstances when determining the legal sufficiency of a State party's actions or omissions in this regard.

In the Eurasian context, the two key regional treaties related to terrorism, the Treaty on Cooperation Among the States Members of the CIS in

---

[80] *Ibid.* at Art. 5(1).

[81] *Ibid.* at Art. 7(1).

[82] *Ibid.* at Art. 12; *ibid.* at Art. 13.

[83] *See* SAARC Regional Convention on Suppression of Terrorism, Kathmandu, 4 November 1987, Art. 4. The SAARC Regional Convention has since been amended by the Additional Protocol to the SAARC Regional Convention on Suppression of Terrorism, Islamabad, 6 January 2004.

[84] *Ibid.* at Art. 6.

[85] *Ibid.* at Art. 8(1).

[86] *Ibid.* at Art. 8(2).

Combating Terrorism (CIS Convention) and, under the auspices of the SCO, the Shanghai Convention on Combating Terrorism, Separatism, and Extremism (Shanghai Convention), reflect overlapping obligations of some States parties.

Few provisions in the CIS Convention seem to warrant an assessment under the due diligence principle.[87] Article 5 requires cooperation and assistance by States parties on such matters as the exchange of information and preventive measures, the treaty language affording no discretion or consideration of the particular facts and circumstances to States parties in this regard.[88] Strict compliance in the same sense is also required as regards cooperation and assistance between States parties under the Shanghai Convention.[89]

Two opposing interpretations can be given to the provisions in the CIS and Shanghai Conventions that do not seem to warrant an assessment under the due diligence principle. The most straightforward interpretation is that a strict liability standard informs assessments of States parties' compliance with their obligations and that considerations of reasonableness are inappropriate. A contrasting interpretation, however, is that States parties are judged not by a strict liability standard but, rather, by an assessment of how a reasonable State could be expected to act on the particular facts and circumstances.[90]

The EU's Council Framework Decision of 13 June 2002 on Combating Terrorism (Framework Decision on Combating Terrorism) distinguishes itself among the regional instruments related to terrorism in that it clearly

---

[87] For examples of provisions that do, see Treaty on Cooperation Among the States Members of the CIS in Combating Terrorism, Minsk, 4 June 1999, Art. 8(1); *ibid.* at Art. 8(6). It is interesting that executive branch interference with the judiciary is required under the Shanghai Convention as a matter of due diligence, "as can prove necessary, including, as appropriate, in the field of their domestic legislation, in order to ensure that in no circumstances acts referred to in Article 1(1) of this Convention should be subject to acquittal based upon exclusively political, philosophical, ideological, racial, ethnic, religious or any other similar considerations and that they should entail punishment proportionate to their gravity." Shanghai Convention on Combating Terrorism, Separatism, and Extremism, Shanghai, 15 June 2001, Art. 3.

[88] *See* CIS Convention, *supra* note 87, at Art. 5.

[89] *See* Shanghai Convention, *supra* note 87, at Art. 6.

[90] An ICSID Tribunal took a similar approach in *Noble Ventures, Inc.* v. *Romania*. *See Noble Ventures, Inc.* v. *Rom.*, ICSID Case No. ARB/01/11, 105-06 (2005).

and expressly focuses on human rights.[91] Technically-speaking, it is not a treaty, but it is the most relevant instrument within the context of the EU, and because of this, it is worth examining.[92] To ensure that certain acts are recognised as "terrorist offences,"[93] member States must take "necessary measures."[94] The same standard applies for offences related to a terrorist group[95] and activities related to terrorism,[96] as well as for inciting, aiding or abetting, and attempt.[97] The Framework Decision on Combating Terrorism also holds member States to a due diligence standard as regards the liability of legal persons.[98] Similar penalty requirements apply to both natural and legal persons: "necessary measures[, . . . tending toward] effective, proportionate and dissuasive [punishment]."[99] Other examples of provisions that operate according to the due diligence principle concern the extradite or prosecute principle[100] and assistance to victims' families.[101]

B. Security Council Resolutions

Security Council Resolutions also place great emphasis on the due diligence principle in obliging States to confront non-State actors that engage in terrorism. This section concentrates on three Resolutions that establish committees related to terrorism within the Security Council, namely Resolutions 1267,[102] 1373,[103] and 1540,[104] in this regard. At the same time,

---

91 For example, see Council Framework Decision of 13 June 2002 on Combating Terrorism, 2002/475/JHA, Art. 1(2), 2002 O.J. (L 164) 3, 4.

92 On the European arrest warrant as relates to terrorism, see Council Framework Decision of 13 June 2002 on the European Arrest Warrant and the Surrender Procedures Between Member States, 2002/584/JHA, Art. 2(2), 2002 O.J. (L 190) 1, 3.

93 Framework Decision on Combating Terrorism, *supra* note 91, at Arts. 1(1), 4.

94 *Ibid.* at Arts. 1(1), 4.

95 *See ibid.* at Arts. 2(2), 5.

96 *See ibid.* at Arts. 3, 5.

97 *See ibid.* at Arts. 4, 5.

98 *See ibid.* at Arts. 7, 5.

99 *Ibid.* at Arts. 5(1), 5; *ibid.* at Arts. 8, 6. It should be noted, however, that only natural persons can be subjected to criminal punishment.

100 *See ibid.* at Arts. 9(3), 6.

101 *See ibid.* at Arts. 10(2), 6.

102 S.C. Res. 1267, U.N. SCOR, U.N. Doc. S/RES/1267 (1999).

103 S.C. Res. 1373, U.N. SCOR, U.N. Doc. S/RES/1373 (2001).

104 S.C. Res. 1540, U.N. SCOR, U.N. Doc. S/RES/1540 (2004). For a brief overview of Security Council Resolutions in the context of non-State actors and terrorism, see Bertrand

however, this section acknowledges that other Security Council Resolutions also speak to the due diligence obligation of States in the context of non-State actors that engage in terrorism.

Before exploring these standard-setting Resolutions, it is important to appreciate how the Security Council understands terrorism within the larger context of international peace and security. The Security Council has issued numerous condemnatory Resolutions in response to particular terrorist acts. These are noteworthy because they reveal the Security Council's priorities and provide perspective and context. The Security Council has, for example, issued declarative Resolutions regarding the "terrorist assassination attempt" on Egyptian President Hosni Mubarak's life in June 1995 in Addis Ababa;[105] "terrorist bomb attacks in Nairobi, Kenya and Dar-es-Salaam, Tanzania on 7 August 1998 which claimed hundreds of innocent lives, injured thousands of people and caused massive destruction to property;"[106] 11 September's "horrifying terrorist attacks;"[107] attacks in Bali;[108] hostage taking in Moscow;[109] destruction in Kenya;[110] violence in Bogota;[111] separate terrorist incidents in Istanbul five days apart in November 2003;[112] "in the strongest terms the bomb attacks in Madrid, Spain, perpetrated by the terrorist group ETA [i.e., Basque Homeland and Freedom] on 11 March 2004, in which many lives were claimed and people injured;"[113] the London bombings;[114] and terrorism in Iraq.[115]

G. Ramcharan, *Terrorism and Non-State Organizations,* in TOWARDS WORLD CONSTITUTIONALISM: ISSUES IN THE LEGAL ORDERING OF THE WORLD COMMUNITY 681, 687-89 (Ronald St. John Macdonald & Douglas M. Johnston eds., 2005).

105 *See* S.C. Res. 1044, U.N. SCOR, U.N. Doc. S/RES/1044 (1996).

106 S.C. Res. 1189, U.N. SCOR, at 2, U.N. Doc. S/RES/1189 (1998).

107 S.C. Res. 1368, U.N. SCOR, at 1, U.N. Doc. S/RES/1368 (2001). On this Resolution, see Bardo Fassbender, *The UN Security Council and International Terrorism,* in ENFORCING, *supra* note 1, at 83, 86-89.

108 *See* S.C. Res. 1438, U.N. SCOR, U.N. Doc. S/RES/1438 (2002).

109 *See* S.C. Res. 1440, U.N. SCOR, U.N. Doc. S/RES/1440 (2002).

110 *See* S.C. Res. 1450, U.N. SCOR, U.N. Doc. S/RES/1450 (2002).

111 *See* S.C. Res. 1465, U.N. SCOR, U.N. Doc. S/RES/1465 (2003).

112 *See* S.C. Res. 1516, U.N. SCOR, U.N. Doc. S/RES/1516 (2003).

113 S.C. Res. 1530, U.N. SCOR, at 1, U.N. Doc. S/RES/1530 (2004). In the days after the Madrid attacks, attention quickly shifted away from ETA. On this, see Saul, *supra* note 42, at 162.

114 *See* S.C. Res. 1611, U.N. SCOR, U.N. Doc. S/RES/1611 (2005).

115 *See* S.C. Res. 1618, U.N. SCOR, U.N. Doc. S/RES/1618 (2005). Challenging the notion that they were somehow justifiable, the Security Council condemned "without res-

While these condemnatory Resolutions identify what the Security Council regards as terrorism on particular facts and circumstances, it is not only the acts identified therein that are of international significance. Recent years have seen the Security Council regularising its approach to determining whether acts of terrorism amount to threats to international peace and security.[116] As Allain notes, "[n]o longer is the Security Council willing to deliberate as to whether a terrorist act is to be considered a threat. It now consider[s] that such acts are, *ipso facto*, threats to international peace and security."[117] It is also revealing that the Security Council frequently condemns terrorism generally in Resolutions that it adopts in response to particular terrorist acts.[118]

The Security Council adopted the first standard-setting Resolution to be explored in this section, Resolution 1267, in a context in which the Taliban's Afghanistan had largely ignored several earlier Resolutions directed at it.[119] Resolution 1267 required that Afghanistan enact "appropriate effective measures to ensure that the territory under its control is not used for terrorist installations and camps, or for the preparation or organization of terrorist acts against other States or their citizens, and cooperate with efforts to bring indicted terrorists to justice."[120] According to this "appropriate effective measures" standard, only "effective" measures are contemplated, "ef-

---

ervation and in the strongest terms the terrorist attacks that have taken place in Iraq, and regards any act of terrorism as a threat to peace and security." *Ibid.* at 1. It specifically cited the "shameless and horrific attacks in recent weeks which have resulted in over one hundred deaths, including thirty-two children, employees of the Independent Electoral Commission of Iraq, and a member and an expert adviser of the Commission charged with drafting a permanent constitution for a new, democratic Iraq, Mijbil Sheikh Isa and Dhamin Hussin Ubaidi[, . . . and] attacks on foreign diplomats in Iraq [that] have increased in number, and have resulted in the murder or kidnapping of such diplomats." *Ibid.* at 1-2.

[116] *See* Allain, *supra* note 20, at 108-11.

[117] *Ibid.* at 111. Bassiouni argues that this attention is unhelpfully disproportionate to that given to other crimes. *See* M. Cherif Bassiouni, *The Regression of the Rule of Law Under the Guise of Combating Terrorism,* 76(1-2) REV. INT'L DROIT PÉNAL 17, 20-21 (2005).

[118] *See, e.g.,* S.C. Res. 1440, *supra* note 109, at 1 (condemning "in the strongest terms the heinous act of taking hostages in Moscow, the Russian Federation, on 23 October 2002, as well as other recent terrorist acts in various countries, and regards such acts, like any act of international terrorism, as a threat to international peace and security."). Saul suggests that such Security Council condemnations reveal how what might initially be perceived to be terrorism solely of a domestic concern can impinge upon the international. *See* Saul, *supra* note 42, at 161-62.

[119] *See, e.g.,* S.C. Res. 1214, U.N. SCOR, U.N. Doc. S/RES/1214 (1998).

[120] S.C. Res. 1267, *supra* note 102, at 2.

fectiveness" suggesting that the measures taken must tend toward a particular result. "Appropriate" in front of "effective measures" indicates that "effective measures" could potentially be either appropriate or inappropriate but that the due diligence principle dictates only the appropriate kind, namely "appropriate effective measures."

In order to pressure the Taliban to extradite Osama bin Laden,[121] Resolution 1267's Paragraph 4 ordered States to prohibit the use of their airspace for aircraft related to the Taliban regime and to freeze all Taliban-related assets,[122] and the standard that applied was one of "effectively implementing."[123] Most importantly, Resolution 1267 established a committee to monitor States' compliance with their obligations under the Resolution (1267 Committee).[124]

The Security Council expanded the 1267 Committee's mandate in Resolution 1333.[125] More was also expected of States. In particular, Paragraph 5 of Resolution 1333 prohibited any sort of military cooperation with the Taliban regime,[126] and Paragraph 8(c) penetrated particularly deeply in requiring States to "freeze without delay funds and other financial assets of Usama bin Laden and individuals and entities associated with him as designated by the Committee, including those in the Al-Qaida organization."[127]

11 September demonstrated terrorism's awesome power, both literally and in its ability to radically transform the international agenda in a single morning, and triggered what former Judge of the Appeals Chamber of the International Criminal Tribunal for the former Yugoslavia Georges Abi-Saab has called a "shock of recognition."[128] Less than three weeks after 11 September, the Security Council set out a large number of obligations related to terrorism that States must satisfy in sweeping language in Resolution 1373.[129] As regards the due diligence principle, States are required to

---

121 On this obligation, see *ibid.* at 2.

122 *See ibid.* at 2-3.

123 *Ibid.* at 3-4.

124 *See ibid.* at 3. On the 1267 Committee, see Ramcharan, *supra* note 104, at 682-85.

125 *See* S.C. Res. 1333, U.N. SCOR, at 5-6, U.N. Doc. S/RES/1333 (2000).

126 *See ibid.* at 3.

127 *Ibid.* at 4.

128 Georges Abi-Saab, *The Proper Role of International Law in Combating Terrorism,* 1(1) CHIN. J. INT'L L. 305, 306 (2002) (stating that "[a] shock of recognition is very important in that it literally 'brings home' to the collective psyche, as an immediate reality, what may have existed until then merely as an esoteric hypothesis verging on science fiction.").

129 *See* S.C. Res. 1373, *supra* note 103, at 2-3. On this Resolution, see Fassbender,

"[t]ake the necessary steps to prevent the commission of terrorist acts,"[130] "[a]fford one another the greatest measure of assistance in connection with criminal investigations or criminal proceedings relating to the financing or support of terrorist acts,"[131] and establish "effective border controls and controls on issuance of identity papers and travel documents."[132] To ensure that a screening process is implemented to bar those asylum seekers who have terrorist ties, the Resolution requires that States "[t]ake appropriate measures."[133]

The obligations that Resolution 1373 imposes upon States with regard to terrorism are sweeping, the Security Council having taken it upon itself a "quasi-legislative role."[134] To monitor State compliance, the Resolution established the Counter-Terrorism Committee (CTC).[135] Although the CTC and the 1267 Committee both relate to terrorism, they are "different but complementary."[136]

The 1267 Committee and the CTC, according to the Security Council, do not suffice as institutional frameworks to counter the threat posed by terrorism to international peace and security. In April 2004, the Security Council established in Resolution 1540 what has become known as the 1540 Committee to monitor States' compliance with that Resolution.[137] Resolution 1540 addresses the nuclear, chemical, and biological threat posed by non-State actors that engage in terrorism and sets up a number of clear obligations for States in this regard.[138] States must prevent through "appropriate effective laws"[139] non-State actors from being able to "manufacture,

---

supra note 107, at 89; Saul, *supra* note 42, at 156-57; Bianchi, *supra* note 2, at 517; Surya P. Subedi, *The UN Response to International Terrorism in the Aftermath of the Terrorist Attacks in America and the Problem of the Definition of Terrorism in International Law,* 4(3) INT'L L. FORUM DROIT INT'L 159, 160 (2002).

130 S.C. Res. 1373, *supra* note 103, at 2.

131 *Ibid.*

132 *Ibid.*

133 S.C. Res. 1373, *supra* note 103, at 3.

134 Bianchi, *supra* note 2, at 498.

135 *See* S.C. Res. 1373, *supra* note 103, at 3. *See also* Ramcharan, *supra* note 104, at 685.

136 *Distinctions Between Security Council Committees Dealing with Terrorism* (*1267 Committee and Counter-Terrorism Committee*), Press Release SC/7827, 28 July 2003, *available at* http://www.un.org/News/Press/docs/2003/sc7827.doc.htm.

137 *See* S.C. Res. 1540, *supra* note 104, at 3.

138 On Resolution 1540, see Saul, *supra* note 42, at 164.

139 S.C. Res. 1540, *supra* note 104, at 2.

acquire, possess, develop, transport, transfer or use nuclear, chemical or biological weapons and their means of delivery, in particular for terrorist purposes."[140] The Resolution also imposes preventative measures upon States with regard to weapons of mass destruction, specifically that they use "appropriate effective measures to account for and secure such items in production, use, storage or transport,"[141] "appropriate effective physical protection measures,"[142] "appropriate effective border controls and law enforcement efforts to detect, deter, prevent and combat, including through international cooperation when necessary, the illicit trafficking and brokering in such items,"[143] and "appropriate effective national export and trans-shipment controls over such items [. . . and] appropriate criminal or civil penalties for violations of such export control laws and regulations."[144] Each of these obligations requires an assessment according to the due diligence principle.

IV. Conclusion

Thus, that many of the counterterrorism provisions under treaty law and in Security Council Resolutions impose obligations upon States that operate within a due diligence framework is clear. It should also be stressed, however, that States' counterterrorism obligations under international law do not limit themselves to treaties and Security Council Resolutions. Ramcharan, for example, argues that the post-11 September international legal order includes a "duty to prevent terrorist acts from being committed in one's territory [that is] an obligation under international customary law the breach of which would entail the responsibility of the State."[145] In its *Congo* decision, furthermore, the ICJ stated that certain provisions of General Assembly Resolution 2625 that deal with States' counterterrorism obligations amount to customary international law.[146]

---

[140] *Ibid.* at 2-3.

[141] *Ibid.* at 3.

[142] *Ibid.*

[143] *Ibid.* (continuing by stating that this must be done "in accordance with their national legal authorities and legislation and consistent with international law.").

[144] *Ibid.*

[145] Ramcharan, *supra* note 104, at 691.

[146] *See* Congo, *supra* note 9, at Para. 162 (stating that "the Declaration on Principles of International Law Concerning Friendly Relations and Co-operation Among States in accor-

States' counterterrorism obligations may also amount to peremptory norms of general international law, or *jus cogens*.[147] The prohibitions of the use of force, genocide, and torture are examples of such norms.[148] Should States' counterterrorism obligations be recognised as *jus cogens*, the most important, and radical, legal consequence of this under treaty law would be that treaties that would conflict with those obligations would have to be set aside.[149] Although the author makes no conclusion on the matter, this is an area in need of further study.[150]

---

dance with the Charter of the United Nations (hereinafter 'the Declaration on Friendly Relations') provides that: 'Every States has the duty to refrain from organizing, instigating, assisting or participating in acts of civil strife or terrorist acts in another State or acquiescing in organized activities within its territory directed towards the commission of such acts, when the acts referred to in the present paragraph involve a threat or use of force.' (General Assembly resolution 2625 (XXV), 24 October 1970.) The Declaration further provides that, 'no State shall organize, assist, foment, finance, incite or tolerate subversive, terrorist or armed activities directed towards the violent overthrow of the regime of another State, or interfere in civil strife in another State.' *(ibid.)*. These provisions are declaratory of customary international law.").

[147] According to the Vienna Convention on the Law of Treaties, such a norm is a "norm accepted and recognized by the international community of States as a whole as a norm from which no derogation is permitted and which can be modified only by a subsequent norm of general international law having the same character." Vienna Convention on the Law of Treaties, Vienna, 23 May 1969, Art. 53. On peremptory norms, see JAMES CRAWFORD, THE CREATION OF STATES IN INTERNATIONAL LAW 99-105 (2nd ed. 2006).

[148] On the prohibition of the use of force in this regard, see Military and Paramilitary Activities in and Against Nicaragua (*Nicar.* v. *U.S.*), 1986 I.C.J. 14, 153 (Nagendra Singh, J., separate); *ibid.* at 199 (Sette-Camara, J., separate); Legal Consequences of the Construction of a Wall in the Occupied Palestinian Territory (Advisory Opinion), 2004 I.C.J., at Para. 3.1 (Elaraby, J., separate); Oil Platforms (*Iran* v. *U.S.*), 2003 I.C.J. 161, 327 (Simma, J., separate). On genocide, see Application of the Convention on the Prevention and Punishment of the Crime of Genocide (*Bosn. & Herz.* v. *Serb. & Mont.*), 2007 I.C.J., at Para. 161. On torture, see *Prosecutor* v. *Furundzija* (IT-95-17/1-T), Trial Chamber, 1998 I.C.T.Y., at 55. For further examples of *jus cogens*, see FRAGMENTATION OF INTERNATIONAL LAW, *supra* note 63, at 188-90. Also helpful is David S. Mitchell, *The Prohibition of Rape in International Humanitarian Law as a Norm of* Jus Cogens: *Clarifying the Doctrine,* 15(2) DUKE J. COMP. & INT'L L. 219, 228-34 (2005).

[149] *See* Vienna Convention, *supra* note 147, at Art. 53; *ibid.* at Art. 64. On these articles, see FRAGMENTATION OF INTERNATIONAL LAW, *supra* note 63, at 183-88.

[150] The same can be said for obligations *erga omnes* in this regard. *See* Vincent-Joel Proulx, *Babysitting Terrorists: Should States Be Strictly Liable for Failing to Prevent Transborder Attacks?,* 23(3) BERKELEY J. INT'L L. 615, 650 (2005).

Chapter 5
ASSESSING THE DUE DILIGENCE OBLIGATION OF STATES IN THE CONTEXT OF NON-STATE ACTORS THAT ENGAGE IN TERRORISM: THEORETICAL ISSUES

Chapter 5
ASSESSING THE DUE DILIGENCE OBLIGATION OF STATES IN THE CONTEXT OF NON-STATE ACTORS THAT ENGAGE IN TERRORISM: THEORETICAL ISSUES

I. INTRODUCTION

Previous chapters have shown that the due diligence principle under international law operates in diverse areas, imposes a "best effort" obligation on States,[1] and informs assessments of State responsibility in the context of non-State actors that engage in terrorism. While it is a principle that is relatively straightforward in the abstract, it is a surprisingly complex principle that, as has been previously mentioned, scholars have largely neglected and underappreciated.

This chapter explores theoretical issues that the due diligence principle raises, particularly as regards its operation in the counterterrorism context. Hart argues that, "[i]n all fields of experience, not only that of rules, there is a limit, inherent in the nature of language, to the guidance which general language can provide."[2] This chapter examines the implications of what Hart suggests about the inherent limit of language in light of the flexible reasonableness standard adaptable to particular facts and circumstances that is the due diligence principle.[3] By exploring these theoretical issues, it raises

---

[1] On the "best effort" obligation, see Pierre-Marie Dupuy, *Reviewing the Difficulties of Codification: On Ago's Classification of Obligations of Means and Obligations of Result in Relation to State Responsibility,* 10(2) EUR. J. INT'L L. 371, 379 (1999) (stating that "[*w*]*hat counts here is the violation of the best effort obligation, not the end result actually achieved*."). *See also* International Law Commission, *Commentaries*, *Articles on Prevention of Transboundary Harm from Hazardous Activities*, in REPORT OF THE INTERNATIONAL LAW COMMISSION ON THE WORK OF ITS FIFTY-THIRD SESSION 377, 391-92, U.N. Doc. A/56/10 Supp. No. 10 (2001).

[2] H.L.A. HART, THE CONCEPT OF LAW 126 (2nd ed. 1994).

[3] On flexibility and the due diligence principle, see Pierre-Marie Dupuy & Cristina Hoss, Trail Smelter *and Terrorism: International Mechanisms to Combat Transboundary Harm*, in TRANSBOUNDARY HARM IN INTERNATIONAL LAW: LESSONS FROM THE *TRAIL SMELTER* ARBITRATION 225, 226 (Rebecca M. Bratspies & Russell A. Miller eds., 2006).

the fundamental question whether the due diligence principle possesses sufficient clarity and predictability to satisfy the requirement of legality, whether it reflects, and acts as a vehicle for facilitating, political struggle, or whether an alternative framework for understanding can be, and should be, identified.[4]

II. Theoretical Issues

Since the due diligence principle resembles a flexible reasonableness standard adaptable to particular facts and circumstances, at the outset it can be criticised, or at least noted, for its subjectivity, in much the same way as Judge Rosalyn Higgins, now President of the International Court of Justice (ICJ), has discussed reasonableness as relates to equity.[5] Dupuy similarly argues that judging State behaviour according to a "good government" stan-

---

[4] These questions are not unrelated to Franck's discussion of determinacy, coherence, symbolic validation, and adherence in the context of "rule legitimacy." Thomas M. Franck, *The Power of Legitimacy and the Legitimacy of Power: International Law in an Age of Power Disequilibrium*, 100(1) AM. J. INT'L L. 88, 93 (2006). According to him, determinacy is seminal, it "being that quality of a norm that generates an ascertainable understanding of what it permits and what it prohibits." *Ibid.* (continuing by stating that, "[w]hen that line becomes unascertainable, states are unlikely to defer opportunities for self-gratification. The rule's compliance pull evaporates."). Franck further argues that "it is usually achieved by a rule text's explicit statement of a boundary between the permissible and the impermissible, or by the designation of a process for clarifying, in a contested instance, the meaning of a rule." *Ibid.* at 94. *Cf.* JAMES CRAWFORD, THE CREATION OF STATES IN INTERNATIONAL LAW 711 (2nd ed. 2006) (stating that "[i]nternational law is normativity in collision with history; if it is to be of any value it must give guidance to persons at the time of the events and, prima facie at least, acts which were valid or produced legal effects at a particular time should not retroactively be treated as void.").

[5] *See* ROSALYN HIGGINS, *Oiling the Wheels of International Law: Equity and Proportionality*, in PROBLEMS AND PROCESS: INTERNATIONAL LAW AND HOW WE USE IT 219, 221 (1994). "The requirements of justice are, in my view, a subjective concept, of essentially the same kind as 'equitable result'. To label something as the result of 'justice requires', or the 'equitable result', is merely to avoid justifying and making specific certain policy objectives." *Ibid.* at 220. Koskenniemi defines equity as "an undifferentiated sense of justice." Martti Koskenniemi, *The Politics of International Law,* 1(1-2) EUR. J. INT'L L. 4, 18 (1990). For another definition of equity, see Sambiaggio (*Italy* v. *Venez.*), 10 R.I.A.A. 499, 509 (1903) (defining it as "nothing more than the natural application of those rules of reason and justice which nations recognize as surest and which international law recommends in cases submitted for consideration.").

dard "entails its assessment by reference to a certain standard, which contains an undeniable degree of subjectivity and whose different elements vary according to the epoch, the circumstances and the particular situation of the authorities of the State in question."[6] Pisillo Mazzeschi notes that the due diligence principle necessarily references itself against an international objective standard but that its interpretation in light of particular facts and circumstances renders it "undoubtedly [of] an elastic and relative nature."[7] In short, the due diligence principle means, or at least can be construed to mean, everything to everyone and nothing to no one.

It is to this idea of subjectivity in the law that ICJ Judge Philadelpho Azevedo alluded to in his separate opinion in the *Conditions of Admission of a State to Membership in the United Nations* (*Admissions*) case when he stated that the admission conditions of Article 4 of the United Nations Charter (Charter) "are so broad and flexible that the recommendations and decisions relating thereto necessarily contain a strong arbitrary element. It would be difficult to say that any one of the required conditions has a purely objective character, and that it could be appraised algebraically."[8] Certainly, the due diligence principle, in that it does not allow for the methodical inputting of facts and circumstances into a preset formula to determine whether a particular rule of due diligence has been breached, does not operate along the lines of an algebraic equation.[9] As Hart would say, ours is not

---

[6] Pierre Dupuy, *Due Diligence in the International Law of Liability*, in LEGAL ASPECTS OF TRANSFRONTIER POLLUTION 369, 372 (Organisation for Economic Co-operation and Development ed., 1977). Dupuy defines "good government" as a "government mindful of its international obligations." *Ibid.* at 369.

[7] Riccardo Pisillo Mazzeschi, *The Due Diligence Rule and the Nature of the International Responsibility of States,* 35 GERM. Y.B. INT'L L. 9, 44 (1992). *See ibid.* at 45 (asserting that, "[o]n a more general level, we can say that, as the content of certain obligations of diligent conduct becomes more specific and more detailed, also the concept of due diligence becomes more specific and tends to lose its characteristics of a general and flexible norm of behavior.").

[8] Conditions of Admission of a State to Membership in the United Nations (Advisory Opinion), 1948 I.C.J. 57, 77 (Azevedo, J., separate). According to Art. 4 of the Charter, "1. Membership in the United Nations is open to all other peace-loving states which accept the obligations contained in the present Charter and, in the judgment of the Organization, are able and willing to carry out these obligations. 2. The admission of any such state to membership in the United Nations will be effected by a decision of the General Assembly upon the recommendation of the Security Council." U.N. CHARTER Art. 4.

[9] According to Dupuy and Hoss, "[i]t is [. . .] difficult to establish a clear line between legal and illegal behavior from the states with regard to their obligation of due diligence." Dupuy & Hoss, *supra* note 3, at 235.

a "world fit for 'mechanical jurisprudence."[10] This is clearly the case with the due diligence principle.

According to Hart, a tension exists in the law between the general and the specific, the specific corresponding to "fact-situations, continually thrown up by nature or human invention, which possess only some of the features of the plain cases but others which they lack."[11] The plain case corresponds to the prototypical, expected case, the case that can be easily disposed of and that presents little in the way of interpretative challenge.[12] In contrast to the plain case, which Hart also refers to as the "authoritative example"[13] and the "paradigm, clear case[ ],"[14] there is the "unenvisaged case."[15] Although the former will suffice as a guide in most instances, there inevitably arises interpretative confusion, this being due to language's "*open texture*."[16]

An example of a plain case would be when a State, for whatever reason, deliberately and indisputably ignores its due diligence obligation under treaty law and Security Council Resolutions that deal with non-State actors that engage in terrorism. In such a situation, the State would not be acting diligently as a matter of law, much less with the diligence that is due, according to the due diligence principle. A dicier situation, an example of an unenvisaged case, would be when reasonable arguments can be made for

---

[10] HART, *supra* note 2, at 128 (describing a "world fit for 'mechanical jurisprudence'" as "[i]f the world in which we live were characterized only by a finite number of features, and these together with all the modes in which they could combine were known to us, then provision could be made in advance for every possibility. We could make rules, the application of which to particular cases never called for a further choice. Everything could be known, and for everything, since it could be known, something could be done and specified in advance by rule.").

[11] *Ibid.* at 126.

[12] *See ibid.* (stating that "[t]he plain case, where the general terms seem to need no interpretation and where the recognition of instances seems unproblematic or 'automatic', are only the familiar ones, constantly recurring in similar contexts, where there is general agreement in judgments as to the applicability of the classifying terms."). *Cf.* David Kairys, *Legal Reasoning*, in THE POLITICS OF LAW: A PROGRESSIVE CRITIQUE 11, 17 n. 6 (David Kairys ed., 1982).

[13] HART, *supra* note 2, at 127.

[14] *Ibid.* at 129.

[15] *Ibid.* "There will indeed be plain cases constantly recurring in similar contexts to which general expressions are clearly applicable ('If anything is a vehicle a motor-car is one') but there will also be cases where it is not clear whether they apply or not. ('Does "vehicle" used here include bicycles, airplanes, roller skates?')." *Ibid.* at 126.

[16] *Ibid.* at 128.

and against a State's having acted with due diligence and when the opposing sides in the dispute only agree that the particular facts and circumstances do not lend themselves to evaluation according to the parameters of the plain case, although it is likely that this, too, will be in dispute.[17] The intrusion of politics in the counterterrorism discourse renders corresponding due diligence rules particularly indeterminate and troublesome and not always capable of being easily and uncontroversially interpreted in all situations that call for legal judgment.[18]

A. Interpretative Tools

International law and the scholarship that it has generated provide a number of interpretative tools that can assist in understanding treaty provisions and Security Council Resolutions that operate according to the due diligence principle, both generally and as regards the counterterrorism context in particular. Although they have their limitations, in much the same way as "[c]anons of 'interpretation' cannot eliminate, though they can diminish, these uncertainties; for these canons are themselves general rules for the use of language, and make use of general terms which themselves require interpretation. They cannot, any more than other rules, provide for their own interpretation,"[19] they are worth exploring to arrive at a better understanding of the texture of the due diligence principle.

Treaty law provides a number of interpretative tools. The *pacta sunt servanda* principle, for example, recognises the binding effect of treaties and requires States to act with good faith in carrying out their obligations.[20]

---

[17] "Particular fact-situations do not await us already marked off from each other, and labelled as instances of the general rule, the application of which is in question; nor can the rule itself step forward to claim its own instances." *Ibid.* at 126. Compare these examples of plain and unenvisaged cases with Proulx's model. *See* Vincent-Joel Proulx, *Babysitting Terrorists: Should States Be Strictly Liable for Failing to Prevent Transborder Attacks?*, 23(3) BERKELEY J. INT'L L. 615, 662-66 (2005).

[18] *See* TAL BECKER, TERRORISM AND THE STATE: RETHINKING THE RULES OF STATE RESPONSIBILITY 151 (2006) (arguing that, "despite the capacity to articulate counter-terrorism obligations in theory, establishing their violation in practice can be hotly contested. This is especially the case when the State is charged with failing to prevent or tolerating the terrorist activity through acts of omission.").

[19] HART, *supra* note 2, at 126.

[20] *See* Vienna Convention on the Law of Treaties, Vienna, 23 May 1969, Art. 26. *See also* V. S. Mani, *Future Strategies in the War Against Terrorism and Proliferation of Weap-*

A good faith standard, a standard that the ICJ has recognised as being a "well-established principle of international law,"[21] informs the interpretation of a treaty "in accordance with the ordinary meaning to be given to the terms of the treaty in their context and in the light of its object and purpose."[22] Mani refers to good faith when he states that the test for international counterterrorism laws "stand[s] or fall[s] on the bedrock of the principle of good faith, which is in turn conditioned by mutuality of trust and confidence."[23] Thus, the good faith principle can be used to provide a degree of clarity to the due diligence principle.

Zegveld's inquiry into available means and foreseeable harm in her study of armed opposition groups and State responsibility is also worth examining in the context of the due diligence principle.[24] As to available means, she argues that the "administrative means or resources that are at the state's disposal determine the due diligence obligation of the state to take action against armed opposition groups."[25] The frequency of attacks informs foreseeability and, as a result, how the due diligence principle applies to particular facts and circumstances.[26] While this emphasis on frequency certainly

---

ons of Mass Destruction: An Indian Perception, 44(2) INDIAN J. INT'L L. 221, 245 (2004). In *Gabčíkovo-Nagymaros*, the ICJ found that the good faith principle as regards the treaty at issue "obliges the Parties to apply it in a reasonable way and in such a manner that its purpose can be realized." Gabčíkovo-Nagymaros (*Hung.* v. *Slovk.*), 1997 I.C.J. 7, 79.

[21] Land and Maritime Boundary Between Cameroon and Nigeria, Preliminary Objections (*Cameroon* v. *Nig.*), 1998 I.C.J. 275, 296. On good faith, see International Law Commission, *Commentaries*, *Articles on Prevention of Transboundary Harm, supra* note 1, at 396-97.

[22] Vienna Convention on the Law of Treaties, *supra* note 20, at Art. 31(1). This reflects customary international law. *See* Legal Consequences of the Construction of a Wall in the Occupied Palestinian Territory (Advisory Opinion), 2004 I.C.J., at Para. 94.

[23] Mani, *Future Strategies*, *supra* note 20, at 245. "States remain the final individual arbiters, at any point in time, to determine how much of power of restraint they consider themselves to have conceded to the world order." V.S. Mani, *Centrifugal and Centripetal Tendencies in the International System: Some Reflections,* in TOWARDS WORLD CONSTITUTIONALISM: ISSUES IN THE LEGAL ORDERING OF THE WORLD COMMUNITY 241, 247 (Ronald St. John Macdonald & Douglas M. Johnston eds., 2005).

[24] *See* LIESBETH ZEGVELD, ACCOUNTABILITY OF ARMED OPPOSITION GROUPS IN INTERNATIONAL LAW 191 (2002); *ibid.* at 192 n. 82.

[25] *Ibid.* at 192. Arguably, it would be more accurate to say that the means or resources that are *or should be* at the disposal of the State set the standard for analysis. Farrior makes a similar argument in a related context. *See* Stephanie Farrior, *State Responsibility for Human Rights Abuses by Non-State Actors*, 1998 A.S.I.L. PROC. 299, 302-03.

[26] *See* ZEGVELD, *supra* note 24, at 194.

extends to the due diligence principle in the counterterrorism context, it should be stressed that the Security Council's consistent practice in recent years of referring to "any act of terrorism as a threat to peace and security"[27] and of the "need to combat by all means, in accordance with the Charter of the United Nations, threats to international peace and security caused by terrorist acts"[28] has had the effect on foreseeability of having alerted States to the threat of terrorism and, as such, of having triggered a heightened due diligence obligation for them.[29]

In addition to treaty law rules and a focus on foreseeability, a further interpretative tool that can assist in understanding the due diligence principle involves balancing. Hart, for example, in dealing with contentious due diligence cases, would argue that a balance must be struck, "in the light of circumstances, between competing interests which vary in weight from case to case."[30] He proposes a test that stresses questions of close resemblance and relevance.[31] For cases in which the "sphere to be controlled is such that it is impossible to identify a class of specific actions to be uniformly done or forborne and to make them the subject of a simple rule, yet the range of circumstances, though very varied, covers familiar features of common experience,"[32] the law requires that the subject of the obligation, this being the State in the context of the due diligence principle and

[27] S.C. Res. 1618, U.N. SCOR, at 1, U.N. Doc. S/RES/1618 (2005).

[28] *Ibid.* at Preamble.

[29] *Cf.* ZEGVELD, *supra* note 24, at 192-94; International Law Commission, *Commentaries, Articles on Prevention of Transboundary Harm, supra* note 1, at 377 (stating that "[d]ischarge of the duty of prevention or due diligence is all the more required as knowledge regarding the operation of hazardous activities, materials used and the process of managing them and the risks involved it steadily growing."). "The term 'significant', while determined by factual and objective criteria, also involves a value determination which depends on the circumstances of a particular case and the period in which such determination is made. For instance, a particular deprivation at a particular time might not be considered 'significant' because at that specific time scientific knowledge or human appreciation for a particular resource had not reached a point at which much value was ascribed to that particular resource. But some time later that view might change and the same harm might then be considered 'significant.'" *Ibid.* at 389. According to Becker, "[i]n an international atmosphere of heightened terrorist activity, and intensified expectations for compliance with counter-terrorism obligations after September 11th, some level of notice is effectively built into the system." BECKER, *supra* note 18, at 135.

[30] HART, *supra* note 2, at 135.

[31] *See ibid.* at 127.

[32] *Ibid.* at 132.

counterterrorism, make reasonable decisions.[33] In reaching these reasonable decisions, Hart focuses on preventative measures that simultaneously avoid great harm and do not unduly compromise other important interests.[34]

Another balancing test that can be used as an interpretative tool arises in the context of the prevention of transboundary harm from hazardous activities. According to the core prevention provision in the International Law Commission (ILC)'s 2001 *Articles on Prevention of Transboundary Harm from Hazardous Activities* (*Articles on Prevention of Transboundary Harm*), the "State of origin shall take all appropriate measures to prevent significant transboundary harm or at any event to minimize the risk thereof."[35] Article 2's balancing test for "risk of causing significant transboundary harm" requires inquiry for "risks taking the form of a high probability of causing significant transboundary harm and a low probability of causing disastrous transboundary harm."[36] Given this emphasis on probability and magnitude, or risk and harm,[37] and the similar transboundary essence of the threats that pollution and terrorism pose,[38] the *Articles on Prevention of Transboundary Harm's* probability and magnitude balancing test can be used to assist in the interpretation of the due diligence principle in the counterterrorism context.

It is also worth noting that the ILC's *Commentaries* to the *Articles on Prevention of Transboundary Harm* express an understanding of "*'significant' [. . . as being] something more than 'detectable' but [. . . that it] need not be at the level of 'serious' or 'substantial.'*"[39] In the post-11 September counterterrorism context, terrorism is much more than "detectable" and probably also "serious" and "substantial."[40] As the ILC states, "[t]he higher

[33] *See ibid.* (stating that "[t]his technique leaves to individuals, subject to correction by a court, the task of weighing up and striking a reasonable balance between the social claims which arise in various unanticipatable forms.").

[34] *See ibid.* at 132-33.

[35] International Law Commission, *Articles on Prevention of Transboundary Harm from Hazardous Activities,* in REPORT OF THE INTERNATIONAL LAW COMMISSION ON THE WORK OF ITS FIFTY-THIRD SESSION, *supra* note 1, at 370, 372, Art. 3.

[36] *Ibid.* at 371, Art. 2(a).

[37] *See* International Law Commission, *Commentaries, Articles on Prevention of Transboundary Harm, supra* note 1, at 387.

[38] *See* Dupuy & Hoss, *supra* note 3, at 225.

[39] International Law Commission, *Commentaries, Articles on Prevention of Transboundary Harm, supra* note 1, at 388.

[40] Compare this with the ILC's description of "ultra-hazardous activity[, which] is perceived to be an activity with a danger that is rarely expected to materialize but might as-

the degree of inadmissible harm, the greater would be the duty of care required to prevent it."[41]

Thus, as interpretative tools, treaty law, particularly attention to good faith, inquiry into the foreseeability of harm, and balancing tests, including the making of reasonable decisions and a focus on probability and magnitude, can assist in understanding treaty provisions and Security Council Resolutions that operate according to the due diligence principle, both generally and as regards the counterterrorism context in particular. These specific tools seem to be intuitively relevant and appropriate when interpreting the due diligence principle, but they are not exhaustive as guides for understanding. Other interpretative tools can be brought to bear in providing a degree of clarity.

B. The Limitations of Interpretative Tools and Other Thoughts

While interpretative tools can provide a degree of clarity to the due diligence principle, parties in an unenvisaged case, like opposing counsel in an adversarial criminal justice system, will argue that the other side's interpretation of the law opens itself to reasonable debate and thoughtfully considered doubt, or as Kennedy states, they will "plead the most favourable interpretations of vague or uncertain rules."[42] Some of this has to do with uncertainty as to whether a single violation of a particular due diligence rule triggers State responsibility or whether more than one violation must be shown,[43] but the problem is actually more fundamental and cannot be easily dismissed. It is simply no small challenge to conclude, as Proulx does, that the "[*o*]*nly* margin for polemic with regard to this duty pertains to

---

sume, on that rare occasion grave (more than significant, serious or substantial) proportions." *Ibid.* at 381.

[41] *Ibid.* at 396. "The required degree of care is proportional to the degree of hazard involved. The degree of harm itself should be foreseeable and the State must know or should have known that the given activity has the risk of significant harm." *Ibid.*

[42] DAVID KENNEDY, OF WAR AND LAW 36 (2006). *Cf.* Nico Krisch, *International Law in Times of Hegemony: Unequal Power and the Shaping of the International Legal Order*, 16(3) EUR. J. INT'L L. 369, 387 (2005) (arguing that, "[i]n the earlier periods of modern international law, rules were mostly customary and so vague that dominant states had great latitude in applying them, and withdrawal and interpretation were hardly distinguishable.").

[43] *See* Farrior, *supra* note 25, at 302. This begs the question, of course, of the meaning of "violation." *Cf.* Michael J. Glennon, *How International Rules Die*, 93(3) GEO. L.J. 939, 972 n. 161 (2005).

the actual content of the obligation, especially when contemplating the vast range or shades of state passiveness, inaction, or 'willful blindness' vis-a-vis terrorist activities taking root within a given territory."[44]

The fundamental problem with interpretative tools in the due diligence context, as well as more generally, is that "people view the normative consequences of social process through different criteria and arrive at irreconcilable conclusions even when using the same criteria."[45] Judge Higgins, in fact, has highlighted the imprecision of good faith by itself.[46]

When a State stands accused of having breached a due diligence obligation, it will, understandably, argue that the interpretative tool being brought to bear on the underlying rule in light of the particular facts and circumstances is either inappropriate, is being misunderstood, or is being misapplied. Kennedy refers to this idea in a related context as legal elasticity that provides for "diverse interpretations."[47] "You can argue whatever you like," he notes, "but within the constraints of this common language of civilization."[48]

In addition to disputing the proper application of interpretative tools to the underlying due diligence rule in light of the particular facts and circumstances, the accused State, the State that has been thrust into a corner and on the defensive, will also likely contest the basics of the dispute. In presenting their arguments as to legality and illegality, the opposing sides, as well as those parties who position themselves at various points in between, will

---

44 Proulx, *supra* note 17, at 647 (emphasis added).

45 Koskenniemi, *The Politics of International Law*, *supra* note 5, at 16. "Between the form of the law and a decision to project on it meaning 'x' instead of 'y', is a professional technique that excludes no interpretation *a priori*, that enables stakeholders to articulate their grievances as legal claims on conditions of equality, including them in the normative universe as subjects of rights and duties or carriers of distinct identities." Martti Koskenniemi, *What Is International Law For?*, in INTERNATIONAL LAW 89, 102 (Malcolm D. Evans ed., 2003). According to Williamson, the "application of law to a particular set of international events may be selective, as may be the decision of which legal bases to assert." Edwin D. Williamson, *Realism and Legalism: Realism Versus Legalism in International Relations*, 2002 A.S.I.L. PROC. 262, 262.

46 *See* HIGGINS, *supra* note 5, at 222.

47 KENNEDY, *supra* note 42, at 39. Of international humanitarian law, Kennedy argues that, "[a]lthough any of us might well disagree with one or another interpretation, we must recognize that the legal materials are elastic enough to enable diverse interpretations. [. . .] The astonishing thing is that these are differences in *perspective* on a quite similar set of legal doctrines and political considerations." *Ibid.*

48 *Ibid.* at 82.

act toward "facts" as "historians," in the sense that, as Carr recognises, "facts speak only when the historian calls on them: it is he who decides to which facts to give the floor, and in what order or context."[49] In this context, Charlesworth's point about "[t]he negotiability of facts"[50] and the political implications of choices of facts[51] and Koskenniemi's emphasis on "political preference, including the question of what element of a many-faceted 'reality' should be chosen as the starting point of one's analysis,"[52] are particularly relevant.

How are the proper application of interpretative tools and the basics of the dispute to be resolved, by whom, and on what authority? There are no straightforward answers.

The ICJ explored the relationship between law and politics and the proper role of politics in legal interpretation in its first advisory opinion, the *Admissions* case.[53] As regards Article 4 of the Charter, the ICJ adopted a series of tools to assist it in its interpretative task. Among these were a focus on the "natural meaning of the words"[54] and consideration of "any factor which it is possible reasonably and in good faith to connect with the conditions laid down."[55] Given that, according to the ICJ, the Charter expresses the conditions of admission in language that can be characterised as being of a "very wide and very elastic nature[, . . . it was held that] no relevant

---

[49] E. H. CARR, *The Historian and His Facts,* in WHAT IS HISTORY?: THE GEORGE MACAULAY TREVELYAN LECTURES DELIVERED IN THE UNIVERSITY OF CAMBRIDGE JANUARY-MARCH 1961 7, 11 (1970). "The facts are really not at all like fish on the fishmonger's slab. They are like fish swimming about in a vast and sometimes inaccessible ocean; and what the historian catches will depend, partly on chance, but mainly on what part of the ocean he chooses to fish in and what tackle he chooses to use – these two factors being, of course, determined by the kind of fish he wants to catch. By and large, the historian will get the kind of facts he wants. History means interpretation." *Ibid.* at 23.

[50] Hilary Charlesworth, *International Law: A Discipline of Crisis*, 65(3) MOD. L. REV. 377, 382 (2002).

[51] *See ibid.* at 383-84. *See also* Kairys, *supra* note 12, at 17.

[52] Koskenniemi, *What Is International Law For?*, *supra* note 45, at 93.

[53] According to the ICJ, "[t]he question put is in effect confined to the following point only: are the conditions stated in paragraph 1 of Article 4 exhaustive in character in the sense that an affirmative reply would lead to the conclusion that a Member is not legally entitled to make admission dependent on conditions not expressly provided for in that Article, while a negative reply would, on the contrary, authorize a Member to make admission dependent also on other conditions." Admissions, *supra* note 8, at 61.

[54] *Ibid.* at 62.

[55] *Ibid.* at 63.

political factor – that is to say, none connected with the conditions of admission – is excluded."[56]

Although the ICJ in the *Admissions* case limited its examination to the conditions of admission, its interpretative approach seems applicable in the context of the due diligence principle because, like the conditions of admission, the due diligence principle involves general language of a potentially limitless scope that must be given legal substance through interpretation in light of particular facts and circumstances. At the same time, there are inherent problems with this approach, whether in the context of the conditions of admission or the due diligence principle. On what basis, for example, and with regard to which criteria and for what reasons can a "natural meaning of the words" test actually circumscribe, in a tangible way, permissible legal interpretation of the due diligence principle embodied in Security Council Resolution 1373's requirement that States "[t]ake the necessary steps to prevent the commission of terrorist acts"?[57] The task is circular, definitionally nebulous and question-begging, and ultimately vacuous, as are interpretative approaches generally when applied to particular facts and circumstances.[58] Furthermore, how can the permitted consideration of "any factor which it is possible reasonably and in good faith to connect with the conditions laid down" be practically useful as guidance in the context of the due diligence principle and counterterrorism?[59]

Consider how the due diligence principle has operated in post-occupation Iraq[60] with regard to terrorist atrocities committed there.[61] The Secu-

---

56 *Ibid.* "In this case, the limits of this freedom are fixed by Article 4 and allow for a wide liberty of appreciation." *Ibid.* at 64.

57 S.C. Res. 1373, U.N. SCOR, at 2, U.N. Doc. S/RES/1373 (2001).

58 *Cf.* Duncan Kennedy, *Legal Education as Training for Hierarchy*, in THE POLITICS OF LAW, *supra* note 12, at 40, 48 (asserting that "[r]ights discourse is internally inconsistent, vacuous, or circular. Legal thought can generate equally plausible rights justifications for almost any result."). The same thinking would apply to Dinstein's finding of legal comfort in the due diligence principle and good faith when assessing military objectives under international humanitarian law. *See* Yoram Dinstein, *Collateral Damage and the Principle of Proportionality*, in NEW WARS, NEW LAWS?: APPLYING THE LAWS OF WAR IN 21ST CENTURY CONFLICTS 211, 220 (David Wippman & Matthew Evangelista eds., 2005).

59 Compare this with Koskenniemi's allusion to politics informing legal discourse in the context of the "late modern turn to doctrinal pragmatism." Koskenniemi, *The Politics of International Law*, *supra* note 5, at 14.

60 According to the Security Council, the occupation of Iraq ended in late-June 2004. It noted this prospectively and also acknowledged this after the fact. *See* S.C. Res. 1546, U.N. SCOR, at 2, U.N. Doc. S/RES/1546 (2004) (stating that it was "[*a*]*cting* under Chapter VII

rity Council has "[*c*]*ondemn*[*ed*] without reservation and in the strongest terms the terrorist attacks that have taken place in Iraq."[62]

The United States has levelled charges against Iran for its role in supporting groups in Iraq. According to the Iraq Study Group (ISG), the Supreme Council for the Islamic Revolution in Iraq (SCIRI)-affiliated militia the Badr Brigade has "long-standing ties with the Iranian Revolutionary Guard Corps,"[63] and SCIRI, for its part, has "close ties with Iran."[64] Furthermore, according to the ISG, Iran has "provided arms, financial support, and training for Shiite militias within Iraq, as well as political support for Shia parties."[65] In a January 2007 address to the nation, United States Presi-

---

of the Charter of the United Nations, [. . .] 2. *Welcomes* that, also by 30 June 2004, the occupation will end and the Coalition Provisional Authority will cease to exist, and that Iraq will reassert its full sovereignty."); S.C. Res. 1637, U.N. SCOR, at 1, U.N. Doc. S/RES/1637 (2005) (noting its "[*w*]*elcoming* [of] the assumption of full governmental authority by the Interim Government of Iraq on 28 June 2004, the direct democratic elections of the Transitional National Assembly on 30 January 2005, the drafting of a new constitution for Iraq and the recent approval of the draft constitution by the people of Iraq on 15 October 2005."). *See also ibid.* at Annex II, at 6 (stating United States Secretary of State Condoleezza Rice's position that, "[s]ince the end of the occupation on 28 June 2004, the Government of Iraq and the MNF [(i.e., Multinational Force)] have developed an effective and cooperative security partnership to address the evolving nature of Iraq's security environment, including the continuing need to prevent and deter acts of terrorism."). *But see* Andrea Carcano, *End of the Occupation in 2004?: The Status of the Multinational Force in Iraq After the Transfer of Sovereignty to the Interim Iraqi Government,* 11(1) J. CONFLICT & SECURITY L. 41 (2006).

61 A virtually unlimited number of cases could be examined in light of the numerous due diligence rules in the counterterrorism context, and the post-occupation Iraq example is given as but one instance. As another example, consider the United States' porous and heavily-trafficked, in both drugs and people, southwestern border with Mexico. On this border, see Sara A. Carter, *Of Special Interest: Links Between Illegal Immigration, Terrorism, Drug Trade Worry U.S. Officials*, SAN BERNARDINO SUN, 29 December 2006, *available at* http://www.sbsun.com/portlet/article/html/fragments/print_article.jsp?articleId=4917114&siteId=208. Security Council Resolution 1373 states that "all States shall [. . .] (g) Prevent the movement of terrorists or terrorist groups by effective border controls and controls on issuance of identity papers and travel documents, and through measures for preventing counterfeiting, forgery or fraudulent use of identity papers and travel documents." S.C. Res. 1373, *supra* note 57, at 2.

62 S.C. Res. 1618, *supra* note 27, at 1.

63 THE IRAQ STUDY GROUP REPORT 11, *available at* http://www.usip.org/isg/iraq_study_group_report/report/1206/iraq_study_group_report.pdf (2006).

64 *Ibid.* at 17.

65 *Ibid.* at 25. "Iran backs Shia claims and supports various Shia militias in Iraq, but it also supports other groups in order to enhance its influence and hedge its bets on possible outcomes." *Ibid.* at 35.

dent George W. Bush cited Iran, along with Syria, as "allowing terrorists and insurgents to use their territory to move in and out of Iraq. Iran is providing material support for attacks on American troops."[66]

As historical context, it is revealing that Iraq's report to the Security Council's Counter-Terrorism Committee (CTC) of 13 August 2002 accused Iran of providing safe haven to militias and dissident elements, "which are under the supervision of Iranian military secret agencies and are known to the international community through their terrorist acts both in the Arab world and elsewhere,"[67] and of having created these groups.[68] Unsurprisingly, Iran rejected these accusations in its report to the CTC of 19 February 2003.[69] It continues to publicly condemn sectarian strife and instability in post-occupation Iraq.[70]

As to the legal context, Iran remains bound by treaty law and Security Council Resolutions that impose counterterrorism obligations upon it.[71]

---

[66] THE WHITE HOUSE, *President's Address to the Nation* (10 January 2007), *available at* http://www.whitehouse.gov/news/releases/2007/01/print/20070110-7.html. *See* Philip Sherwell, *US Forces Turn on Iranians*, SUN. TELEGRAPH, 15 January 2007, *available at* http://www.telegraph.co.uk/core/Content/displayPrintable.jhtml;jsessionid=RIB4UNO4N0IBHQFIQMGSFFWAVCBQWIV0?xml=/news/2007/01/14/wirq114.xml&site=5&page=0.

[67] NOTE VENABLE DATED 14 AUGUST 2002 FROM THE CHAIRMAN OF THE SECURITY COUNCIL COMMITTEE ESTABLISHED PURSUANT TO RESOLUTION 1373 (2001) CONCERNING COUNTER-TERRORISM ADDRESSED TO THE PRESIDENT OF THE SECURITY COUNCIL, U.N. SCOR, Annex, at 9, U.N. Doc. S/2002/943 (2002).

[68] *See ibid.*

[69] *See* LETTER DATED 3 MARCH 2003 FROM THE CHAIRMAN OF THE SECURITY COUNCIL COMMITTEE ESTABLISHED PURSUANT TO RESOLUTION 1373 (2001) CONCERNING COUNTER-TERRORISM ADDRESSED TO THE PRESIDENT OF THE SECURITY COUNCIL, U.N. SCOR, Annex, at 6-7, U.N. Doc. S/2003/266 (2003).

[70] According to Iran's permanent representative to the United Nations, Mohammad-Javad Zarif, "[w]e strongly condemn all these terrorist acts, and reject all attempts that promote sectarian division in Iraq." *Iranian Envoy Criticizes Ineffective Attitude of SC*, ISLAMIC REPUBLIC NEWS AGENCY, 13 December 2006, *available at* http://www.irna.com/index2.php?option=com_news&task=print&code=0612130850140221&Itemid=&lang=en. *But see* Traci Carl, *Iran Leader Courts Latin American Allies*, N.Y. SUN, 15 January 2007, *available at* http://hosted.ap.org/dynamic/stories/N/NICARAGUA_IRAN?SITE=NYNSN&SECTION=HOME&TEMPLATE=DEFAULT.

[71] Iran is a State party to the Convention on Offences and Certain Other Acts Committed on Board Aircraft, Tokyo, 14 September 1963; Convention for the Suppression of Unlawful Seizure of Aircraft, The Hague, 16 December 1970; Convention for the Suppression of Unlawful Acts Against the Safety of Civil Aviation, Montreal, 23 September 1971; Convention on the Prevention and Punishment of Crimes Against Internationally Protected Per-

The Security Council has required States generally to "[r]efrain from providing any form of support, active or passive, to entities or persons involved in terrorist acts, including by suppressing recruitment of members of terrorist groups and eliminating the supply of weapons to terrorists,"[72] and it has also spoken specifically of States' obligations with regard to ending terrorism in post-occupation Iraq. As regards the latter, for example, Resolution 1723 reiterates that terrorist acts "must not be allowed to disrupt Iraq's political and economic transition, and *further reaffirm*[*s*] the obligations of Member States under Resolution 1618 (2005) of 4 August 2005 and other relevant resolutions and international conventions with respect, inter alia, to terrorist activities in and from Iraq or against its citizens."[73]

Has Iran violated its obligation to act with due diligence by its actions or omissions with regard to terrorist atrocities committed in post-occupation Iraq? In addition to the fact that the Security Council has failed to specifically condemn Iran in this regard, interpreting the law in light of the contested facts and circumstances does not seem to lead to a clear, undisputed legal conclusion on the matter. What legal meaning can be, and should be, attached to the ISG's finding that the Badr Brigade has "long-standing ties with the Iranian Revolutionary Guard Corps" and that SCIRI has "close ties with Iran"? Does the ISG's assertion that Iran has "provided arms, financial support, and training for Shiite militias within Iraq, as well as political support for Shia parties" trigger attribution of those groups' conduct

---

sons, Including Diplomatic Agents, New York, 14 December 1973; and Protocol for the Suppression of Unlawful Acts of Violence at Airports Serving International Civil Aviation, Supplementary to the Convention for the Suppression of Unlawful Acts Against the Safety of Civil Aviation, Montreal, 24 February 1988. *See Status of Participation by States in the 13 Universal Instruments Related to the Prevention and Suppression of Terrorism, available at* http://www.un.org/sc/ctc/documents/treatytable.pdf (last visited 25 January 2007).

[72] S.C. Res. 1373, *supra* note 57, at 2.

[73] S.C. Res. 1723, U.N. SCOR, at 2, U.N. Doc. S/RES/1723 (2006). Security Council Resolution 1618 "[*r*]*eaffirms* the obligations of Member States under resolutions 1373 (2001) of 28 September 2001, 1267 (1999) of 15 October 1999, 1333 (2000) of 19 December 2000, 1390 (2002) of 16 January 2002, 1455 (2003) of 17 January 2003, 1526 (2004) of 30 January 2004, and 1617 (2005) of 29 July 2005 and other relevant international obligations with respect, inter alia, to terrorist activities in and from Iraq or against its citizens, and specifically strongly *urges* Member States to prevent the transit of terrorists to and from Iraq, arms for terrorists, and financing that would support terrorists, and *re-emphasizes* the importance of strengthening the cooperation of the countries in the region, particularly neighbours of Iraq, in this regard." S.C. Res. 1618, *supra* note 27, at 2.

to Iran under Article 8 of the *Articles on Responsibility of States for Internationally Wrongful Acts*?[74] If so, would this be on the basis of the ICJ's test of "effective control"[75] or the International Criminal Tribunal for the former Yugoslavia's test of "overall control"?[76] If the conduct of those responsible for terrorist atrocities committed in post-occupation Iraq cannot be attributed to Iran as a matter of State responsibility, can it be shown that Iran has violated a due diligence rule through its actions or omissions?[77]

Even if the opposing sides in such a dispute, for example, the United States and Iran, only disagreed as to whether Iran had violated a due diligence rule through its actions or omissions, much would remain unresolved from a legal point of view. Debate would shift to what Koskenniemi calls a

---

[74] International Law Commission, *Articles on Responsibility of States for Internationally Wrongful Acts*, in JAMES CRAWFORD, THE INTERNATIONAL LAW COMMISSION'S ARTICLES ON STATE RESPONSIBILITY: INTRODUCTION, TEXT AND COMMENTARIES 61, 62, at Art. 8 (2003) (2001) (stating that "[t]he conduct of a person or group of persons shall be considered an act of a State under international law if the person or group of persons is in fact acting on the instructions of, or under the direction or control of, that State in carrying out the conduct."). "It is clear [. . .] that a State may, either by specific directions or by exercising control over a group, in effect assume responsibility for their conduct. Each case will depend on its own facts, in particular those concerning the relationship between the instructions given or the direction or control exercised and the specific conduct complained of." International Law Commission, *Commentaries, Articles on Responsibility of States for Internationally Wrongful Acts*, in *ibid.*, at 74, 113.

[75] Case Concerning Military and Paramilitary Activities in and Against Nicaragua (*Nic.* v. *U.S.*), 1986 I.C.J. 14, 65 (stating that, "[f]or this conduct to give rise to legal responsibility of the United States, it would in principle have to be proved that that State had effective control of the military or paramilitary operations in the course of which the alleged violations were committed.").

[76] *Prosecutor* v. *Tadić* (IT-94-1-A), Appeals Chamber, 1999 I.C.T.Y., at 56 (stating that, "[i]n order to attribute the acts of a military or paramilitary group to a State, it must be proved that the State wields overall control over the group, not only by equipping and financing the group, but also by coordinating or helping in the general planning of its military activity. Only then can the State be held internationally accountable for any misconduct of the group. However, it is not necessary that, in addition, the State should also issue, either to the head or to members of the group, instructions for the commission of specific acts contrary to international law."). For a recent ICJ discussion of these tests, see Application of the Convention on the Prevention and Punishment of the Crime of Genocide (*Bosn. & Herz.* v. *Serb. & Mont.*), 2007 I.C.J., at Paras. 396-407.

[77] As Proulx notes, "it is clear that the mechanism of indirect state responsibility has become a sort of 'safety net' to pin responsibility on a host-state should an aggrieved state endeavor to establish direct responsibility but fail to do so." Proulx, *supra* note 17, at 651-52.

"politics of expertise,"[78] with the United States arguing that Iran's actions and omissions are unreasonable and, thus, violative of a due diligence rule and Iran arguing that its actions and omissions are not unreasonable or, if they are, that they do not qualify as an internationally wrongful act of State on the basis of a circumstance precluding wrongfulness.

It is difficult to arrive at a clear, undisputed legal conclusion on the matter. Much of this has to do with the reality of what the ICJ referred to in the *Corfu Channel* case, each State's "exclusive territorial control."[79] As arbitrator Max Huber noted in the *Island of Palmas* case, State sovereignty means "[i]ndependence in regard to a portion of the globe[, . . .] the right to exercise therein, to the exclusion of any other State, the functions of a State."[80] With this comes an ability to complicate, confuse, and conceal.[81] Difficulties of proof arise because State action is "composed mostly, if not always, of a plurality of acts and attitudes emanating from different organs situated frequently at different levels in the hierarchy of the State's mastodontic structure."[82] When a due diligence paradigm applies, evidence gathering is made still more challenging because non-State actors that engage in terrorism are naturally secretive.[83] Furthermore, as Proulx notes,

---

[78] Martti Koskenniemi, *The Fate of Public International Law: Between Technique and Politics,* 70(1) MOD. L. REV. 1, 10 (2007) (continuing by stating that "what might be 'reasonable' for an environmental expert is not what is 'reasonable' to a chemical manufacturer; what is 'optimal' to development engineer is not what is optimal to the representative of an indigenous population; what is 'proportionate' to a humanitarian specialist is not necessarily what is proportionate to a military expert.").

[79] Corfu Channel (*U.K.* v. *Alb.*), 1949 I.C.J. 4, 18. *See* Request for an Examination of the Situation in Accordance with Paragraph 63 of the Court's Judgment of 20 December 1974 in the Nuclear Tests Case (*N.Z.* v. *Fr.*), 1995 I.C.J. 288, 342 (Weeramantry, J., dissenting).

[80] Island of Palmas, 2 R.I.A.A. 829, 838 (1928).

[81] The Inter-American Court of Human Rights (IACtHR) has recognised this. *See* Velásquez Rodríguez, Ser. C, Case No. 4, Inter-Am. Ct. H.R. 1988, Para. 136. For further on this, see BECKER, *supra* note 18, at 241.

[82] Gaetano Arangio-Ruiz, *State Fault and the Forms and Degrees of International Responsibility: Questions of Attribution and Relevance,* in LE DROIT INTERNATIONAL AU SERVICE DE LA PAIX, DE LA JUSTICE ET DU DÉVELOPPEMENT 25, 35 (Mélanges Michel Virally ed., 1991). Assessing a State's actions and omissions in light of the due diligence principle is much more difficult than corresponding private law assessments. *See ibid.* at 34.

[83] *See* HELEN DUFFY, THE "WAR ON TERROR" AND THE FRAMEWORK OF INTERNATIONAL LAW 57 (2005). *See also* Luigi Condorelli, *The Imputability to States of Acts of International Terrorism,* 19 ISR. Y.B. H.R. 233, 245-46 (1989).

> [w]hether obscured by intricate information networks, new technologies like the Internet, the sophisticated cellular structure of organizations like al Qaeda, complex financial systems, convoluted political realities, or other factors, the level of government involvement in terrorist activities is no longer readily discernible in all instances.[84]

In the *Corfu Channel* case, the ICJ stated that, although "it cannot be concluded from the mere fact of the control exercised by a State over its territory and waters that that State necessarily knew, or ought to have known, of any unlawful act perpetrated therein, nor yet that it necessarily knew, or should have known, the authors,"[85] the complaining State in such situations can benefit from a more lenient standard regarding circumstantial evidence and factual inferences.[86] Nonetheless, a finding of knowledge, according to the ICJ, requires that factual inferences leave "*no room* for reasonable doubt."[87]

How does this more lenient standard of proof regarding circumstantial evidence and factual inferences apply in the context of post-occupation Iraq? Furthermore, although the ICJ has stated that evidence under the more lenient standard "must be regarded as of special weight when it is based on a series of facts linked together and leading logically to a single conclusion,"[88] what exactly is meant by this? It is unclear and seems to be irretrievably so.

---

[84] Proulx, *supra* note 17, at 617.

[85] Corfu Channel, *supra* note 79, at 18.

[86] *See ibid.* According to the IACtHR, in addition to testimonial and documentary direct evidence, "[c]ircumstantial evidence, indicia, and presumptions may be considered, so long as they lead to conclusions consistent with the facts." Velásquez Rodríguez, *supra* note 81, at Para. 130. For commentary on this in the context of counterterrorism and human rights, see DUFFY, *supra* note 83, at 305 (asserting that "[l]inked to the foregoing positive obligations is the onus that lies with the state, in certain circumstances, to demonstrate that it has met those obligations, as opposed to the onus resting with the individual to prove the violation. This is particularly so where – as is not infrequently the situation in human rights cases, and all the more so in the shrouded world of counter-terrorism – the facts lie wholly, or in large part, within the exclusive knowledge of the authorities."). *See also* TRUTH AND RECONCILIATION COMMISSION OF SOUTH AFRICA REPORT 603, *available at* http://www.info.gov.za/otherdocs/2003/trc/rep.pdf (released 21 March 2003).

[87] Corfu Channel, *supra* note 79, at 18. According to Proulx, "[a]s with the Coke bottle manufacturer who has exclusive knowledge over the manufacturing process, the host-state is better positioned than the injured state to know, for example, what logistical, intelligence, police, and military means are at its disposal to eliminate the threat." Proulx, *supra* note 17, at 655.

[88] Corfu Channel, *supra* note 79, at 18.

Since the Security Council has spoken but generally on the matter, whether it can be said as a matter of law that Iran has violated its obligation to act with due diligence vis-à-vis its actions or omissions with regard to terrorist atrocities committed in post-occupation Iraq or, indeed, whether it bears responsibility as a State for terrorism there remains subject to reasonable debate and legally undetermined.

At the same time, however, it can be said that sufficient political will properly channelled could legally transform the situation. This could be done if the Security Council were to adopt a tailored Resolution that would find Iran legally responsible for breach of a due diligence obligation or for responsibility as a State for terrorism in post-occupation Iraq. As Kennedy notes more generally, until that time, "statements about one's entitlements – or an adversary's crimes and misdemeanors – [. . . would be mere] assertions, hypotheses, wagers on how the community of relevant interpreters will react. If they accept the proposition, the entitlement is valid, the violation a crime. If they don't, they aren't."[89]

When the due diligence rule at issue operates within the context of treaty law or Security Council obligation, much of the wrangling as to legality and illegality will take place not in a court of law recognised as such by the opposing sides but, rather, among more obviously political actors who, by their actions and omissions, dynamically inform the substance of the rule.[90] In the treaty law context, these actors include States parties to the applicable treaty, while in the Security Council context, the main political actors that affect legal meaning are the members of the Security Council, particularly the Permanent Five.[91]

---

[89] KENNEDY, *supra* note 42, at 93. "Conversing before the court of world public opinion, statesmen not only assert their prerogatives, they also test and establish those prerogatives through action. [. . .] As lawyers must harness enforcement to their norms, states must defend their prerogatives to keep them – must back up their assertions with action to maintain their credibility. A great many military campaigns have been undertaken for just this kind of credibility. Missiles become missives." *Ibid.* at 159.

[90] *Cf.* Anthony D'Amato, *Trashing Customary International Law*, 81 AM. J. INT'L L. 101, 104 (1987) (expressing a similar idea in the context of customary international law by arguing that "[c]ustomary rules [. . .] are not static. They change in content depending upon the amplitude of new vectors (state interests). [. . .] Another way of phrasing this result is to use Darwinian terms: the customary rules that survive the legal evolutionary process are those that are best adapted to serve the mutual self-interest of all states.").

[91] For Mani, power disparities between States have effectively ensured a top-heavy international relations in which powerful States "hold[] the entire world of small powers to

The due diligence principle gestates, morphs, and comes into its own in the legal sense not because of anything obvious or natural but because of the meaning that dominant political actors choose to externally impose upon it in the particular context of the dispute.[92] As Kairys notes in a related context, "[t]here is no *legal* explanation in any of this; the law has provided a falsely legitimizing justification for a decision that is ultimately social and political."[93]

Clearly, power plays a key role in the legal meaning that is given to due diligence rules in the counterterrorism context. Even though most critical legal scholarship targets the judiciary in the municipal law context and does not address the dynamics of international law *per se*, much less the due diligence principle in particular, this school of thinking provides some insight. Kairys, for example, critiquing American constitutional law, asserts that:

> Our legal norms are broadly and vaguely stated. They do not logically lead to particular results or rationales concerning most important or difficult issues. A wide variety of interpretations, distinctions, and justifications are available; and judges have the authority and power to choose the issues they will address and to ignore constitutional provisions, statutes, precedents, evidence, and the best legal arguments.[94]

"Judges," to use Kairys' language, are those political actors at international level who have a stake in the legal content that is given to a due diligence rule in a particular context and the ability and desire to assert that stake in a way that can be said to have legal effect. Through force of arms, clever legal persuasion, diplomacy, bribery, or a combination of these methods and others, they "judge," as it were. These political actors distinguish precedent and State practice and argue away their opposition.[95]

---

ransom." Mani, *Centrifugal, supra* note 23, at 249. According to Fassbender, the Security Council is "really fifteen governments agreeing, or disagreeing, on something – according to what they perceive to be their respective 'national interest' (and sometimes also according to the interest of the international community), and always under the shadow of the veto power of five of them." Bardo Fassbender, *The UN Security Council and International Terrorism,* in ENFORCING INTERNATIONAL LAW NORMS AGAINST TERRORISM 83, 85 (Andrea Bianchi ed., 2004).

[92] *Cf.* Koskenniemi, *The Fate of Public International Law, supra* note 78, at 8.

[93] Kairys, *supra* note 12, at 14.

[94] *Ibid.* at 13.

[95] *Cf. ibid.* at 11-12.

Appreciating this key role of power in legal interpretation requires the questioning of some basic jurisprudential assumptions. A power understanding is necessarily sceptical of Judge Manfred H. Lachs' assertion in his separate opinion in *Case Concerning Military and Paramilitary Activities in and Against Nicaragua* that "[a] judge – as needs no emphasis – is bound to be impartial, objective, detached, disinterested and unbiased."[96] Whether it be an ICJ judge or a State manoeuvring at international level in a manner that it views as legally relevant and as most conducive to its national interest, "judges" are necessarily partial, subjective, attached, interested, and biased.[97] It is simply too much to assert that "whatever philosophy [. . .] judges may confess they are bound to 'master the facts' and then apply to them the law with utmost honesty"[98] and that, "[b]y applying an objective criterion faithfully, any legal question can be examined without considering the political elements which may, in some proportion, be involved."[99] Interpreting the law, pinpointing the law, is necessarily political, wilful blindness and recourse to "objectivity" notwithstanding.[100]

Thus, while interpretative tools can assist at an abstract level in understanding the due diligence principle in the counterterrorism context, their limitations inevitably arise when they are applied to particular facts and

---

96 Nicaragua, *supra* note 75, at 158 (Lachs, J., separate).

97 On States' consideration of the conditions of admission in Art. 4 of the Charter in the *Admissions* case, Judge Azevedo stated that "[m]otives of all kinds, tending to unite or separate men and countries, will slip through the remaining loopholes; all kinds of prejudices, and even physical repugnance will find a way of influencing the decision, either by an act of the will or even through the action of the subconscious. Each appraisal will be psychologically determined according to the criterion applied by each voter." Admissions, *supra* note 8, at 78 (Azevedo, J., separate).

98 Nicaragua, *supra* note 75, at 159 (Lachs, J., separate). For a critical account of politics in the ICJ, see Davis R. Robinson, *The Role of Politics in the Election and the Work of Judges of the International Court of Justice*, 2003 A.S.I.L. PROC. 277.

99 Admissions, *supra* note 8, at 75 (Azevedo, J., separate).

100 "It is impossible to make substantive decisions within the law which would imply no political choice. The late modern turn to equity in the different realms of international law is, in this sense, a healthy admission of something that is anyway there: in the end, legitimizing or criticizing state behaviour is not a matter of applying formally neutral rules but depends on what one regards as politically right, or just." Koskenniemi, *The Politics of International Law*, *supra* note 5, at 31. As Said notes more generally, "[p]olitics is everywhere; there can be no escape into the realms of pure art and thought or, for that matter, into the realm of disinterested objectivity or transcendental theory." EDWARD W. SAID, *Representations of the Intellectual*, in REPRESENTATIONS OF THE INTELLECTUAL: THE 1993 REITH LECTURES 3, 21 (1996).

circumstances. Instead of relying on legal language to provide a ready-made answer to all permutations of cases, it would be better to recognise that political actors largely use the due diligence principle in the counterterrorism context in what Kennedy calls "an open-ended social and political conversation,"[101] as part of "law's contemporary function as a vernacular of political judgment."[102] According to him:

> In the court of world public opinion, the laws in force are not necessarily the rules that are *valid*, in some technical sense, but the rules that are persuasive to relevant political constituencies. Whether a norm is or is not legal is a function not of its origin or pedigree, but of its effects. Law has an effect – is law – when it *persuades* an audience with political clout that something someone else did, or plans to do, is or is not legitimate. The point is no longer the validity of distinctions, but the persuasiveness of arguments.[103]

This thinking is particularly relevant to understanding the due diligence principle in the counterterrorism context.[104]

III. CONCLUSION

In assessing the due diligence obligation of States in the context of non-State actors that engage in terrorism and theoretical issues that this raises, international lawyers must appreciate the importance of the language that

---

[101] KENNEDY, *supra* note 42, at 154.

[102] *Ibid.* at 46. According to Reus-Smit, "[t]he discourse of politics is now replete with the language of law and legitimacy as much as realpolitik, lawyers are as central to military campaigns as strategists, legal right is as much a power resource as guns and money, and juridical sovereignty, grounded in the legal norms of international society, is becoming a key determinant of state power." Christian Reus-Smit, *Introduction*, in THE POLITICS OF INTERNATIONAL LAW 1, 2 (Christian Reus-Smit ed., 2004).

[103] KENNEDY, *supra* note 42, at 96. *Cf.* Ulf Linderfalk, *Is the Hierarchical Structure of Articles 31 and 32 of the Vienna Convention Real or Not?: Interpreting the Rules of Interpretation*, 54(1) NETH. INT'L L. REV. 133, 134 (2007) (contending that "[t]he result of an interpretation process is correct when it can be successfully defended as being in accordance with the provisions of Vienna Convention Articles 31-33. The result is incorrect when it cannot be so defended.").

[104] *Cf.* KENNEDY, *supra* note 42, at 91-92 (discussing a similar issue in the context of proportionality and necessity under international humanitarian law). On the hairy nature of proportionality, see Dinstein, *supra* note 58, at 215-17.

they use. They play a key role in an international order that increasingly sees international law as an "ongoing conversation about the legitimacy of state behavior – legitimacy judged by [. . .] compatibility with UN Charter principles."[105]

Through their use of language, international lawyers bestow legitimacy and cordon off as illegitimate. When, as an example, United Nations Special Rapporteur on the Situation of Human Rights in the Palestinian Territories Occupied Since 1967 John Dugard contrasted Israel's actions in a statement before the General Assembly's Third Committee on 19 October 2006 with "civilized legal values"[106] and described its "brutal assault[, . . .] savage response[, . . .] shelling [. . . that] has been unrelenting[, and . . .] reign of aerial terror,"[107] he demonstrated this, law's political potential, the "other" being for him the uncivilised Israeli, a brutal assailant, a savage, an unrelenting sheller of ordnance, a terrorist. There is great power and authority in invoking international legal language.

Interpretation, and the politics inherent in it, is inevitable in the law. This is only so much the case with the due diligence principle in the counter-terrorism context.

---

[105] KENNEDY, *supra* note 42, at 159.

[106] Statement by Prof. John Dugard, Special Rapporteur on the Situation of Human Rights in the Occupied Palestinian Territory, Third Committee of the General Assembly (19 October 2006) (on file with author).

[107] *Ibid.*

Chapter 6
SHOULD NATIONAL SECURITY TRUMP HUMAN RIGHTS IN THE FIGHT AGAINST TERRORISM?

Chapter 6
SHOULD NATIONAL SECURITY TRUMP HUMAN RIGHTS IN THE FIGHT AGAINST TERRORISM?

I. INTRODUCTION

It is unsurprising that the role of human rights in the counterterrorism discourse has become an issue of major concern to those broadly associated with human rights. In securing the right to life in their fight against non-State terrorists, States cannot act in a vacuum. International human rights law, involving as it does positive and negative State obligations, requires a delicate juggling act by States when fighting terrorism.[1]

This chapter addresses some important issues in the context of human rights and counterterrorism. It begins by exploring the applicable legal framework in the current counterterrorism context, with particular emphasis on the United States' engagement with Al Qaeda. Arguing that an armed conflict model is the most convincing approach, it then asks how international human rights law applies during armed conflicts and looks at how international actors have attempted to frame human rights in a way that appeals to States' self-interest. This chapter then critically engages in the debate by exploring whether human rights observance is necessary to effectively fight terrorism and whether States can effectively fight terrorism while at the same time not violating human rights.[2] It should be stressed that this chapter's insights are relevant to counterterrorism obligations that operate according to the due diligence principle and also to those that operate according to other principles of responsibility.

---

[1] For a discussion by Duffy on international human rights law in the context of terrorism, see HELEN DUFFY, THE "WAR ON TERROR" AND THE FRAMEWORK OF INTERNATIONAL LAW 301-32 (2005).

[2] Dunér addresses similar concerns. *See* Bertil Dunér, *Disregard for Security: The Human Rights Movement and 9/11,* 17(1-2) TERRORISM & POL. VIOLENCE 89, 91 (2005) (assessing the "question of a *trade-off* between security and human rights [. . .] and [. . .] the *instrumentality* of human rights for security.").

II. The Applicable Legal Framework

Given that the law acts as an overarching framework that provides a reference point for judgment, human rights analysis must begin by identifying the applicable legal framework. Once this is done, the identified regime can be applied to particular facts and circumstances, and conclusions can be drawn as to the legality or illegality of a State's actions or omissions. This, of course, presumes that the relevant legal framework can be identified with some degree of predictability and certainty. This section focuses in particular on the United States' engagement with Al Qaeda.

Taft sketches as potentially applicable to the United States' engagement with Al Qaeda the legal regimes that have historically applied during wartime and peacetime, or, respectively, international humanitarian law and criminal law, yet argues that the preferred approach would involve a "new system whose rules are well understood and take account of both the need to protect our citizens and assure that we accurately identify, effectively deter, and appropriately punish those who pose threats to our society or have committed criminal acts."[3] As a non-State terrorist organisation, he notes that Al Qaeda cannot be considered to be bound by the Geneva Conventions as a matter of treaty law because it does not have the capacity to enter into such agreements.[4] However, given the gravity of the terrorist threat and the inherently political nature of Al Qaeda's agenda and choice of means, Taft argues for a framework rooted in the "law of armed conflict modified to adapt to those unconventional aspects."[5]

Posner's argument broadly resembles Taft's.[6] The former's approach, however, acknowledges a greater number of legal permutations potentially applicable in the current counterterrorism context, namely international humanitarian law, criminal law, a lacuna in which international humanitarian law does not apply, and an altered international humanitarian law.[7]

---

3 William H. Taft, Keynote Address, 21(2) Am. U. Int'l L. Rev. 149, 149 (2005).

4 *See ibid.* at 154. Of the Geneva Conventions, Judge Rosalyn Higgins of the International Court of Justice (ICJ) has said that "[i]t does remain an area where some of the provisions sit very awkwardly with non-state actors and with actors who even if states are not parties." A Conversation with Secretary of State Condoleezza Rice, Centennial Annual Meeting of the American Society of International Law (29 March 2006), *available at* http://www.state.gov/secretary/rm/2006/63855.htm.

5 Taft, *supra* note 3, at 150.

6 Eric A. Posner, *Terrorism and the Laws of War*, 5(2) Chi. J. Int'l L. 423 (2005).

7 *See ibid.*; *ibid.* at 423 n. 1.

According to Posner, applying the laws of war completely to Al Qaeda could potentially mean granting its captured combatants widespread protection.[8] He is critical of another potentially applicable legal framework, criminal law, because it ignores the inherently political raison d'être of Al Qaeda and its ability to act coherently and strategically.[9] At the same time, Posner recognises that two philosophical underpinnings of the laws of war, namely symmetry and reciprocity, which he defines, respectively, as the "condition [that] requires that the laws of war generate military advantages for neither belligerent [. . . and t]he [. . .] condition [that] requires that each belligerent have the ability to retaliate when the other belligerent violates the laws of war,"[10] sit uneasily in the current environment, which Pfanner describes as asymmetrical warfare,[11] and thus, Posner favours an approach that appreciates this dynamic.[12] Casey and Rivkin pick up on the reciprocity issue and argue that wilful blindness to its place in the current environ-

[8] *See ibid.* at 431.

[9] *See ibid.* at 431-32. Osama bin Laden coherently laid out Al Qaeda's political manifesto in his "*Letter to America*," in which, to name a few of his demands, he insisted upon conversion to Islam, criticised the notion of secular politics, gambling, homosexuality, and interest on investments, and blamed the United States for the spread of AIDS. *See Full Text: Bin Laden's "Letter to America,"* OBSERVER, at (Q2)(1)-(7) (24 November 2002), *available at* http://observer.guardian.co.uk/worldview/story/0,11581,845725,00.html. Egyptian militant Islamist Sayyid Qutb saw in usury an "aim [. . . to ensure] that all the wealth of mankind end up in the hands of Jewish financial institutions which run on interest." SAYYID QUTB, MILESTONES 111 (2005).

[10] Posner, *supra* note 6, at 424. *See* Toni Pfanner, *Asymmetrical Warfare from the Perspective of Humanitarian Law and Humanitarian Action*, 87(857) INT'L REV. RED CROSS 149, 161 (2005).

[11] *See* Pfanner, *supra* note 10, at 150 (defining asymmetrical warfare as that in which "the parties are unequal and the principle of equality of arms no longer holds true. The belligerents have disparate aims and employ dissimilar means and methods to pursue their tactics and strategies.").

[12] *See* Posner, *supra* note 6, at 427-34. *See also* Lee A. Casey & David B. Rivkin, Jr., *Rethinking the Geneva Conventions*, in THE TORTURE DEBATE IN AMERICA 203, 204 (Karen J. Greenberg ed., 2006) (asserting that "[o]ne potential solution, both in terms of applying the Geneva Conventions in instances where the United States engages a noncompliant Geneva party and vis-à-vis al Qaeda, would be adoption of a reciprocity rule. This need not involve resort to tit-for-tat reprisals, but could be a flexible approach whereby the United States takes account of its opponent's compliance record in its own interpretation and application of the treaties.").

ment can be likened to "sending a gambler to the tables with an ironclad guarantee that he's 'covered.'"[13]

Across the Atlantic Ocean, Greenwood, writing in 2002, sits uncomfortably with the characterisation as mere crime, however serious, of the threat posed by Al Qaeda terrorism.[14] He cites the Security Council's classification of terrorism as a threat to international peace and security,[15] something which with regard to non-State actors International Court of Justice (ICJ) Judge Pieter Hendrik Kooijmans recognised in his separate opinion during the summer of 2004 in the *Legal Consequences of the Construction of a Wall in the Occupied Palestinian Territory* (*Wall*) case as a "completely new element[, . . .] the legal implications of which cannot as yet be assessed but which marks undeniably a new approach to the concept of self-defence."[16] Greenwood asserts a need for international law to appreciate in its threat perception that modern terrorism in the form of Al Qaeda involves a "terrorist organization operating outside the control of any state [that] is capable of causing death and destruction on a scale comparable with that of regular military action by a state."[17] The classical notion of a power hierarchy between States and non-State actors, with the former in a horizontal relationship with each other and in an overbearing vertical relationship with

---

[13] Casey & Rivkin, *supra* note 12, at 205. Neuman also discusses reciprocity. *See* Gerald L. Neuman, *Humanitarian Law and Counterterrorist Force*, 14(2) EUR. J. INT'L L. 283, 283-87 (2003).

[14] Christopher Greenwood, *International Law and the "War Against Terrorism,"* 78(2) INT'L AFF. 301 (2002).

[15] *See ibid.* at 306-07. *See also* Yoram Dinstein, *Ius Ad Bellum Aspects of the "War on Terrorism,"* in TERRORISM AND THE MILITARY: INTERNATIONAL LEGAL IMPLICATIONS 13, 15-16 (Wybo P. Heere ed., 2003).

[16] Legal Consequences of the Construction of a Wall in the Occupied Palestinian Territory (Advisory Opinion), 2004 I.C.J., at Para. 35 (Kooijmans, J., separate). The General Assembly Resolution asked for an advisory opinion regarding "the legal consequences arising from the construction of the wall being built by Israel, the occupying Power, in the Occupied Palestinian Territory, including in and around East Jerusalem, as described in the report of the Secretary-General, considering the rules and principles of international law, including the Fourth Geneva Convention of 1949, and relevant Security Council and General Assembly resolutions." G.A. Res. ES-10/14, U.N. GAOR, at 3, U.N. Doc. A/RES/ES-10/14 (2003).

[17] Greenwood, *supra* note 14, at 307. *See* Ruth Wedgwood, *Al Qaeda, Terrorism, and Military Commissions*, 96(2) AM. J. INT'L L. 328, 328 (2002); REPLY OF THE GOVERNMENT OF THE UNITED STATES OF AMERICA TO THE REPORT OF THE FIVE UNCHR SPECIAL RAPPORTEURS ON DETAINEES IN GUANTANAMO BAY, CUBA, 45(3) I.L.M. 742, 751 (2006).

the latter, Greenwood argues, may be outdated and in need of adaptation.[18]

These arguments favouring an international humanitarian law perspective toward Al Qaeda broadly resemble the United States' position since 11 September.[19] According to the *Reply of the Government of the United States of America to the Report of the Five UNCHR Special Rapporteurs on Detainees in Guantanamo Bay, Cuba*, there exists an armed conflict, as international humanitarian law understands that legally-loaded term, between the United States and Al Qaeda, the applicable legal framework existing outside treaty law in the realm of customary international humanitarian law.[20] The key point is "the existence of an armed conflict[, . . .] determined *inter alia* by the intensity, and scope and duration of hostilities, not by whether the situation is afforded Geneva Convention protection."[21] While it is true that the United States Supreme Court's June 2006 decision in *Hamdan* v. *Rumsfeld* held that common Article 3 of the Geneva Conventions applies to the United States' engagement with Al Qaeda,[22] it should be stressed that,

---

[18] *See* Greenwood, *supra* note 14, at 301. *See also* Pfanner, *supra* note 10, at 158. According to Pfanner, "[a]symmetrical wars fit in neither with Clausewitz's concept of war nor with the traditional concept of international humanitarian law." *Ibid.* at 173.

[19] The United States' position can be contrasted with the European approach. *See* Alix Kroeger, *New Challenges Strain EU-US Ties*, BBC NEWS, 1 June 2006, *available at* http://news.bbc.co.uk/go/pr/fr/-/1/hi/world/europe/5036282.stm.

[20] *See* REPLY, *supra* note 17, at 748. Recourse to customary international humanitarian law as a controlling legal framework obviates the limited State-to-State nature that generally obtains under treaty-based international humanitarian law and focuses attention on the nature of the interaction between the United States and Al Qaeda, not the fact that Al Qaeda, as a non-State actor, is not bound by those international humanitarian law rules that exist only in treaty law. *See* Greenwood, *supra* note 14, at 314; *ibid.* at 314 n. 44; REPLY, *supra* note 17, at 752 (stating that "[o]ur fight against Al Qaida is different from traditional armed conflicts in that it is not a state-to-state conflict, in which there generally is an identifiable conclusion of hostilities, after which each side releases those combatants it has detained.").

[21] REPLY, *supra* note 17, at 749. This argument is strengthened by the fact that Al Qaeda's Osama bin Laden has clearly recognised an armed conflict posture. Over three and a half years before 11 September, for example, he publicly stated that "[a]ll these crimes and sins committed by the Americans are a clear declaration of war on God, his messenger, and Muslims." Shaykh Usamah Bin-Muhammad Bin-Ladin et al., *Jihad Against Jews and Crusaders: World Islamic Front Statement*, WASH. POST (23 February 1998), *available at* http://www.washingtonpost.com/ac2/wp-dyn/A4993-2001Sep21?language=printer (2001). *See* Pfanner, *supra* note 10, at 155-56.

[22] *Hamdan* v. *Rumsfeld*, No. 05-184, slip op. at 66-69 (U.S. S. Ct. 29 June 2006). On this case, see John R. Crook, *Contemporary Practice of the United States Relating to International Law*, 100(4) AM. J. INT'L L. 918, 918-22 (2006).

since common Article 3 itself only operates within an armed conflict paradigm, this decision, while disappointing to the executive branch,[23] does not fundamentally question the applicability of international humanitarian law and an armed conflict paradigm.

It should be noted that an international humanitarian law framework brings with it a number of strategic advantages to the United States in combating Al Qaeda, including combatant detention, non-coercive interrogation and intelligence gathering, and a clear set of guidelines for combatants.[24] It can also be pointed out that the United States' peacetime criminal justice system failed to stymie Al Qaeda's ambitions and avert 11 September.[25] Referring to the United States' attack on Al Qaeda operatives in Yemen in 2002, Pejic argues that a non-armed conflict paradigm could have sufficed in that example, although she concedes that such a framework would have required individualised evidence of an imminent and serious threat to life, the attack having been done as a last resort and with the consent of the target State, and that there have been an investigation with review provision after the fact.[26] Furthermore, again referring to the same example, Pejic asserts that "the suspects' mere 'membership' in al-Qaeda (whatever that may mean) would clearly not have been a sufficient reason to kill them."[27] Outside of armed conflict, she is generally correct, but within an armed conflict framework, "mere 'membership'" suffices to ensure a legitimate military target on the battlefield. If one were to apply Pejic's criteria to the fatal bombing by air of Al Qaeda's Abu Musab al-Zarqawi,[28]

---

[23] Rivkin and Casey call the decision "a setback with a sterling silver lining. [. . .] Together with the Supreme Court's 2004 decision in *Hamdi* v. *Rumsfeld* – directly affirming the government's right to capture and detain, without criminal charge or trial, al Qaeda and allied operatives until hostilities are concluded – *Hamdan* vindicates the basic legal architecture relied upon by the administration in prosecuting this war." David B. Rivkin, Jr., & Lee A. Casey, *Hamdan: What the Ruling Says – And What It Doesn't Say*, WALL ST. J., 3 July 2006, *available at* http://www.opinionjournal.com/extra/?id=110008599.

[24] *See* Taft, *supra* note 3, at 150-52. *But see* Jelena Pejic, *Terrorist Acts and Groups: A Role for International Law?*, 75 BRIT. Y.B. INT'L L. 71, 89 (2004) (stating that "law enforcement standards do not necessarily prevent states from dealing with the gravest terrorist acts, and recourse to international humanitarian law rules on the conduct of hostilities in fighting 'terrorism' is neither inevitable nor necessarily advantageous.").

[25] *See* Casey & Rivkin, *supra* note 12, at 210; Wedgwood, *Al Qaeda, supra* note 17, at 329-30.

[26] *See* Pejic, *supra* note 24, at 90-91.

[27] *Ibid.* at 91.

[28] On this incident, see *How Zarqawi Was Found and Killed*, BBC NEWS, *available at* http://news.bbc.co.uk/2/hi/middle_east/5060468.stm (last updated 9 June 2006).

a strong case can be made that several of her criteria would not have been met. This suggests the strategic advantages of an international humanitarian law framework.

A fundamentally contrasting perspective to the question of the applicable legal framework in the current counterterrorism context is that a war mentality does not apply.[29] According to Paust, the very fact that Al Qaeda cannot be considered a State, belligerent nation, or insurgency means that, *ipso facto*, international humanitarian law does not apply to its engagement with States, including its engagement with the United States.[30] Nonetheless, although he argues that the non-State, non-belligerent, non-nation, and non-insurgency nature of Al Qaeda generally precludes the triggering of international humanitarian law, Paust distinguishes those situations in which Al Qaeda is involved in a conflict in which States are on opposing sides, such as Afghanistan post-11 September and Iraq after the United States-led invasion of March 2003.[31] In a statement issued just days after 11 September, Schabas also reflected a State-centric understanding of international law, stating that, "according to [. . . it], we must know what State committed it. A group of individuals, even numbering in the hundreds, cannot commit an 'act of war.'"[32]

Pejic also generally rejects the applicability of international humanitarian law to States' engagements with Al Qaeda: "[n]ot only is the violence not inter-state, it is also clear that states would never 'legitimise' the non-state 'adversary' by granting groups perpetrating terrorist acts [. . .] status and rights in combat and upon capture."[33] According to her, because Al Qaeda is not sufficiently cohesive as a non-State organisation and because the actions taken against it do not trigger the law of armed conflict, a criminal law framework, not an armed conflict framework, applies.[34]

---

[29] *See International Humanitarian Law and the Challenges of Contemporary Armed Conflicts: Excerpt of the Report Prepared by the International Committee of the Red Cross for the 28th International Conference of the Red Cross and Red Crescent, Geneva, December 2003*, 86(853) INT'L REV. RED CROSS 213, 232-33 (2004).

[30] *See* Jordan J. Paust, *Post-9/11 Overreaction and Fallacies Regarding War and Defense, Guantanamo, the Status of Persons, Treatment, Judicial Review of Detention, and Due Process in Military Commissions*, 79(4) NOTRE DAME L. REV. 1335, 1340-42 (2004).

[31] *See ibid.* at 1342.

[32] William A. Schabas, *Statement of 17 September 2001*, *available at* http://www.nuigalway.ie/human_rights/Docs/Press%20Releases/170901%20PR.doc.

[33] Pejic, *supra* note 24, at 81.

[34] *See ibid.* at 87-88; *ibid.* at 90.

While the International Committee of the Red Cross (ICRC) is clearly correct in noting that "international humanitarian law is applicable when the 'fight against terrorism' amounts to, or involves, armed conflict,"[35] the fundamental disagreement between those who argue that a customary international humanitarian law framework governs the relationship between the United States and Al Qaeda and those who prefer a criminal law model relates to whether it can legally be said that an armed conflict exists between the United States and Al Qaeda.[36] Rona concedes the definitionally problematic and indeterminate nature of the legal concept of armed conflict[37] but suggests that any armed conflict properly so called must have identifiable parties, take place in a particular geographical space, be distinguishable from unrelated acts of violence, have a defined start and finish, and involve hostilities of a certain minimal intensity.[38] After assessing these five criteria, he concludes that there does not exist an armed conflict between the United States and Al Qaeda, thus precluding the application of international humanitarian law.[39]

This conclusion, however, whether by Rona or other like-minded individuals, does not, and cannot, definitively settle the matter. To deal with each of Rona's five criteria in turn, for example, one could argue that: while Rona is undoubtedly correct that "'[t]error' or 'terrorism' cannot be a party to the conflict,"[40] it could be said that Al Qaeda's history of intense and frequent acts of violence and the concerted international effort, particularly

---

[35] *International Humanitarian Law and the Challenges of Contemporary Armed Conflicts*, *supra* note 29, at 233.

[36] *See* Pejic, *supra* note 24, at 76; *International Humanitarian Law and the Challenges of Contemporary Armed Conflicts*, *supra* note 29, at 231. Related questions follow if it can legally be said that an armed conflict exists between the United States and Al Qaeda, namely whether customary international humanitarian law applies and, if so, its content and application to particular facts and circumstances. For critical perspectives on recourse to customary international humanitarian law, see Gabor Rona, *Interesting Times for International Humanitarian Law: Challenges from the "War on Terror,"* 27(2) FLETCHER FORUM WORLD AFF. 55, 68-69 (2003); Pejic, *supra* note 24, at 81-82.

[37] *See* Rona, *supra* note 36, at 62-63; *ibid.* at 74 n. 63.

[38] *See ibid.* at 60-63. *See also International Humanitarian Law and the Challenges of Contemporary Armed Conflicts*, *supra* note 29, at 234-35.

[39] *See* Rona, *supra* note 36, at 60-63.

[40] *Ibid.* at 60. *See* Pejic, *supra* note 24, at 88 (stating that "'[t]errorism' is a phenomenon. Both practically and as a matter of law, war cannot be waged against a phenomenon."); Dinstein, *Ius Ad Bellum Aspects*, *supra* note 15, at 22 (asserting that "[t]he expression 'war on terrorism' by itself is a figure of speech or a metaphor.").

in the Security Council, that has been directed at it has imposed upon it some degree of international status, thereby meaning that there are identifiable parties to a conflict;[41] the requirement that the conflict take place in a particular geographical space has yielded in an era in which a non-State actor such as Al Qaeda can pose a global threat and in which States open themselves to attacks on their own territory if they fail to act with due diligence as required by international law;[42] admittedly, disparate acts of violence by Al Qaeda across the world make the task of distinguishing the conflict from unrelated acts of violence a more taxing exercise, but this blurring along the edges should not lead one to ignore Al Qaeda's proud and public claims of responsibility after its violent engagements; Rona is correct to highlight difficulties related to the start and finish of an armed conflict with Al Qaeda,[43] but presumably, one could look at the first Al Qaeda-acknowledged attack or the first attack that could be attributed to the group and proceed from there; and finally, as to the last criterion, hostilities of a certain minimal intensity, the thousands of casualties, in dozens of countries but particularly in Afghanistan and Iraq, that have resulted from the engagement between the United States and Al Qaeda suggest the inappropriateness of a peacetime paradigm.

Furthermore, the argument that the mere failure of the United States to have formally derogated from its non-derogable obligations under international human rights law means that, *ipso facto*, an armed conflict, and a corresponding international humanitarian law framework, cannot be said to exist, as rapporteurs of the United Nations Human Rights Commission

---

[41] *But see* Pejic, *supra* note 24, at 87 n. 78 (stating that, "[w]hile all the terrorist acts that have occurred since September 11th have been labelled as being in some way 'linked' to al-Qaeda, very little about the exact nature of such a 'link' is ever provided, except that the suspects are usually Muslim men.").

[42] Dinstein alludes to this. *See* Dinstein, *Ius Ad Bellum Aspects, supra* note 15, at 20-21. On the due diligence obligation and non-State terrorist organisations, see Robert P. Barnidge, Jr., *States' Due Diligence Obligations with Regard to International Non-State Terrorist Organisations Post-11 September 2001: The Heavy Burden That States Must Bear*, 16 IR. STUD. INT'L AFF. 103 (2005).

[43] Taft discusses this in the context of detainees. *See* Taft, *supra* note 3, at 153. Dinstein interprets the law of international armed conflict as allowing the detention of Al Qaeda unlawful combatants at Guantánamo Bay until the cessation of hostilities with that non-State actor, but he leaves unaddressed attendant dilemmas associated with the end of what he terms "hostilities in which Al Qaeda is involved." YORAM DINSTEIN, THE CONDUCT OF HOSTILITIES UNDER THE LAW OF INTERNATIONAL ARMED CONFLICT 50 (2004).

(UNHRC) seemed to imply in February 2006,[44] is equally problematic and unsustainable, preferring as it does form over substance.[45] While it is technically required that States issue official derogations under international human rights law, an armed conflict is an armed conflict, with or without a formal derogation, when the facts and circumstances suggest as much, and armed conflict necessarily triggers international humanitarian law. Bassiouni is correct to note, albeit in the context of torture, that semantics only go so far and that "a rose by any other name is still a rose."[46]

Unlike a judgment of, for example, the United States Supreme Court, which has an acknowledged authority as a legally binding and definitive interpretation of the law as applied to particular facts and circumstances under the municipal law of the United States, international law has yet to conclusively determine whether an armed conflict exists between the United States and Al Qaeda.[47] According to the ICRC, "there is no uniform answer,"[48] as "international opinion – both governmental and expert, as well as public opinion – remains largely divided on how to deal with new forms of violence, primarily acts of transnational terrorism, in legal terms."[49]

Having said that, it should be noted that the present author's approach to the relationship between the United States and Al Qaeda is largely influenced by international humanitarian law, draws heavily on the insights and justifications of Taft and others with similar perspectives, and favours a description, however inartfully, of the relationship between the two actors, the United States and Al Qaeda, as a transnational international armed conflict.[50] The ICRC's concern that "[i]t is doubtful, absent further factual

---

[44] *See* SITUATION OF DETAINEES AT GUANTÁNAMO BAY, U.N. ESCOR, at 36, U.N. Doc. Future E/CN.4/2006/120 (2006).

[45] Wedgwood argues along comparable lines with regard to formal declarations of war. *See* Wedgwood, *Al Qaeda, supra* note 17, at 335.

[46] M. Cherif Bassiouni, *Great Nations and Torture*, in THE TORTURE DEBATE, *supra* note 12, at 256, 259. According to Bassiouni, "[t]he position of the United States is that torture called by another name is permissible and that torture which does not cause the risk of death is considered only coercive – ignoring the obvious conclusion that a rose by any other name is still a rose. In this case, torture by any other name is still torture." *Ibid.*

[47] Rona makes a similar point with regard to aggression. *See* Rona, *supra* note 36, at 67.

[48] *International Humanitarian Law and the Challenges of Contemporary Armed Conflicts*, *supra* note 29, at 231.

[49] *Ibid.* at 214.

[50] The concept of a "transnational international armed conflict" seeks to convey by its use of "transnational" the armed conflict's cross-border nature and involvement of a non-

evidence, whether the totality of the violence taking place between States and transnational networks can be deemed to be armed conflict in the legal sense"[51] should be acknowledged, but recent events, it is asserted, have provided the necessary "further factual evidence." At the same time, Neuman's point that all State uses of force against terrorists may not amount to armed conflict in the international humanitarian law sense[52] remains, in principle, valid and unassailable.

III. Applying International Human Rights Law

Thus, while international law has yet to definitively settle the question whether an armed conflict exists between the United States and Al Qaeda, reasonable arguments being able to be made in favour of and against an armed conflict paradigm, this chapter proceeds taking for granted the applicability of international humanitarian law. What role, if any, then, does international human rights law play in such a context?

The emerging consensus is that international human rights law continues to have legal effect, *mutatis mutandis*, during situations of armed conflict.[53] As the ICJ stated in the *Wall* case, "the protection offered by human rights conventions does not cease in case of armed conflict, save through the effect of provisions for derogation of the kind to be found in Article 4 of the International Covenant on Civil and Political Rights."[54] The ICJ went on in the same paragraph of that advisory opinion to say that the reality of armed conflict requires that, with respect to the *lex specialis derogat legis generalis* maxim, international human rights law be considered the *legis*

State actor, Al Qaeda, and by its use of "international" the involvement of a State actor, the United States, as an opposing party in the conflict. On the interplay between the transnational and the international and the argument that an armed conflict paradigm applies, see *ibid.* at 231-32. For a theoretical discussion, see Anthea Roberts, *Righting Wrongs or Wronging Rights?: The United States and Human Rights Post-September 11*, 15(4) Eur. J. Int'l L. 721, 741 (2004); *ibid.* at 746-48.

[51] *International Humanitarian Law and the Challenges of Contemporary Armed Conflicts*, *supra* note 29, at 234.

[52] *See* Neuman, *supra* note 13, at 290-91.

[53] *See* Noam Lubell, *Challenges in Applying Human Rights Law to Armed Conflict*, 87(860) Int'l Rev. Red Cross 737, 737-39 (2005). *See also* Dinstein, Conduct, *supra* note 43, at 20-25.

[54] Wall, *supra* note 16, at Para. 106.

generalis and international humanitarian law be treated as the *lex specialis*.[55] In late-2005, the ICJ, although failing to expressly mention the *lex specialis derogat legis generalis* rule, substantially reiterated this position in *Armed Activities on the Territory of the Congo* (*Congo*).[56] Rapporteurs of the UNHRC, after the ICJ had rendered its decisions in the *Wall* and *Congo* cases, described the relationship between the two regimes as "not mutually exclusive, but [. . .] complementary."[57] In this sense, the ICJ and these rapporteurs clearly reject the position to these two areas of law, a stance advanced by the United States, which would see them as hermetically sealed from one another.[58]

While clarity that the *lex specialis derogat legis generalis* rule applies in situations of armed conflict is helpful in allowing State and non-State actors to adjust their actions accordingly, it is the interaction between international humanitarian law and international human rights law on particular facts and circumstances that poses the most difficulties in practice.[59] Complexities arise, and there is a pressing need for practical guidance and precision. If one accepts, for example, Heintze's assertion that the trend is toward more "than mere complementarity and aims at providing the greatest effective protection of the human being through the cumulative application of both bodies of law"[60] and that the ICJ "regard[s] the *protection* granted by international humanitarian law and human rights law as a single unit and [appreciates a need] to harmonize the two sets of international rules,"[61] serious, and crippling, questions still remain, such as the meaning of and standard against which "greatest effective protection" is to be interpreted and the nature of the mechanism through which harmonisation is to occur, this harmonisation presumably occurring without simultaneously under-

---

[55] *See ibid. See also* Hans-Joachim Heintze, *On the Relationship Between Human Rights Law Protection and International Humanitarian Law*, 86(856) INT'L REV. RED CROSS 789, 793 (2004) (making a similar point by stating that "the law of peace and the law of war overlap but also that, when examining which duties are incumbent on a State in times of armed conflict, it is not possible to avoid taking international human rights law into consideration.").

[56] *See* Armed Activities on the Territory of the Congo (*Congo* v. *Uganda*), 2005 I.C.J., at Para. 216.

[57] SITUATION OF DETAINEES, *supra* note 44, at 10.

[58] On the United States' position in this regard, see Heintze, *supra* note 55, at 789-93.

[59] *See* Lubell, *supra* note 53, at 738.

[60] Heintze, *supra* note 55, at 794.

[61] *Ibid.* at 797.

mining the integrity and effectiveness of international humanitarian law and international human rights law. Dinstein categorises international humanitarian law as containing rights that operate to the benefit of States and individuals, although he acknowledges that the provisions of this area of law are not always clear as to whether they benefit States or individuals,[62] and argues that international humanitarian law may provide greater protections to individuals in certain cases than international human rights law.[63] With this borne in mind, adjudicating on the basis of "greatest effective protection" is particularly problematic.

The ICJ did little to resolve these complexities in noting that a particular legal question during armed conflict may involve international humanitarian law alone, international human rights law alone, or a combination of both areas of law.[64] It probably would have been unrealistic to have expected a more unambiguous, nuanced approach, however. The United States' fears expressed to the UNCHR in March 2006 that a legal perspective that would allow international human rights law to be considered during armed conflict would necessarily mean that captured enemy combatants would be entitled to the full panalopy of legal rights afforded criminal defendants under international human rights law[65] is an alarming and extreme interpretation that may be unwarranted, but at the same time, ICJ Judge Christopher Gregory Weeramantry's statement in his dissenting opinion in the 1996 *Legality of the Threat or Use of Nuclear Weapons* (*Nuclear Weapons*) case that, "[i]ndeed, so well are human rights norms and standards ingrained today in global consciousness, that they flood through into every corner of humanitarian law"[66] provides little in the way of practical interpretative assistance. In this context, Lubell's encouragement of sensitivity to the distinct legal languages of international humanitarian law and international human rights law as a way to negotiate impasses that may arise may be a useful and promising approach.[67]

That having been said, the Security Council has clearly stressed a role for international human rights law in its Resolutions related to terrorism. In

---

[62] *See* DINSTEIN, CONDUCT, *supra* note 43, at 20-22.

[63] *See ibid.* at 24-25.

[64] *See* Wall, *supra* note 16, at Para. 106.

[65] *See* REPLY, *supra* note 17, at 752.

[66] Legality of the Threat or Use of Nuclear Weapons (Advisory Opinion), 1996 I.C.J. 226, 491 (Weeramantry, J., dissenting).

[67] *See* Lubell, *supra* note 53, at 744-46.

an annexed declaration in January 2003, for example, it expressly stated that "[s]tates must ensure that any measure taken to combat terrorism comply with all their obligations under international law, and should adopt such measures in accordance with international law, in particular international human rights, refugee, and humanitarian law."[68] In its Resolution dealing with incitement of terrorism, which was adopted in September 2005, the Security Council again stressed the necessity of States' compliance with "all of their obligations under international law, in particular international human rights law, refugee law, and humanitarian law."[69]

The Security Council has been far from alone within the United Nations system in emphasising the necessary role of human rights in counter-terrorism, as this focus has been the thrust of the United Nations generally.[70] The General Assembly, for example, has used language similar to that used by the Security Council in highlighting human rights. In a Resolution adopted in December 2002, it affirmed that "[s]tates must ensure that any measure taken to combat terrorism complies with their obligations under international law, in particular international human rights, refugee and humanitarian law."[71] The General Assembly used virtually identical language in adopting the 2005 World Summit Outcome.[72]

United Nations Secretary General Kofi Annan has also made similar arguments. To consider but one of his remarks on the subject, he stressed at the International Summit on Democracy, Terrorism, and Security in Madrid in March 2005 that "human rights and the rule of law must always be respected [. . . and that u]pholding human rights is not merely compatible with [a] successful counter-terrorism strategy. It is an essential element."[73] Annan would likely have agreed with the holistic strategy advocated by Sri Lankan President Chandrika Bandaranaike Kumaratunga in her address at the 2005 World Summit.[74]

---

68 S.C. Res. 1456, U.N. SCOR, Annex, at 3, U.N. Doc. S/RES/1456 (2003).

69 S.C. Res. 1624, U.N. SCOR, at 3, U.N. Doc. S/RES/1624 (2005).

70 *See* Alex P. Schmid, *Terrorism and Human Rights: A Perspective from the United Nations,* 17(1-2) TERRORISM & POL. VIOLENCE 25, 29 (2005); SITUATION OF DETAINEES, *supra* note 44, at 7.

71 G.A. Res. 57/219, U.N. GAOR, at 2, U.N. Doc. A/RES/57/219 (2002).

72 *See* G.A. Res. 60/1, U.N. GAOR, at 22, U.N. Doc. A/RES/60/1 (2005).

73 Kofi Annan, A Global Strategy for Fighting Terrorism: Keynote Address to the Closing Plenary of the International Summit on Democracy, Terrorism, and Security (10 March 2005), *available at* http://www.un.org/apps/sg/printsgstats.asp?nid=1345.

74 *See* Chandrika Bandaranaike Kumaratunga, Address by Her Excellency Chandrika Bandaranaike Kumaratunga, President of the Democratic Socialist Republic of Sri Lanka,

The activities of the United Nations treaty bodies related to human rights, the European Court of Human Rights, the African Commission on Human and Peoples' Rights, the Inter-American Commission on Human Rights, and the Inter-American Court of Human Rights (IACtHR) also evidence a human rights imperative.[75] For example, the IACtHR's jurisprudence recognises the unquestionable right of States to security but says that the means to be used are necessarily limited by legal and moral considerations.[76]

IV. Marketing Human Rights to States Fighting Terrorism

While international law does not permit States to blind themselves to human rights when confronting terrorist threats from non-State actors, reality demonstrates that they often subject international legal considerations to a calculus that favours expediency and stability during times of crisis.[77] Ewing, for example, decries the lack of judicial activism in defence of individual human rights, both historically and specifically since the Human Rights Act 1998, when national security concerns have been raised in the United Kingdom.[78] States often ignore, if not purposely and disdainfully reject, what they perceive to be the legal platitudes of external actors in such situations. This is perhaps especially the case given that international human

at the High-Level Plenary Meeting of the General Assembly of the United Nations 5 (15 September 2005), *available at* http://www.un.org/webcast/summit2005/statements15/sri050915l5eng.pdf (stating that, "[i]f we are to fight global terrorism, poverty and disease, we must take an integrated approach to security, human rights and development, both nationally and internationally.").

[75] *See* Office of the United Nations High Commissioner for Human Rights, Digest of Jurisprudence of the United Nations and Regional Organizations on the Protection of Human Rights While Countering Terrorism, U.N. Sales No. HR/PUB/03/1 (2003).

[76] *See* Velásquez Rodríguez, Ser. C, Case No. 4, Inter-Am. C.H.R. 1988, Para. 154.

[77] *See* Roberts, *supra* note 50, at 730-35. On this since 11 September, with particular emphasis on the United States, see M. Cherif Bassiouni, *The Regression of the Rule of Law Under the Guise of Combating Terrorism,* 76(1-2) Rev. Int'l Droit Pénal 17 (2005). According to Bassiouni, "[i]t is truly extraordinary to have witnessed in a relatively short period of three years, and as a result of an incident that pales in comparison to the many tragedies the world has suffered over the last half century, the transformation of the international rule of law and human rights into a trend of repressiveness and regression from the rule of law." *Ibid.* at 24.

[78] *See* K.D. Ewing, *The Futility of the Human Rights Act*, Pub. L. 829 (Winter 2004). He describes the post-11 September era as "in effect the sixth cycle of restraint." *Ibid.* at 851.

rights law imposes obligations upon States that it does not, and cannot, impose upon non-State terrorist organisations.[79]

State practice with regard to counterterrorism and human rights supports this submission of human rights.[80] The Office of the United Nations High Commissioner for Refugees has expressed its concern at the possible victimisation of asylum seekers and has argued that counterterrorism efforts may jeopardise the prohibition on *refoulement* and the basic right to seek asylum.[81] Similar fears have been raised about human rights generally by the Office of the United Nations High Commissioner for Human Rights (OHCHR)[82] and the then UNHRC.[83] High Commissioner for Human Rights Louise Arbour, who heads the OHCHR, recently referred to some counterterrorism tactics as forming part of a "vicious circle of illegality."[84] Judge

---

79 On this disparity in obligations, see Joan Fitzpatrick, *Speaking Law to Power: The War Against Terrorism and Human Rights,* 14(2) EUR. J. INT'L L. 241, 243 (2003).

80 According to Annan, "international human rights experts, including those of the UN system, are unanimous in finding that many measures which States are currently adopting to counter terrorism infringe on human rights and fundamental freedoms." Annan, *supra* note 73. Also of relevance are Richard Goldstone, *The Tension Between Combating Terrorism and Protecting Civil Liberties,* in HUMAN RIGHTS IN THE "WAR ON TERROR" 157, 165-66 (Richard Ashby Wilson ed., 2005) (making Annan's point with reference to the United States, the United Kingdom, India, South Africa, Zimbabwe, Liberia, and Indonesia); Mary Robinson, *Connecting Human Rights, Human Development, and Human Security,* in HUMAN RIGHTS, *ibid.*, at 308, 310 (noting a "subtle – or not so subtle – change of emphasis in many parts of the world: order and security have become priorities that trump all other concerns."); PROTECTING HUMAN RIGHTS AND FUNDAMENTAL FREEDOMS WHILE COUNTERING TERRORISM: REPORT OF THE SECRETARY-GENERAL, U.N. GAOR, at 8, U.N. Doc. A/60/374 (2005); PROMOTION AND PROTECTION OF HUMAN RIGHTS: PROTECTION OF HUMAN RIGHTS AND FUNDAMENTAL FREEDOMS WHILE COUNTERING TERRORISM: REPORT OF THE HIGH COMMISSIONER FOR HUMAN RIGHTS, U.N. ESCOR, at 6, U.N. Doc. E/CN.4/2005/100 (2004). The disparity between human rights rhetoric and action is common to human rights generally. *See* V.S. Mani, *Centrifugal and Centripetal Tendencies in the International System: Some Reflections,* in TOWARDS WORLD CONSTITUTIONALISM: ISSUES IN THE LEGAL ORDERING OF THE WORLD COMMUNITY 241, 251 (Ronald St. John Macdonald & Douglas M. Johnston eds., 2005).

81 *See* LETTER DATED 3 FEBRUARY 2005 FROM THE CHAIRMAN OF THE SECURITY COUNCIL COMMITTEE ESTABLISHED PURSUANT TO RESOLUTION 1373 (2001) CONCERNING COUNTER-TERRORISM ADDRESSED TO THE PRESIDENT OF THE SECURITY COUNCIL, U.N. SCOR, Annex, at 94, U.N. Doc. S/2005/87 (2005).

82 *See ibid.* at Annex, at 95; Rama Mani, *The Root Causes of Terrorism and Conflict Prevention,* in TERRORISM AND THE UN: BEFORE AND AFTER SEPTEMBER 11 219, 233 (Jane Boulden & Thomas G. Weiss eds., 2004).

83 *See* Mani, *supra* note 82, at 233.

84 Louise Arbour, Address by Louise Arbour, UN High Commissioner for Human Rights at Chatham House and the British Institute of International and Comparative Law (16 February

Rosalyn Higgins of the ICJ, referring to the 1966 International Covenant on Civil and Political Rights (ICCPR) and the 1966 International Covenant on Economic, Social, and Cultural Rights (ICESCR), should be commended for her candour in noting that "many, many States are not in compliance with their obligations under the two Covenants."[85]

Amnesty International and Human Rights Watch have also documented this State practice.[86] Bassiouni describes what he perceives to be the new reality, a "no-man's land approach where law and due process of law guaranteed by judicial scrutiny have become marginally relevant,"[87] and implies that this may tend toward dictatorship.[88]

The United Nations, to its credit, has recognised this reality, although it has also been criticised for a bias towards human rights over security in cases of terrorist attacks by non-State actors.[89] It has responded by framing the human rights debate so that States can perceive human rights to be in their best interest when countering terrorism. Far from being mere legal niceties, according to the United Nations, human rights play an essential role in the effective combating of terrorism.[90]

To give some examples, Annan has argued that States that compromise human rights actually help terrorists.[91] The OHCHR has stressed that State

---

2006), *available at* http://www.unhchr.ch/huricane/huricane.nsf/view01/E60AF3995B87D7EDC1257117005711E8?opendocument.

[85] Wall, *supra* note 16, at Para. 27 (Higgins, J., separate).

[86] *See* IRENE KHAN, AMNESTY INTERNATIONAL, *Foreword, available at* http://web.amnesty.org/web/web.nsf/print/4C6D9C974BE73CA880256FE7005A49C7 (last visited 12 April 2007) (stating that, "[f]rom Israel to Uzbekistan, Egypt to Nepal, governments have openly defied human rights and international humanitarian law in the name of national security and 'counter-terrorism.'"); HUMAN RIGHTS WATCH, *Human Rights Watch World Report 2006: U.S. Policy of Abuse Undermines Rights Worldwide,* 18 January 2006, *available at* http://hrw.org/english/docs/2006/01/13/global12428_txt.htm.

[87] Bassiouni, *Regression, supra* note 77, at 21.

[88] *See ibid.* at 24. He also notes that "[t]he disparity between proclamations of adherence to the international rule of law, due process and human rights, and the actions of certain governments is widening." *Ibid.* at 25.

[89] *See* Gerald M. Steinberg, *The UN, the ICJ and the Separation Barrier: War by Other Means,* 38(1-2) ISR. L. REV. 331, 337 (2005) (stating that, "[w]hen terror attacks are conducted or supported by non-state actors, and the defensive response of the state under attack encroaches on civil liberties and human rights, the existing international legal framework is more likely to condemn the defensive actions than the perpetrators of the violence, particularly given the anti-state bias that permeates post-modern ideology.").

[90] *See* Edward J. Flynn, *Counter-Terrorism and Human Rights: The View from the United Nations,* 1 EUR. HUM. RTS. L. REV. 29, 30 (2005).

[91] *See* Annan, *supra* note 73 (stating that "compromising human rights [. . .] facilitates achievement of the terrorist's objective – by ceding to him the moral high ground, and

fidelity to human rights when fighting terrorism means that "terrorism can be effectively countered without infringing on fundamental freedoms."[92] According to Arbour, "respect for human rights is – not an obstacle – but rather an essential element in effective counter-terrorism strategies."[93] Mary Robinson and Sergio Vieire de Mello, two of Arbour's predecessors, also made such arguments,[94] as did Annan in his 2006 *Uniting Against Terrorism: Recommendations for a Global Counter-Terrorism Strategy: Report of the Secretary-General* (*Uniting Against Terrorism*).[95] Higgins has referred to States' fidelity to the related field of international humanitarian law as "the price of our hopes for the future."[96]

Outside the United Nations, the Council of Europe (CE) has argued that satisfying human rights law while fighting terrorism is both "possible [. . . and] absolutely necessary."[97] CE Secretary General Terry Davis asserted in March 2005 that States need not fear that the effectiveness of counter-terrorism will be compromised by incorporating human rights because "the need to respect human rights is not an obstacle to the effective fight against terrorism."[98]

President of the Supreme Court of Israel Aharon Barak, Irish Minister for Foreign Affairs Dermot Ahern, and India's National Human Rights

---

provoking tension, hatred and mistrust of government among precisely those parts of the population where he is most likely to find recruits.").

92 DIGEST, *supra* note 75, at 1.

93 LETTER DATED 3 FEBRUARY 2005, *supra* note 81, at Annex, at 95. *See* Louise Arbour, Security Under the Rule of Law, Address of Louise Arbour UN High Commissioner for Human Rights to the Biennial Conference of the International Commission of Jurists (Berlin) (27 August 2004), *available at* http://www.unhchr.ch/huricane/huricane.nsf/view01/3485B28EDDA173F0C1256EFD0035373C?opendocument.

94 *See* Flynn, *supra* note 90, at 49.

95 UNITING AGAINST TERRORISM: RECOMMENDATIONS FOR A GLOBAL COUNTER-TERRORISM STRATEGY: REPORT OF THE SECRETARY-GENERAL, U.N. GAOR, at 2, U.N. Doc. A/60/825 (2006) (arguing that "[e]ffective counter-terrorism measures and the protection of human rights are not conflicting goals, but complementary and mutually reinforcing ones. Accordingly, the defence of human rights is essential to the fulfilment of all aspects of a counter-terrorism strategy.").

96 Wall, *supra* note 16, at Para. 14 (Higgins, J., separate).

97 Council of Europe, *Guidelines of the Committee of Ministers of the Council of Europe on Human Rights and the Fight Against Terrorism,* adopted 11 July 2002, in COUNCIL OF EUROPE, HUMAN RIGHTS AND THE FIGHT AGAINST TERRORISM: THE COUNCIL OF EUROPE GUIDELINES 7, 7, Preamble(d) (2005). On this, see C. A. Gearty, *Terrorism and Human Rights,* 1 EUR. HUM. RTS. L. REV. 1, 4 (2005).

98 Terry Davis, *Preface*, in COUNCIL OF EUROPE, *supra* note 97, at 5, 5.

Commission have also argued that upholding human rights while countering terrorism serves a crucial instrumental value.[99] In agreement with this are many scholars, such as Gearty.[100] Non-governmental organisations have also generally "maintained [. . .] that there is in reality no goal conflict between security and human rights – even that human rights fulfil a considerable instrumental function with respect to freedom from terrorism."[101]

To assert, as Annan does in *Uniting Against Terrorism*, that "in the fight against terrorism, we must never sacrifice our values and lower our standards to those of the terrorists"[102] presumes both that international standards are sufficient to effectively fight terrorism and that, even if they are not, "our values and [. . .] standards" must not yield. Whether a State can simultaneously ensure human rights for all of those within its jurisdiction and provide effective security from terrorism, however, remains an open question.

To that end, the following sections explore whether human rights observance is necessary to effectively fight terrorism and whether States can effectively fight terrorism while at the same time not violating human rights. Essentially, this involves evaluating whether what Posner concludes about international humanitarian law, that "[t]he laws may make war more humane by depriving soldiers of destructive weapons and tactics; but they may make war less humane by prolonging it, and they may make the world

---

99 *See* Aharon Barak, *A Judge on Judging: The Role of a Supreme Court in a Democracy,* 116(1) HARV. L. REV. 16, 148 (2002) (citing H.C. 5100/94, *Pub. Comm. Against Torture in Isr.* v. *Gov't of Israel*, 53(4) P.D. 817, 845) (stating that, "[s]ometimes, a democracy must fight with one hand tied behind its back. Nonetheless, it has the upper hand."); Dermot Ahern, Address by the Minister for Foreign Affairs to the Royal Irish Academy Marking 50 Years of UN Participation (18 November 2005), *available at* http://foreignaffairs.gov.ie/Press_Releases/20051118/1915.htm (asserting that "[t]he violation of such norms is not only wrong in itself but it is also counterproductive as it can be used to justify further atrocities."); V. Vijayakumar, *Legal and Institutional Responses to Terrorism in India,* in GLOBAL ANTI-TERRORISM LAW AND POLICY 351, 356 (Victor V. Ramraj et al. eds., 2005).

100 *See* Gearty, *Terrorism and Human Rights, supra* note 97, at 6 (asserting that, without an "overarching human rights dimension, counterterrorism law is not only immoral and subversive of the values which it purports to defend, but it is also certain to fail.").

101 Dunér, *supra* note 2, at 97. *See* Roberts, *supra* note 50, at 738 (asserting that "[h]uman rights NGOs often argue that trade-offs between human rights and national security will result in more rather than less terrorism and that terrorism can be effectively countered without restricting human rights.").

102 UNITING AGAINST TERRORISM, *supra* note 95, at 22.

less secure by making war more attractive,"[103] extends to international human rights law in the context of non-State terrorism.

V. Is Human Rights Observance Necessary to Effectively Fight Terrorism?

History is replete with examples of States that have effectively destroyed their political opposition through an overwhelming show of force that has relegated human rights to, at best, a matter of secondary importance.[104] While some of these State responses have amounted to State terrorism, this has not always been the case. As the following historical examples suggest, States that prioritise military success over individual human rights in confronting dissident elements frequently achieve their objectives.

To give an example, the United States, preferring a swift end to the Second World War, got it when the Enola Gay emptied its atomic payload on Hiroshima and when Nagasaki was hit soon thereafter. Although there is continuing debate on the subject, a strong case can be made that the nuclear

---

[103] Posner, *supra* note 6, at 427. *See* Thomas Sowell, *Pacifists Versus Peace*, JEWISH WORLD REV., 21 July 2006, *available at* http://jewishworldreview.com/cols/sowell072106.asp. According to Lindley-French, "[t]he Israeli military was put in an untenable position: It was not permitted to take risks with its personnel, and it had the wrong equipment, training and way of doing things to win such a conflict. Consequently, Israel could only attack Hezbollah indirectly, increasing the risk to Lebanese civilians and decreasing any chance of success." Julian Lindley-French, *The Use of Force: Western Military Power Is in Crisis*, INT'L HERALD TRIB., 26-27 August 2006.

[104] *See* ALAN M. DERSHOWITZ, WHY TERRORISM WORKS: UNDERSTANDING THE THREAT, RESPONDING TO THE CHALLENGE 105-30 (2002); Goldstone, *supra* note 80, at 161 (stating that "oppressive societies which, by definition, do not respect the civil rights of their citizens [. . .] have all the machinery they might need to put down attacks from within and outside their borders."). *See also* Steven Plaut, *The Anti-Terror Campaign That Succeeded*, JEWISH PRESS, 27 June 2007, *available at* http://www.jewishpress.com/page.do/21967/The_Anti%2DTerror_Campaign_That_Succeeded.html. Lindley-French, adopting a realist perspective, rhetorically asks "[w]hy [. . .] the best armies in the world [are] in difficulty against adversaries that 19th-century colonial officers would have defeated [. . .] Israel has been much criticized for using excessive force in trying to defeat Hezbollah. In fact, military logic would have suggested not only a far more ruthless use of military force to defeat such an enemy, but a very different use. Israel had the power, but used it in the wrong way. [. . .] Western military power must be sharper at the point of contact with the likes of the Taliban and Hezbollah, and yet deeper if it is thereafter to create the security space in which peace can truly be established." Lindley-French, *supra* note 103.

bombings of Hiroshima and Nagasaki, while obviously killing and maiming tens of thousands of Japanese people, civilians included, avoided what would have been an even larger bloodbath had Allied forces had to invade Japan as they did at Normandy.[105] Hiroshima and Nagasaki demonstrate that overwhelming force can bring a State's enemies to their knees.

States need not necessarily observe human rights, at least not completely, to effectively fight terrorism and maintain their control. There is also evidence to the contrary, to the effect that "a little repression increases instability whereas a great deal of it has the opposite effect."[106] Essentially, these latter types of regimes are those which Feinstein and Slaughter refer to as those which are governed by "rulers whose power over their own people and territory is so absolute that no matter how brutal, aggressive, or irrational they become, no force within their own society can stop them."[107]

Contrasting the experiences of Czechoslovakia, Albania, and Algeria with those of Spain, Italy, and West Germany on the question of human rights and the incidence of terrorism, for example, supports this.[108] Furthermore, the lack of significant non-State terrorism in China, Cuba, North Korea, and the communist States of the former Soviet Union and central and eastern Europe can be contrasted with experiences in democracies, defining democracies broadly, such as Greece, Argentina, Canada, the United States, the United Kingdom, Turkey, Mexico, the Philippines, Israel, India, France, Japan, Italy, Russia, Spain, Indonesia, and Sri Lanka.[109] In this sense, Falk's contention that "there is no evidence to support the claim that the abridgement of human rights and the abuse of detainees and suspects enhances security"[110] is misleading because it is empirically contradictory.

It is useful here to refer to the ICJ's recent jurisprudence, particularly the *Wall* case. That case was decided in the context of the Second Intifada and

---

[105] *See* Posner, *supra* note 6, at 426.

[106] H.B. MISHRA, TERRORISM: THREAT TO PEACE AND HARMONY 27 (1999). *See ibid.* at 31 (stating that, "[w]herever the means of repression have been most complete and perfected, there has been no terrorism at all. These facts are not in dispute, but there is psychological resistance to accepting the obvious. Seldom has it been admitted that virtue in politics is not always rewarded.").

[107] Lee Feinstein & Anne-Marie Slaughter, *A Duty to Prevent*, 83(1) FOREIGN AFF. 136, 143 (2004).

[108] *See* MISHRA, *supra* note 106, at 44.

[109] *See* Dunér, *supra* note 2, at 91-92.

[110] Richard Falk, *Human Rights: A Descending Spiral,* in HUMAN RIGHTS, *supra* note 80, at 225, 236.

a seemingly intractable level of violence between Israelis and Palestinians that, by the admission of Fatah's Ziyad Abu'Ein, was in part facilitated by the Oslo Accords.[111] Israeli historian Benny Morris expressed the frustration and anger of many of his compatriots in stating about the Palestinians, "Something like a cage has to be built for them. I know that sounds terrible. It is really cruel. But there is no choice. There is a wild animal there that has to be locked up in one way or another."[112]

In the *Wall* case, the ICJ considered public international law in its broadest sense.[113] In particular, it regarded as binding law the Hague Regulations,[114] the Fourth Geneva Convention,[115] the ICCPR,[116] the ICESCR,[117] and the 1989 Convention on the Rights of the Child.[118]

In concluding that the separation barrier was "contrary to international law,"[119] the ICJ cited "substantial restrictions on [. . .] freedom of movement[, . . .] serious repercussions for agricultural production[, and . . .] increasing difficulties for the population concerned regarding access to health services, educational establishments and primary sources of water."[120] The ICJ was clear in its condemnation, expressly declaring Israel's actions to be "breaches [. . .] of various of its obligations under the applicable international humanitarian law and human rights instruments."[121]

---

111 According to Abu'Ein, "there would have been no resistance in Palestine if not for Oslo. It was Oslo that strongly embraced the Palestinian resistance. All the occupied territories – and I was one of the activists in the first and second Intifadas, and I was arrested by Israel several times [. . .] If not for Oslo, there would have been no resistance. Throughout the occupied territories, we could not move a single pistol from one place to another. If not for Oslo, the weapons we got through Oslo, and if not for the 'A' areas of the Palestinian Authority, if not for the training, the camps, the protection provided by Oslo, and if not for the release of thousands of Palestinian prisoners through Oslo – this Palestinian resistance could not have carried out this great Palestinian Intifada, with which we confronted the Israeli occupation." Interview on Al-Alam TV with Ziyad Abu'Ein, *If Not for the Oslo Accords, There Would Have Been No Intifada*, MEMRI (4 July 2006), *available at* http://www.memritv.org/Transcript.asp?P1=1205.

112 Ari Shavit, *Survival of the Fittest,* HAARETZ, *available at* http://www.haaretz.com/hasen/objects/pages/PrintArticleEn.jhtml?itemNo=380984 (last updated 1 September 2004).

113 *See* Wall, *supra* note 16, at Para. 86.

114 *See ibid.* at Para. 89.

115 *See ibid.* at Para. 101.

116 *See ibid.* at Para. 111.

117 *See ibid.* at Para. 112.

118 *See ibid.* at Para. 113.

119 *Ibid.* at Para. 142.

120 *Ibid.* at Para. 133.

121 *Ibid.* at Para. 137. *See ibid.* at Para. 134.

Given that international actors have, as referred to above, asserted a necessarily symbiotic relationship between human rights and effective counterterrorism, one might naturally be led to believe that the separation barrier has been no more effective in frustrating terrorism than a sieve is in preventing an inevitable breach and torrent of water. One might be particularly led to believe this given Palestine's assertion in its written statement to the ICJ in the *Wall* case that Israel's motives were actually nothing more than "bald assertions of its security interest."[122] The evidence suggests, however, that what the ICJ essentially regarded as a human rights monstrosity has been effective in combating terrorism.

Israel argues that the separation barrier is an integral part of its counterterrorism strategy, that it is a "temporary and non-violent measure to counter a murderous threat directed at the softest of targets"[123] and that it "enable[s] it effectively to combat terrorist attacks launched from the West Bank."[124] In its written statement to the ICJ in the *Wall* case, Israel cited fewer attacks, although acknowledging that the number of attempts remained consistent at approximately fifty each week, and credited the separation barrier as being "a significant factor in this respect."[125] Comparing an area

[122] Written Statement Submitted by Palestine, Legal Consequences of the Construction of a Wall in the Occupied Palestinian Territory (Advisory Opinion), 2004 I.C.J., at Para. 460.

[123] Written Statement of the Government of Israel on Jurisdiction and Propriety, Legal Consequences of the Construction of a Wall in the Occupied Palestinian Territory (Advisory Opinion), 2004 I.C.J., at Para. 3.74.

[124] Wall, *supra* note 16, at Para. 116. For critical positions on this justification, see PALESTINIAN CENTRE FOR HUMAN RIGHTS, SECURING THE WALL FROM INTERNATIONAL LAW: AN INITIAL RESPONSE TO THE ISRAELI STATE AUTHORITY 6-7, *available at* http://www.pchrgaza.org/Interventions/Securing%20the%20Wall.pdf (2005); BIMKOM & B'TSELEM, UNDER THE GUISE OF SECURITY: ROUTING THE SEPARATION BARRIER TO ENABLE THE EXPANSION OF ISRAELI SETTLEMENTS IN THE WEST BANK 9-18, *available at* http://www.btselem.org/Download/200512_Under_the_Guise_of_Security_eng.pdf (2005).

[125] Written Statement of the Government of Israel, *supra* note 123, at Para. 3.66. "Statistical data indicates a 30% drop in the number of terrorist attacks that took place in 2003 compared to 2002. Similarly, there has been a 50% decrease in the number of victims murdered by terrorists in 2003 compared to the previous year." Israel Ministry of Foreign Affairs, *Saving Lives: Israel's Anti-Terrorist Fence – Answers to Questions*, *available at* http://www.mfa.gov.il/mfa/mfaarchive/2000_2009/2003/11/saving%20lives-%20israel-s%20anti-terrorist%20fence%20-%20answ (1 January 2004). *See* Israel Ministry of Foreign Affairs, *2005 Terrorism Review*, *available at* http://www.mfa.gov.il/MFA/Terrorism-+Obstacle+to+Peace/Terrorism+and+Islamic+Fundamentalism-/2005+Terrorism+Review.htm (2 January 2006) (stating that, "during the 34 months of confrontation (beginning on 29 September 2000) up until the establishment of the security fence in July 2003, operational infrastruc-

in the West Bank with the separation barrier with one without it also supports this conclusion.[126] Higgins, in her separate opinion in the *Wall* case, also acknowledged the effectiveness of the separation barrier, stating that it "does seem to have resulted in a diminution on attacks on Israeli civilians."[127] The separation barrier between Israel and Gaza, furthermore, has shown its effectiveness: no Palestinian suicide bombers have crossed into Israel from Gaza because of it.[128]

Gearty usefully notes that the apologists of counterterrorism and those who prioritise human rights couch their agendas in moral terms.[129] Who is to judge which morality should be given greater weight? States have shown themselves quite capable of carpet bombing their opposition into submis-

---

tures in Samaria perpetrated 73 deadly large-scale terrorist attacks (suicide attacks and/or car bombs) inside Israel, in which 293 Israelis were murdered and 1,950 were wounded. In the 28 months following August 2003 and up to December 2005, they succeeded in perpetrating 11 such attacks inside Israel, in which 54 Israelis were murdered and 358 were wounded."). According to Krauthammer, "[t]he success of this fence plus unilateral-withdrawal strategy is easily seen in the collapse of the intifada. Palestinian terror attacks are down 90 percent." Charles Krauthammer, *The Legacy of Ariel Sharon: What's Ahead for the State of Israel?: Sharon Put Israel on a Strategic Path out of the Wreckage of the Post-Oslo World,* CHI. TRIB., 9 January 2006. *See* Tarik Kafala & Martin Asser, *Analysis: Palestinian Suicide Attacks,* BBC NEWS, *available at* http://news.bbc.co.uk/2/hi/middle_east/3256858.stm (last updated 17 April 2006) (stating that "[t]he number of attacks fell as Israel besieged Palestinian towns and pressed ahead with its barrier in and around the occupied West Bank."); Irshad Manji, *How I Learned to Love the Wall*, N.Y. TIMES, 18 March 2006 (noting that, "[s]ince the barrier went up, suicide attacks have plunged, which means innocent Arab lives have been spared along with Jewish ones.").

126 *See* Israel Ministry of Foreign Affairs, *Israel's Anti-Terrorist Fence: The Anti-Terrorist Fence – An Overview, available at* http://securityfence.mfa.gov.il/mfm/Data/48152.doc (last visited 12 April 2007). For similar evidence, see Ministry of Defence, *Israel's Security Fence: Questions and Answers, available at* http://www.securityfence.mod.gov.il/Pages/ENG/questions.htm (last updated 22 February 2004) (stating that "[t]he first stage of the Security Fence (from Salem to Elkana) which has been operational since July 2003, is already proving itself as an effective defensive deterrent which prevents the repeated attempts to enter Israel and carry out terror attacks.").

127 Wall, *supra* note 16, at Para. 35 (Higgins, J., separate).

128 *See* Israel Ministry of Foreign Affairs, *Israel's Anti-Terrorist Fence, supra* note 126. Israel has also cited a less categorical statistic, see Ministry of Defence, *Israel's Security Fence, supra* note 126 (stating that "the security fence between Israel and the Gaza Strip that has existed since 1996 has proven its effectiveness and [that] the vast majority of terrorist attempts have been discovered and thwarted."), but the point is still convincingly made.

129 *See* Gearty, *Terrorism and Human Rights, supra* note 97, at 1. *See also* Fitzpatrick, *supra* note 79, at 246 (describing this as a "clash of moral absolutes.").

sion with sufficient political will and when committed to using "both [. . . their] hands, [. . .] fingernails, [. . .] teeth, and [. . .] feet, without following the Marquess of Queensberry rules."[130] This suggests that human rights observance may not be necessary, at least not in all cases, to effectively fight terrorism.

VI. Can States Effectively Fight Terrorism While at the Same Time Not Violating Human Rights?

While human rights observance may not be necessary, at least not in all cases, to effectively fight terrorism, the related question whether States can effectively fight terrorism while at the same time not violating human rights must be addressed. Essentially, this involves critically examining Mishra's contention that, "[i]f terrorism has had any success at all, it has been against democratic governments and ineffective, obsolete or half-hearted dictatorships."[131] Wedgwood notes the vulnerability of democratic States to international non-State terrorist organisations,[132] and former Justice of the Constitutional Court of South Africa Richard Goldstone makes a similar point.[133]

Alex P. Schmid, Senior Crime Prevention Officer at the United Nations' Vienna Office on Drugs and Crime, recently dealt with this issue in an article written in a personal capacity.[134] Because Schmid's argument goes

---

130 DERSHOWITZ, *supra* note 104, at 3. According to Ethiopian Emperor Haile Sellassie I, Italy's mustard gassing of Ethiopia just prior to the Second World War achieved its objective of domination and conquest, but the means used were immoral. *See* HAILE SELLASSIE I, MY LIFE AND ETHIOPIA'S PROGRESS: VOLUME ONE: 1892-1937: THE AUTOBIOGRAPHY OF EMPEROR HAILE SELLASSIE I: KING OF KINGS AND LORD OF LORDS 263 (Edward Ullendorff trans., Frontline Dist. Int'l, Inc. 2003) (1976) (stating that, "[a]lthough they may destroy the Ethiopian army with this instrument of poison, yet when it is reported in future history that they wiped out with poison a defenceless people, it is not to be doubted that this will forever be a burden of shame and humiliation for Fascist Italy."). For a disturbing description, see *ibid.* at 263-64.

131 MISHRA, *supra* note 106, at 49.

132 *See* Ruth Wedgwood, *Countering Catastrophic Terrorism: An American View,* in ENFORCING INTERNATIONAL LAW NORMS AGAINST TERRORISM 103, 117 (Andrea Bianchi ed., 2004); Wedgwood, *Al Qaeda, supra* note 17, at 329.

133 *See* Goldstone, *supra* note 80, at 161.

134 *See* Schmid, *supra* note 70, at 25.

to the core of the idea that terrorism can be most effectively defeated when it is rooted in human rights, it is worth citing his position at length:

> There are four pillars on which successful antiterrorist measures should build:
> I. Good Governance
> II. Democracy
> III. Rule of Law
> IV. Social Justice
> Why these four? The reason for this is simple:
> (i) When governance is bad, resistance against corrupt rule gains followers and support.
> (ii) When unpopular rulers cannot be voted away in democratic procedures, advocates of political violence find a wide audience.
> (iii) When rulers stand above the law and use the law as a political instrument against their opponents, the law loses its credibility.
> (iv) When long-standing injustices in society are not resolved but allowed to continue for years without any light in sight at the end of the tunnel, we should not be amazed that desperate people – and others championing their cause – are willing to die and to kill for what they perceive to be a just cause.[135]

Despite the fact that Schmid leaves unaddressed the meaning of certain definitionally nebulous terms in his four pillars, it is helpful to critically evaluate each of his pillars and their related reasoning.

The first pillar argues that poor governance breeds resistance. Fundamentally, this claim presumes that those living under poorly-governed regimes both desire good governance and that, if they do, they are able to resist the status quo. To take an example, one presumes that Soviet Premier Joseph Stalin's Soviet Union, with its gulag system and numerous other depravities, qualified as a poorly-governed regime. While the Soviet people may have desired good governance in such a context, they were certainly not in a position to resist Stalin's totalitarian State in any significant way. Totalitarian terror, which Arendt described as that which "threatens [. . .] authentic opponents [. . . and] harmless citizens without political opinions,"[136] assures this.

Schmid's second claim, that governments that lack democratic accountability necessarily spur on grassroots violent opposition movements, seems dubious as a general principle. Resistance, whether violent or non-violent,

---

[135] *Ibid.* at 29-30.
[136] HANNAH ARENDT, THE ORIGINS OF TOTALITARIANISM 322 (1966).

essentially roots itself in ideological commitment.[137] Opposition to unpopular leaders can take a variety of forms, no single form being preordained.

The religious ideology of the Society of Friends, for example, forbids Quakers from engaging in armed struggle, regardless whether they live under democratic government. Those living in the communist States of central and eastern Europe largely reacted to undemocratic rule through non-violent protest on the eve of the end of the Cold War. The example of Solidarity in Poland is particularly noteworthy. Similarly, the inability of Cubans to engage in genuine multi-party elections after almost fifty years of communism does not seem to have triggered a significant indigenous violent backlash against Cuban President Fidel Castro's regime.

Schmid is undoubtedly correct in concluding under his third pillar that the law's credibility is diminished when politicians abuse the law.[138] The possible effect that the mere existence of a corrupt leadership may have in dampening a State's effort to destroy its political opposition, however, does not necessarily follow. It is unclear why a leadership that violates, to whatever extent, the rule of law as Schmid defines it[139] should be impotent in the face of terrorism. Indeed, unconstrained by checks and balances, such leaders may be more likely to exert overwhelming force, without regard to human rights, that may prove to be of great utility.[140]

---

137 Dershowitz makes a similar point in arguing that groups' decisions to use terrorism have "far less to do with the legitimacy of their causes or the suffering of their people [i.e., 'root causes'] than with religious, cultural, political, and ethical differences." DERSHOWITZ, *supra* note 104, at 25. For an interesting fictional exchange between bin Laden and Mahatma Gandhi on the question of terrorism as a method of political change, see Bhikhu Parekh, *Why Terror?*, PROSPECT, April 2004.

138 On the importance of the rule of law, see Bertrand G. Ramcharan, *The United Nations and New Threats, Challenges and Change: The Report of the High-Level Panel,* in TOWARDS WORLD CONSTITUTIONALISM: ISSUES IN THE LEGAL ORDERING OF THE WORLD COMMUNITY 911, 912 (Ronald St. John Macdonald & Douglas M. Johnston eds., 2005) (asserting that "[t]he key to the security of nations and to the success of the United Nations is the international rule of law.").

139 *See* Schmid, *supra* note 70, at 27-28. Koskenniemi refers to the rule of law as "yet another reformulation of the liberal impulse to escape politics." Martti Koskenniemi, *The Politics of International Law,* 1(1-2) EUR. J. INT'L L. 4, 6 (1990). Expressing a similar understanding to Koskenniemi's, Klabbers defines the rule of law as "the rule of humanity, privileging some while oppressing others." Jan Klabbers, *The Right to Be Taken Seriously: Self-Determination in International Law*, 28(1) HUM. RTS. Q. 186, 200 (2006).

140 According to Warbrick, "[t]he rule of law requires that we take the risk that the law may not protect perfectly, that the bomber will get through when a more unconstrained security policy would have prevented him." Colin Warbrick, *The European Response to Terrorism in an Age of Human Rights,* 15(5) EUR. J. INT'L L. 989, 1016 (2004).

Schmid's final pillar makes a "root causes" argument. Essentially, the "root causes" debate relates to the "belief that, despite all the differences, there is something that connects all or most of the heterogeneous cases of terrorism and thus it is possible to find the common characteristics of the terrorists or the 'root cause' of terrorism (e.g. in poverty)."[141] A number of perspectives toward "root causes" can be identified.

According to one view, condemning as terrorist those acts that breach certain clearly-defined norms regardless of the underlying "root causes" makes sense on a number of levels as a matter of policy. It can generally be said that applying a legal rule, such as the prohibition of terrorist acts, to particular facts and circumstances without having to address the legitimacy of political motivations or weigh their merits is fairer and at least suggests objectivity.[142]

To completely disregard the question of "root causes," however, risks ignoring those grievances that may be legitimate and need to be addressed. It also precludes an holistic approach to international peace and security according to which "development, peace, security and human rights are mutually reinforcing."[143] Barber, echoing this language, argues for the addressing of resentment's "facilitating environment."[144] Even if this approach to "root causes" is accepted, however, one should bear in mind the impor-

---

[141] Jitka Malečková, *Impoverished Terrorists: Stereotype or Reality?*, in ROOT CAUSES OF TERRORISM: MYTHS, REALITY AND WAYS FORWARD 33, 39 (Tore Bjørgo ed., 2005).

[142] According to Dershowitz, "[t]he search for 'root causes' smacks more of after-the-fact political justification than inductive scientific inquiry." DERSHOWITZ, *supra* note 104, at 25.

[143] G.A. Res. 60/1, *supra* note 72, at 21.

[144] Benjamin R. Barber, *Democracy and Terror in the Era of Jihad vs. McWorld,* in WORLDS IN COLLISION: TERROR AND THE FUTURE OF GLOBAL ORDER 245, 248 (Ken Booth & Tim Dunne eds., 2002). Barber favours a "new commitment to distributive justice: a readjudication of north-south responsibilities, a redefinition of the obligations of global capital as it faces the claims of global justice and comity, a repositioning of democratic institutions as they follow markets from the domestic to the international sector, a new recognition of the place and requirements of faith in an aggressively secular market society. The war against Jihad will not, in other words, succeed unless McWorld is also addressed." *Ibid.* at 247. Bassiouni stresses the importance of addressing "root causes" to the effective prevention of terrorism. *See* M. Cherif Bassiouni, *Legal Control of International Terrorism: A Policy-Oriented Assessment*, 43(1) HARV. INT'L L.J. 83, 103 (2002). On the classic "root causes" argument, see Walter Laqueur, *Left, Right, and Beyond: The Changing Face of Terror,* in UNDERSTANDING THE WAR ON TERROR 154, 154-55 (James F. Hoge, Jr., & Gideon Rose eds., 2005).

tant distinction that Falk makes between legitimate and illegitimate "root causes."[145]

A contextual approach to the "root causes" question may also make sense from a practical viewpoint, as the Security Council has noted.[146] As Russian President Vladimir V. Putin stressed at the 2005 World Summit, attention must be given to the "long-lasting regional conflicts that terrorists and extremists of all sorts 'parasitize' on using the historic burden of religious, ethnic and social confrontation."[147] Annan refers to this idea as "conditions conducive to exploitation by terrorists to create or increase their power base."[148]

Chomsky asserts that "[j]ust about every crime – whether a robbery in the streets or colossal atrocities – has reasons, and commonly we find that some of them are serious and should be addressed."[149] An-Na'im argues for the indispensability of such an approach, as one that is "essential for a reasoned and sustainable response [. . . and that it] should not be seen as condoning the crime or blaming the victim."[150] The International Commis-

---

145 *See* Falk, *supra* note 110, at 239. For a similar point, see Laqueur, *supra* note 144, at 164 (asserting that "[s]ome of these grievances will be justified and will also be open to a political solution. Others will be justified but may collide with the equally justified claims of another group. And still others may simply be beyond rational discourse and any known approach of conflict resolution.").

146 *See* S.C. Res. 1625, U.N. SCOR, Annex, at 1, U.N. Doc. S/RES/1625 (2005) (recognising the "need to adopt a broad strategy of conflict prevention, which addresses the root causes of armed conflict and political and social crises in a comprehensive manner, including by promoting sustainable development, poverty eradication, national reconciliation, good governance, democracy, gender equality, the rule of law and respect for and protection of human rights.").

147 Vladimir V. Putin, Statement by His Excellency Mr. Vladimir V. Putin, President of the Russian Federation, at the High-Level Plenary Meeting of the United Nations General Assembly 3 (15 September 2005), *available at* http://www.un.org/webcast/summit2005/statements15/rfe050915eng.pdf.

148 UNITING AGAINST TERRORISM, *supra* note 95, at 5.

149 NOAM CHOMSKY, *Is the War on Terrorism Winnable?*, in 9-11 23, 24 (2002). *See* Noam Chomsky, "War on Terror," Amnesty International Annual Lecture Hosted by Trinity College 10 (18 January 2006), *available at* http://www.amnesty.ie/user/content/download/3898/20352/file/chomskylecture06.pdf (stating that "[a] serious counter-terror campaign would [. . .] begin by considering the grievances [. . .] and[,] where appropriate, addressing them, as should be done with or without the threat of terror.")

150 Abdullahi Ahmed An-Na'im, *Upholding International Legality Against Islamic and American Jihad,* in WORLDS IN COLLISION, *supra* note 144, at 162, 168.

sion on Intervention and State Sovereignty suggests comprehensive steps that involve politics, economics, the law, and the military.[151]

Causation, a foundational criminal law principle, should be borne in mind when considering the "root causes" question.[152] To what extent can it be said that "root causes," however defined, cause, in the legal sense of the word, people to commit acts of terrorism? Several approaches can be identified.

According to the United Nations, which asserts an "imperative to develop a global strategy of fighting terrorism that addresses root causes and strengthens responsible States and the rule of law and fundamental human rights,"[153] "[w]hile poverty and denial of human rights may not be said to 'cause' civil war, terrorism or organized crime, they all greatly increase the risk of instability and violence."[154] *A More Secure World: Our Shared Responsibility: Report of the Secretary-General's High-Level Panel on Threats, Challenges, and Change* (*A More Secure World*) notes that terrorism "flourishes"[155] in situations of humiliation, despair, extremism, poverty, human rights abuses, and political oppression and contexts of foreign occupation and regional conflict[156] and "profits"[157] in environments in which States cannot properly ensure law and order.[158] As a matter of principle, however,

[151] *See* INTERNATIONAL COMMISSION ON INTERVENTION AND STATE SOVEREIGNTY, THE RESPONSIBILITY TO PROTECT: REPORT OF THE INTERNATIONAL COMMISSION ON INTERVENTION AND STATE SOVEREIGNTY 22-23, *available at* http://www.iciss.ca/pdf/Commission-Report.pdf (2001).

[152] Bjørgo discusses different types of causes, structural, facilitator, motivational, and triggering. *See* Tore Bjørgo, *Introduction*, in ROOT CAUSES OF TERRORISM, *supra* note 141, at 1, 3-4.

[153] A MORE SECURE WORLD: OUR SHARED RESPONSIBILITY: REPORT OF THE SECRETARY-GENERAL'S HIGH-LEVEL PANEL ON THREATS, CHALLENGES, AND CHANGE 48 (2004). Arguing for similar holistic approaches to terrorism, see Jayantha Dhanapala, *The United Nations' Response to 9/11*, 17(1-2) TERRORISM & POL. VIOLENCE 17, 22-23 (2005); Kennedy Graham, *The Security Council and Counterterrorism: Global and Regional Approaches to an Elusive Public Good,* 17(1-2) TERRORISM & POL. VIOLENCE 37, 54 (2005); Georges Abi-Saab, *The Proper Role of International Law in Combating Terrorism,* 1(1) CHIN. J. INT'L L. 305, 312 (2002).

[154] IN LARGER FREEDOM: TOWARDS DEVELOPMENT, SECURITY AND HUMAN RIGHTS FOR ALL: REPORT OF THE SECRETARY-GENERAL, U.N. GAOR, at 5, U.N. Doc. A/59/2005 (2005).

[155] A MORE SECURE WORLD, *supra* note 153, at 47.

[156] *See ibid.*

[157] *Ibid.*

[158] *See ibid.* Abi-Saab defines "root causes" similarly to the way in which they are defined in *A More Secure World. See* Abi-Saab, *supra* note 153, at 312.

A More Secure World states that "terrorism is never an acceptable tactic, even for the most defensible of causes."[159]

The United States' position is similar to that of the United Nations in this respect. In *The National Security Strategy of the United States of America* (*National Security Strategy*), President George W. Bush bluntly stated that "[p]overty does not make poor people into terrorists and murderers. Yet poverty, weak institutions, and corruption can make weak states vulnerable to terrorist networks and drug cartels within their borders."[160] The *National Security Strategy* prioritises fighting the "underlying conditions that spawn terrorism"[161] yet acknowledges that terrorism can be an extension of ideological commitment,[162] an idea that Annan has referred to as "terrorism as a tactic."[163] In his State of the Union Address in January 2006, Bush noted that despair, corruption, and poverty source terrorism.[164]

Another "root causes" approach seriously questions whether poverty and other elements lead to terrorism. Pipes, for example, presents persuasive evidence from the Arab and Muslim worlds that shows the classic "root causes" argument to be misleading.[165] Brooks argues against the conven-

---

[159] A MORE SECURE WORLD, *supra* note 153, at 51.

[160] THE WHITE HOUSE, THE NATIONAL SECURITY STRATEGY OF THE UNITED STATES OF AMERICA, INTRODUCTION (2002). *But see* THE WHITE HOUSE, *President Commemorates Veterans Day, Discusses War on Terror* (11 November 2005), *available at* http://www.whitehouse.gov/news/releases/2005/11/20051111-1.html (stating that "[o]ver the years these extremists have used a litany of excuses for violence [. . .] In fact, we're not facing a set of grievances that can be soothed and addressed. [. . .] No act of ours invited the rage of killers – and no concession, bribe, or act of appeasement would change or limit their plans for murder. On the contrary, they target nations whose behavior they believe they can change through violence. Against such an enemy, there is only one effective response: We will never back down, we will never give in, we will never accept anything less than complete victory.")

[161] THE WHITE HOUSE, NATIONAL SECURITY STRATEGY, *supra* note 160, at 6.

[162] *See ibid.* (stating the importance of "supporting moderate and modern government, especially in the Muslim world, to ensure that the conditions and ideologies that promote terrorism do not find fertile ground in any nation.").

[163] UNITING AGAINST TERRORISM, *supra* note 95, at 2.

[164] *See* George W. Bush, State of the Union Address by the President (31 January 2006), *available at* http://www.whitehouse.gov/stateoftheunion/2006.

[165] *See* DANIEL PIPES, MILITANT ISLAM REACHES AMERICA 52-63 (2002). According to Pipes, "[a] survey finds that militant Islam is not a response to poverty or impoverishment; not only are Chad and Iraq not hotbeds of militant Islam, but militant Islam has often surged in countries experiencing rapid economic growth. The factors that cause militant Islam to decline or flourish appear to have more to do with issues of identity than with economics." *Ibid.* at 52-53.

tional "root causes" wisdom, asserting that "about 75 percent of anti-Western terrorists come from middle-class or upper-middle-class homes. An amazing 65 percent have gone to college, and three-quarters have professional or semiprofessional jobs, particularly in engineering and science."[166] The European Commission has expressed its understandable frustration that the motivations of some terrorists "defy simplistic categorisation; not being socially-excluded, socio-economically disadvantaged, unemployed or living in deprived suburbs of large cities or inner-city housing estates, or from immigrant families."[167] The example of 11 September terrorist Mohammed Atta can be referred to in this regard.[168]

Pipes suggests that "[i]t could be, quite correctly, that militant Islam results from wealth rather than poverty. Possibly."[169] At the very least, he favours expanding the debate on the "root causes" of militant Islam beyond simply economics to other fields, namely politics, religion, and culture.[170] Altruism, interest, idealism, ambition, machismo, and impatience may also be relevant considerations.[171] Studies have also referred to threats to tradition,[172] stressed the importance of the "accidental element,"[173] and emphasised the significant role of "crime and madness."[174] As Commissioner Zuloaga stated in a supplementary opinion in an arbitral award before the Italy-Venezuela Mixed Claims Commission in the early-twentieth century, "[r]evolutions are not here, more than elsewhere, always occasioned by the faults or errors of the government or by a simple spirit of uprising among the revolted. They obey multiple causes."[175]

---

166 David Brooks, *Trading Cricket for Jihad,* N.Y. TIMES, 4 August 2005. *See* Malečková, *supra* note 141, at 41-42.

167 Communication from the Commission to the European Parliament and the Council Concerning Terrorist Recruitment: Addressing the Factors Contributing to Violent Radicalisation, COM(05)313 final Annex at 11.

168 *See* AYAAN HIRSI ALI, THE CAGED VIRGIN: AN EMANCIPATION PROCLAMATION FOR WOMEN AND ISLAM 9-10 (2006).

169 PIPES, *supra* note 165, at 61.

170 *See ibid.* at 63.

171 *See* MISHRA, *supra* note 106, at 23.

172 *See ibid.* at 27.

173 *Ibid.* at 48.

174 Laqueur, *supra* note 144, at 163.

175 Sambiaggio (*Italy* v. *Venez.*), 10 R.I.A.A. 499, 510 (1903) (continuing by stating that "not infrequently there is in the political horizon of a people a condensation of revolutionary clouds that the patriotism of the best citizens of the government or of the opposition is unable to prevent, so deeply is the reason hidden in political or economic causes.").

The conventional "root causes" thesis also seems to be undermined by studies dealing with Latin America, France, and Africa.[176] A more complicated picture is suggested by the fact that terrorism has been a significant issue in what have historically been the comparatively wealthy States of Argentina and Uruguay but not in the less developed Latin American States of Ecuador and Paraguay,[177] as well as a comparison of left-wing violence in West Germany and Italy and the nature of the political parties in power in those respective countries at the time.[178]

According to Dershowitz, to argue based on "root causes" avoids having to face the reality that groups that have had legitimate causes and have undergone tremendous suffering have chosen non-terrorist methods of change.[179] Morris concurs, in particular by contrasting the lack of terrorism in Europe by the former African colonial subjects of the United Kingdom, France, and Belgium and, in light of the Holocaust, by Jews in Germany and the reality of terrorism by Palestinians, and arrives at a cultural or ideological explanation, that "there is something else here, something deeper, that has to do with Islam and Arab culture."[180] On the question of causation between "root causes" and terrorism, Dershowitz asserts that "[t]here has never even been a direct correlation – to say nothing of causation – between the degrees of injustice experienced by a given group and the willingness of that group to resort to terrorism."[181]

As an example of this, consider the tactics used by, mostly black, Americans during the civil rights movement in the United States during the 1950s and 1960s.[182] Martin Luther King, Jr., and his followers consciously and as

---

[176] *See* MISHRA, *supra* note 106, at 26-27; *ibid.* at 30.

[177] *See ibid.* at 50.

[178] *See ibid.* at 38-39.

[179] *See* DERSHOWITZ, *supra* note 104, at 25; *ibid.* at 234 n. 12 (stating that "[t]he vast majority of groups with just causes have not resorted to terrorism. Nor have poverty-stricken groups historically turned to terrorism. Indeed, terrorism has been more closely associated with elite groups promoting questionable causes. In the minds of many, the terrorism itself is what has elevated the cause."). *See also* Alan M. Dershowitz, *The Abuse Excuse: Zacarias Moussaoui's Lawyers Float the "Impoverished French Muslim Syndrome,"* SLATE, 20 April 2006, *available at* http://www.slate.com/id/2140262. Similarly, Mishra argues that "[g]rievances always exist, but in certain cases oppression has been borne without protest, whereas elsewhere and at other times relatively minor grievances have resulted in violent reaction." MISHRA, *supra* note 106, at 23.

[180] Shavit, *supra* note 112.

[181] DERSHOWITZ, *supra* note 104, at 25.

[182] For a similar point, see *ibid.* at 90-91; *ibid.* at 233-34 n. 10.

a matter of ideological commitment embraced non-violent civil disobedience as a form of struggle. Although suffering abuse along the way, they achieved the remarkable goal of desegregation in the American South. What King described as "[*t*]*he marvelous new militancy which has engulfed the Negro community*,"[183] or the rise of black nationalism and racial pride that would surface in such forms as the Black Panthers, however, sometimes chose violence as a means to an end.

Gearty has argued that "terror is the weapon of the weak. The practitioners of this form of violence lash out because they have no other, more efficient, means of fighting."[184] Given the success of King's non-violent movement and militant black nationalism's corresponding failure to achieve radical change, however, Gearty's sentiments seem to be misplaced. Certainly, given the balance of political power in the American South at the time, as well as racially-motivated violence against black Americans, King and his followers were "weak" enough. Indeed, to ironically twist Gearty's expression, non-violent civil disobedience was a "more efficient [. . .] means of fighting." The case of the Palestinians also supports this argument.[185]

A more recent example of the disjuncture that Dershowitz highlights between the degree of oppression that particular groups undergo, the "root causes," and the resort to violence can be found in the response of elements within the Christian and Muslim communities to, respectively, the cinematic début of Dan Brown's bestselling novel from 2003, *The Da Vinci Code*, and the publication of cartoons depicting Mohammed by, among others, Denmark's *Jyllands-Posten*.[186] Many of the ideas presented in *The Da Vinci Code*, ranging from assertions that Jesus Christ and Mary Magdalene had a child together and that much of Christianity, particularly Catholic Christianity, is a conspiracy of lies, and the pictorial renderings of Mohammed in cartoon form are considered heretical under the respective religious tradi-

---

183 THE AUTOBIOGRAPHY OF MARTIN LUTHER KING, JR. 225 (Clayborne Carson ed., 1998).

184 Conor Gearty, *What is Terror?,* THE TIMES, 9 March 1991.

185 *See* Thomas L. Friedman, *Muslims in Danger,* N.Y. TIMES, 9 July 2005 (stating that "[m]any people said Palestinian suicide bombing was the spontaneous reaction of frustrated Palestinian youth. But when Palestinians decided that it was in their interest to have a cease-fire with Israel, those bombings stopped cold."). Furthermore, Annan has stressed that "there exist alternative, non-violent strategies [. . .] that [. . .] have in most cases proved more effective [than terrorism]. Recent history offers numerous examples of non-violent opposition movements leading to significant change." UNITING AGAINST TERRORISM, *supra* note 95, at 4.

186 On the latter, see HIRSI ALI, *supra* note 168, at XIV-XV.

tions. The manner in which elements within the Christian and Muslim communities reacted to these heresies, however, with peaceful protests and boycotts by the former and displays of violence by the latter that resulted in casualties and damage demonstrates that a people's response to offence can often reflect more how it has been ideologically nurtured than an obvious, or inherent, response of nature.

Rice may present the best approach to "root causes," an approach according to which "root causes" are addressed as a matter of policy prerogative, "because it is the right thing to do – and the smart thing to do. We have seen how poor states can become weak or even failed states, vulnerable to hijacking by terrorist networks – with potentially catastrophic consequences."[187] At the same time, however, even her advice may miss the mark in some situations: "the problem of terrorism is complicated, and what can be said without fear of contradiction about a terrorist group in one country is by no means true for other groups at other times and in other societies."[188]

In the final analysis on Schmid's fourth pillar, although there are several approaches to "root causes," it would be unwise to accept an almost scientifically-determined position that would disregard the intervention of volition and ignore particular facts and circumstances. One must avoid the "impression that terrorists are merely passive objects of social, economic and psychological forces: puppets obeying what these 'causes' compel them to do."[189] It is true that the myriad contexts in which contemporary terrorism occurs, in times of economic boom and bust and in cities large and small,[190] may frustrate the policy-maker. There is a need to take seriously the terrorists' alleged grievances and dispassionately assess them in each particular case.

To conclude this section on whether States can effectively fight terrorism while at the same time not violating human rights, consider the Sri Lankan experience with the Liberation Tigers of Tamil Eelam (LTTE), an example of a State that has tried to incorporate human rights when fighting

---

[187] Condoleezza Rice, *The President's National Security Strategy,* in THE NEOCON READER 79, 85 (Irwin Stelzer ed., 2004) (continuing by stating that, "in societies where legal avenues for political dissent are stifled, the temptation to speak through violence grows.").

[188] MISHRA, *supra* note 106, at 23.

[189] Bjørgo, *supra* note 152, at 3.

[190] *See* MISHRA, *supra* note 106, at 40.

terrorism by non-State actors.[191] In her address at the 2005 World Summit, Kumaratunga relayed Sri Lanka's counterterrorism experience with the LTTE.[192] This approach has involved dialogue, a "bold policy of a negotiated settlement in place of conflict, [. . .] a federal solution as against a separate State[, . . .] a broad multi-ethnic coalition of parties[, and . . .] a new more inclusive, political Constitution that would share power with all communities,"[193] as well as an ethnically-sensitive human rights perspective.[194]

After describing the Sri Lankan approach, Kumaratunga noted the continuation of violence and instability.[195] She positioned human rights in a specific setting of unrest and suggested that the integrity of States that scrupulously abide by human rights may be seriously jeopardised.[196] Kumaratunga helpfully contributed to the debate with her realist perspective, a perspective that, incidentally, should never be divorced from legal discourse, and argued that "[v]ulnerable democracies which have undertaken bold, political initiative to address the root causes of terrorism and seek political solutions by engaging ruthless armed groups find themselves in a genuine dilemma as to how to develop a credible and acceptable approach to such negotiations."[197]

---

[191] *See* Shri D.R. Kaarthikeyan, *Root Causes of Terrorism?: A Case Study of the Tamil Insurgency and the LTTE*, in ROOT CAUSES OF TERRORISM, *supra* note 141, at 131, 136 (detailing Kumaratunga's efforts).

[192] *See* Kumaratunga, *supra* note 74.

[193] *Ibid.* at 2.

[194] *See ibid.* at 3.

[195] *See ibid.* (stating that "this process of engagement and accommodation does not seem to have persuaded this Group to move away from terrorism, as is evidenced by their recent killing of my Foreign Minister, their continued recruitment of child soldiers and their killings of political rivals.").

[196] *See ibid.* at 4 (stating the possibility that such a State "weakens as a result of the activities of terrorists [. . . and that] chaos [. . .] and lawlessness will follow. Extremism, fundamentalism and tribalism will reign supreme. As a result, peace and security, within and among States, as well as universally accepted human rights norms and fundamental freedoms will suffer.").

[197] *Ibid.* at 3. Writing in June 2006, Brooks described the situation in Iraq as one in which "virtue seems to be a handicap and barbarism an empowering force." David Brooks, *Savagery's Stranglehold*, N.Y. TIMES, 8 June 2006.

VII. Assessment

It should be reiterated at this point that international law does not permit States to blind themselves to human rights when fighting terrorism. States that do so, particularly when they do so egregiously, violate international law. The substance of international law may or may not be reasonable, but that human rights considerations must be taken on board should be acknowledged as part of the *lex lata*.

That there may sometimes be a trade-off between the effective fighting of terrorism and individual human rights should not necessarily come as a surprise because the law is rife with conflicts of norms and competing objectives.[198] In the context of self-determination, for example, Klabbers recognises "the law's inability to decide whether the right of self-determination of group X should result in the breakup of state Y and whether it should possibly override competing claims from groups residing on territory where X happens to be in the majority (Serbs in Bosnia, for instance)."[199]

State practice demonstrates that States use a balancing test when negotiating between the sometimes conflicting norms of national security and human rights.[200] This is particularly necessary in the United States, where Al Qaeda has historically benefited from divisions of governmental authority in a federal republic and privacy rights.[201] Freedoms in the globalised era, such as the freedom of movement, open opportunities and benefit those who choose to abuse seemingly benign rights.[202] As Wedgwood argues, "[i]n its adaptive style of warfare, Al-Qaeda is willing to use the scientific fruits of a free society and harness them, in a dangerous syncretism, to the purposes of destruction."[203]

---

[198] For an illuminating interview with Lord Chancellor Charles Falconer in which he discusses trade-offs between individuals' human rights and public safety, see *Human Rights*, BBC SUNDAY AM, BBC NEWS, *available at* http://news.bbc.co.uk/2/hi/programmes/how_euro_are_you/4769979.stm (last updated 14 May 2006).

[199] Klabbers, *supra* note 139, at 199.

[200] The fact that States negotiate at all between these sometimes conflicting norms suggests that the necessarily symbiotic relationship between them that international law posits, at least in the sense of utility, may be exaggerated.

[201] *See* Wedgwood, *Countering Catastrophic Terrorism*, *supra* note 132, at 103-04.

[202] *See ibid.* at 104-05.

[203] *Ibid.* Making a similar point, see SAMUEL P. HUNTINGTON, THE CLASH OF CIVILIZATIONS AND THE REMAKING OF WORLD ORDER 217 (2002).

Given that State practice forms one of the two components of customary international law and that customary international law divorced from State practice is unsustainable, it might be supposed that the reality of widespread human rights abuses by States in the context of counterterrorism would inform an evolution of the law related to national security and human rights in situations of terrorism to the "benefit" of the former.[204] Higgins, however, addressing the issue of torture and acknowledging that more States than not engage in it, argues that customary international law continues to so clearly prohibit torture "because *opinio juris* as to its normative status continues to exist. No state, not even a state that tortures, believes that the international law prohibition is undesirable and that it is not bound by the prohibition."[205] This question of belief by States is absolutely essential because, as D'Amato notes, without ascertaining it, international legal analysis "would amount, to the extent of its deviation from actual belief, only to a natural-law prescription of what states ought to believe."[206]

The ICJ's jurisprudence provides some practical guidelines for assessing customary international law. In *Military and Paramilitary Activities in and Against Nicaragua*, for example, it stated that State practice with regard to a particular customary international law norm, in that case, the prohibition on the use of force and the non-intervention rule, does not have to be "perfect,"[207] nor "in absolutely rigorous conformity with the rule."[208]

---

[204] On the evolutionary nature of customary international law, see Anthony D'Amato, *Trashing Customary International Law*, 81 AM. J. INT'L L. 101, 104 (1987) (stating that "[c]ustomary rules [. . .] are not static. They change in content depending upon the amplitude of new vectors (state interests). [. . . T]he customary rules that survive the legal evolutionary process are those that are best adapted to serve the mutual self-interest of all states.").

[205] ROSALYN HIGGINS, *Sources of International Law: Provenance and Problems*, in PROBLEMS AND PROCESS: INTERNATIONAL LAW AND HOW WE USE IT 17, 22 (1994). *See* Roberts, *supra* note 50, at 737 (asserting in the context of human rights generally responses that resemble Higgins', namely "(a) while some states violate human rights some of the time, most states respect human rights most of the time; (b) even when states breach human rights standards, they often deny these breaches rather than endorsing them as official policy; and (c) human rights violations are often met with protest from other states, so they represent breaches of existing law rather than the beginnings of a new or modified law.").

[206] Anthony D'Amato, *On Consensus*, 8 CAN. Y.B. INT'L L. 104, 105 (1970).

[207] Military and Paramilitary Activities in and Against Nicaragua (*Nicar.* v. *U.S.*), 1986 I.C.J. 14, 98.

[208] *Ibid.*

Indeed, the ICJ went on to say that contrary State practice could be "not infrequent."[209]

Despite the fact that State practice does not have to unyieldingly conform to a particular customary international law norm, Higgins' view for a number of reasons seems to be too confident in its insistence that dispositive and conclusive support for a customary international law prohibition on torture can be found in what she presumably refers to, declarations by State representatives in multilateral fora.[210] First, it necessarily downplays, by not addressing, Anderson's argument that "it is not clear whether a statement, the same statement, can be both State practice and *opinio juris*."[211] Second, Higgins' view overlooks Roberts' point that States generally since 11 September have turned a blind eye to human rights abuses and even publicly declared a bias in favour of national security over human rights.[212] Higgins' view also does not speak to D'Amato's critique that relying on United Nations Resolutions as evidence of *opinio juris* results in the hollowing out of State practice and the creation of self-fulfilling rules: "All we need is the original alleged rule and the empty theory that any practice inconsistent with it does not count."[213] As ICJ Judge Stephen M. Schwebel stated in his dissenting opinion in the *Nuclear Weapons* case, "[i]f a [General Assembly] resolution purports to be declaratory of international law, if it is adopted unanimously (or virtually so, qualitatively as well as quantitively) or by consensus, and *if it corresponds to State practice*, it may

---

[209] *Ibid.* at 106.

[210] "Both physical and verbal acts of States constitute practice that contributes to the creation of customary international law." INTERNATIONAL COMMITTEE OF THE RED CROSS, CUSTOMARY INTERNATIONAL HUMANITARIAN LAW: VOLUME 1: RULES XXXII (Jean-Marie Henckaerts & Louise Doswald-Beck eds., 2005).

[211] Susan Anderson, *When the Law Breaker Becomes the Law Maker*, in THE CHALLENGE OF CONFLICT: INTERNATIONAL LAW RESPONDS 413, 428 (Ustinia Dolgopol & Judith Gardam eds., 2006). *See ibid.* at 415 (maintaining that "how one goes about determining whether *opinio juris* is present is not altogether clear."). As Koskenniemi insightfully notes, "[t]here are no independently applicable criteria for ascertaining the presence of the *opinio juris*[, and . . . c]ustomary law doctrine remains indeterminate because it is circular." Martti Koskenniemi, *The Politics of International Law, supra* note 139, at 26. *See ibid.* at 25-27.

[212] *See* Roberts, *supra* note 50, at 737-38.

[213] D'Amato, *Trashing Customary International Law*, *supra* note 204, at 102. On D'Amato on statements versus actions as State practice, see Anderson, *supra* note 211, at 416; *ibid. at* 434.

be declaratory of international law."[214] To suggest that mere words as to legal obligation on torture speak louder than an international State practice that too often reflects an on-the-ground reality of State recourse to torture in its various grisly guises, furthermore, implies that international law can, and should, take refuge in the insincere platitudes of States that publicly insist by their words that international law prohibits torture but that by their actions and omissions suggest that they do not really believe that it does. Arguably, it is more reasonable to concede that customary international law on this and other norms related to national security and human rights in situations of terrorism in light of widespread State violations is complex, stratified, and varied.[215]

It should be stressed that States, particularly liberal democracies, should not completely disregard human rights when fighting terrorism.[216] Such a contention, however, is rooted in values and politics and not necessarily, or at least not always, in an overriding concern for utility.[217] The perspective advanced by Nobel Laureate Milton Friedman regarding government intervention in society, as a "balance sheet, listing separately the advantages and disadvantages. Our principles tell us what items to put on the one side and what items on the other and they give us some basis for attaching importance to the different items,"[218] goes to the core of the human rights issue and provides a useful template for considerations of policy prerogatives.

The best approach to Friedman's concept of a balance sheet in this context may be that which Vijayakumar articulates as relates to India, "an acceptable course between giving too little power to the government so that it is unable to deal with terrorism, and too much power so that an intolerable violation of human rights is risked."[219] These balanced interests naturally

---

[214] Legality of the Threat or Use of Nuclear Weapons, *supra* note 66, at 319 (Schwebel, J., dissenting) (emphasis added).

[215] According to Roberts, "[w]hile it is too early to tell what impact the US actions post-September 11 will ultimately have on human rights, it is clear that these actions have provided conceptual challenges to the structure of international human rights law." Roberts, *supra* note 50, at 748-49.

[216] For Dershowitz's perspective on where the balance should be struck, see DERSHOWITZ, *supra* note 104, at 165-222.

[217] Equating values and politics, see Klabbers, *supra* note 139, at 203.

[218] MILTON FRIEDMAN, CAPITALISM AND FREEDOM 32 (1967).

[219] Vijayakumar, *supra* note 99, at 351. Brooks describes this as a "sweet spot that satisfies both the demands of power and of principle." Brooks, *Savagery's Stranglehold*, *supra* note 197.

open themselves to interpretation, but phrasing the exercise in this way ensures that neither the community's right to security nor individuals' human rights can straightjacket the other. This approach also avoids the dangerous argument put forward by ICJ Judge Hisashi Owada in his separate opinion in the *Wall* case, according to which argument, as a matter of principle and based on the proportionality rule, military exigencies could never, even, presumably, on a scale of certain national annihilation, justify the human rights violations engendered by Israel's separation barrier.[220]

What An-Na'im says about interpretations of the Shari'a, that, "[w]hen all is said and done, the ultimate question would be a moral one, namely what *ought* to be the principle in the particular case or situation,"[221] applies generally in this context.[222] Falk's assumption for the sake of argument that breaching human rights could increase national security but that this "would not [. . .] alone justify official behavior violative of basic rights"[223] is certainly a legitimate position, but it must be seen as an essentially moral choice.[224] It is unclear why his morality, as much as anyone else's, should be considered inherently dispositive on the issue.[225]

It is with this in mind that one can approach Dershowitz's "ticking bomb" hypothetical on torture and the moral dilemmas involved.[226] On the whole, the human rights establishment has dismissed this hypothetical almost outright,[227] the United Nations Committee Against Torture, the United Na-

---

220 *See* Wall, *supra* note 16, at Para. 24 (Owada, J., separate).

221 Abdullahi Ahmed An-Na'im, *Islamic Ambivalence to Political Violence: Islamic Law and International Terrorism,* 31 GERM. Y.B. INT'L L. 307, 334 (1988).

222 According to Gearty, "[t]he twin narratives of counter-terrorism and human rights share an important common feature: they each present themselves as being rooted in morality, as being concerned with either the procurement (human rights) or the defence (counterterrorism) of an objective good." Gearty, *Terrorism and Human Rights, supra* note 97, at 1.

223 Falk, *supra* note 110, at 236.

224 This resembles Koskenniemi's argument about the political nature of legal interpretation: "A court's decision or a lawyer's opinion is always a genuinely political act, a choice between alternatives not fully dictated by external criteria." Martti Koskenniemi, *What Is International Law For?*, in INTERNATIONAL LAW 89, 105 (Malcolm D. Evans ed., 2003).

225 This is particularly the case given the fluid nature of rights. On the fluid nature of rights, see Klabbers, *supra* note 139, at 199-200.

226 *See* DERSHOWITZ, *supra* note 104, at 131-63. For a brief criticism of this hypothetical, see Bassiouni, *Great Nations and Torture, supra* note 46, at 259.

227 As examples, see Bassiouni, *Great Nations and Torture*, *supra* note 46, at 259; Pejic, *supra* note 24, at 99-100.

tions Special Rapporteur on Torture and Other Cruel, Inhuman or Degrading Treatment, the Board of Trustees of the United Nations Voluntary Fund for Victims of Torture, and Arbour jointly stating on United Nations International Day in Support of Victims of Torture on 26 June 2006 that the very idea itself of arguments that seek to justify torture, regardless of context, is "anathema,"[228] as if to suggest that the mere discussion of the appropriateness of a currently-accepted international legal norm, the absolute prohibition of torture, lies outside the boundaries of legitimate discourse.

Likewise, Bassiouni argues that "[t]orture, or torture by any other name, is legally, morally, and ethically reprehensible."[229] Unfortunately, this statement presents itself as an unassailable truism, as something that is sacrosanct and beyond reasoned debate and, in so doing, positions those who might disagree as necessarily supporting a reprehensible sense of legality, morality, and ethics. This is unfortunate, and it is a posture that installs what Fallaci would describe as "fear,"[230] a type of thinking that she would refer to as "intellectual terrorism."[231] One must constantly bear in mind Tomuschat's position that "the philosophical ought must be distinguished from the legal ought."[232]

---

228 United Nations Committee Against Torture, the United Nations Special Rapporteur on Torture and Other Cruel, Inhuman or Degrading Treatment, the Board of Trustees of the United Nations Voluntary Fund for Victims of Torture, and the United Nations High Commissioner for Human Rights, Joint Statement on the Occasion of the United Nations International Day in Support of Victims of Torture (26 June 2006), *available at* http://www.ohchr.org/english/about/funds/torture/docs/JointStatement26.06.06.pdf.

229 Bassiouni, *Great Nations and Torture, supra* note 46, at 259. One can compare this with Hirsi Ali's description of Muslims who thoughtfully criticise the theological status quo. *See* HIRSI ALI, *supra* note 168, at XII (stating that "any Muslim who asks critical questions about Islam is immediately branded a 'deserter.' A Muslim who advocates the exploration of sources for morality, in addition to those of the Prophet Muhammad, will be threatened with death, and a woman who withdraws from the virgins' cage is branded a whore.").

230 ORIANA FALLACI, THE FORCE OF REASON 257-58 (2006) (describing this as "[f]ear of thinking and, in thinking, of reaching conclusions which do not match those of the formulas imposed by the others. Fear of speaking and, in speaking, of reaching a judgement which is different from the judgement accepted by most. Fear of not being sufficiently aligned, obedient, servile, and therefore of being condemned to the civil death with which inert or rather inanimate democracies blackmail the citizens. Fear of being free, in short. Of taking risks, of having courage.").

231 *Ibid.* at 209.

232 CHRISTIAN TOMUSCHAT, HUMAN RIGHTS: BETWEEN IDEALISM AND REALISM 2 (2003).

It should at least be acknowledged that international law, as a construction of world politics and power,[233] may or may not coincide with one's morality and ethics, the content of the latter two elements of which has been debated for millennia.[234] Few, hopefully none, would today agree with United States Supreme Court Chief Justice Roger Brooke Taney's analogy of a black slave in the United States to "an ordinary article of merchandise and property,"[235] yet the legal authority as a matter of positive law of *Dred Scott* v. *Sandford* under the United States' constitutional system at the time was clear.[236] This is not to suggest that international law's current posture on torture is or is not justified: it may or may not be. Rather, there exists a need for reasoned debate on the issue that proceeds from acceptance of the assumption, however contentious, that "[m]en's freedoms can conflict, and when they do, one man's freedom must be limited to preserve another's."[237]

VIII. Conclusion

In conclusion, international law demands much of States in the current counterterrorism context. According to it, States must effectively fight terrorism while at the same time safeguarding the human rights of the general public and, perhaps most precariously of all, those of the terrorists themselves. International actors have attempted to frame human rights in a way that appeals to States' self-interest, but empirical evidence suggests that a community's right to security and individual human rights can conflict. It serves neither security nor human rights to deny this.

---

233 According to Krisch, "acknowledging that power plays a large role does not necessarily have any bearing on the justification *vel non* of an action or development. But it may give us some greater distance in assessing them." Nico Krisch, *International Law in Times of Hegemony: Unequal Power and the Shaping of the International Legal Order*, 16(3) Eur. J. Int'l L. 369, 408 (2005).

234 On a related point, see Robert H. Bork, The Tempting of America: The Political Seduction of the Law 176 (1990) (asserting that "[i]t is essential to bear in mind the distinction between the reality of judicial power and the legitimacy or morality of the use of that power. [. . .] Power alone is not sufficient to produce legitimate authority.").

235 *Dred Scott* v. *Sandford*, 60 U.S. 393, 451 (1857).

236 For a commentary by Bork on the case, see Bork, *supra* note 234, at 28-34.

237 Friedman, *supra* note 218, at 26. *See* Koskenniemi, *What Is International Law For?*, *supra* note 224, at 99 (discussing assessments of security and freedom in the context of the European Convention on Human Rights).

United Nations Special Rapporteur on the Situation of Human Rights in the Palestinian Territories Occupied Since 1967 John Dugard has said that the very question of terrorism involves an "intense conflict in perception."[238] To a large extent, the questions which legal framework applies in the current counterterrorism context and where the balance should be struck between national security and human rights on particular facts and circumstances likewise trigger fundamental issues of perception. Such issues also demonstrate the interplay between the legal and the political and challenge the idea that these realms can be hermetically sealed from one another.[239] Put bluntly, one's legal conclusions on these questions largely reflect whether she agrees with Lord Hoffmann in the House of Lords that Al Qaeda "do[es] not threaten the life of the nation[, . . .] does not threaten our institutions of government or our existence as a civil community"[240] or with Orwell, who, chastising his leftist comrades at the time of the Second World War, recognised that, "[h]owever little we may like it, toughness is the price of survival."[241]

---

[238] John Dugard, *The Problem of the Definition of Terrorism in International Law,* in SEPTEMBER 11, 2001: A TURNING POINT IN INTERNATIONAL AND DOMESTIC LAW? 187, 189 (Paul Eden & Thérèse O'Donnell eds., 2005).

[239] Consider Judge Alejandro Alvarez's revealing comments in his separate opinion in the *Corfu Channel* case. *See* Corfu Channel (*U.K.* v. *Alb.*), 1949 I.C.J. 4, 41-42 (Alvarez, J., separate) (stating that "[t]he law of social interdependence does not place law in opposition to politics, as has been done hitherto; on the contrary, it admits that there are close relations between them. [. . .] pure law does not exist: law is the result of social life and evolves with it; in other words, it is, to a large extent, the effect of politics – especially of a collective kind – as practiced by the States. We must therefore beware of considering law and politics as mutually antagonistic. Each of them should be permeated by the other.").

[240] *A. & Others* v. *Secretary of State for the Home Department*, U.K.H.L. 56, Para. 96 (2004).

[241] GEORGE ORWELL, *The Lion and the Unicorn,* in WHY I WRITE 11, 85 (2004).

Chapter 7
CONCLUSION

Chapter 7
CONCLUSION

This research has examined how international law assesses, and on what grounds and through which mechanisms, how a State can bear responsibility for its actions or omissions with regard to its international legal obligations to act with due diligence in confronting non-State actors that engage in terrorism. The due diligence principle has emerged from the niche field of diplomatic protection to the mainstream of international law. As Dupuy and Hoss note, "[t]he emergence and strengthening of the obligation of due diligence is at the center of the development of international law on transboundary harm."[1] Clearly, it has an important role to play in matters of international peace and security.

While the normative significance of the due diligence principle means that it can function, or at least should function, as a credible reference point for judging State behaviour, admonitions and prohibitions as to international legality have limited purchase on the ground if they blind themselves to reality and the constraints that States face. Theory and practice inform one another, and insensitivity to their dynamic interrelationship in what is asserted to be law risks creating a framework that relevant actors see as being merely cosmic and aspirational, without credibility and relevance. As Franck argues in a related context, the "struggle will be waged with the weaponry of facts, but, more important, with that of perceptions."[2] It is "perceptions" that support or destroy the international law enterprise.[3]

The most important and pressing concern that arises in squaring what is sought to be achieved in theory with what can be achieved in practice is what Zegveld refers to in the context of armed opposition groups and State

---

[1] Pierre-Marie Dupuy & Cristina Hoss, Trail Smelter *and Terrorism: International Mechanisms to Combat Transboundary Harm*, in TRANSBOUNDARY HARM IN INTERNATIONAL LAW: LESSONS FROM THE *TRAIL SMELTER* ARBITRATION 225, 226 (Rebecca M. Bratspies & Russell A. Miller eds., 2006).

[2] Thomas M. Franck, *The Power of Legitimacy and the Legitimacy of Power: International Law in an Age of Power Disequilibrium*, 100(1) AM. J. INT'L L. 88, 91 (2006).

[3] *See ibid.* at 92 (asserting that "it is the perception that law has lost its purchase, not the unlawful behavior itself, that propels the descent into social chaos.").

responsibility, the issue of "factual capability."[4] Factual capability, which she defines as the ability of States to "prevent and repress violent attacks by armed opposition groups,"[5] functions in the context of the due diligence principle and counterterrorism as States' ability to comply with their obligations under relevant treaties and Security Council Resolutions.

To use the language of the International Law Commission (ILC)'s *Commentaries* to the *Articles on Prevention of Transboundary Harm from Hazardous Activities,* factual capability corresponds to each State's "possess[ion of] a legal system and sufficient resources to maintain an adequate administrative apparatus to control and monitor the activities."[6] The ILC refers to "incorporating accepted international standards [. . . as] constitut[ing] a necessary reference point to determine whether measures adopted are suitable."[7] A State's economic underdevelopment may be considered in a due diligence assessment, but according to the ILC and at least in the context of the prevention of transboundary harm from hazardous activities, it cannot shield it from its obligation to act with due diligence.[8]

---

4 LIESBETH ZEGVELD, ACCOUNTABILITY OF ARMED OPPOSITION GROUPS IN INTERNATIONAL LAW 190 (2002). *Cf.* Application of the Convention on the Prevention and Punishment of the Crime of Genocide (*Bosn. & Herz.* v. *Serb. & Mont.*), 2007 I.C.J., at Para. 430 (discussing "capacity" in the context of the due diligence principle and the Convention on the Prevention and Punishment of the Crime of Genocide (Genocide Convention)).

5 ZEGVELD, *supra* note 4, at 190.

6 International Law Commission, *Commentaries, Articles on Prevention of Transboundary Harm from Hazardous Activities,* in REPORT OF THE INTERNATIONAL LAW COMMISSION ON THE WORK OF ITS FIFTY-THIRD SESSION 377, 395, U.N. Doc. A/56/10 Supp. No. 10 (2001). On factual capability in the environmental law context, see ORGANISATION FOR ECONOMIC CO-OPERATION AND DEVELOPMENT SECRETARIAT, *Observations on the Concept of the International Responsibility of States in Relation to the Protection of the Environment,* in LEGAL ASPECTS OF TRANSFRONTIER POLLUTION 380, 384 (Organisation for Economic Co-operation and Development ed., 1977).

7 International Law Commission, *Commentaries, Articles on Prevention of Transboundary Harm, supra* note 6, at 391. Handl argues that the "proliferation of pertinent environmental and technical standards, such as best available technology, best environmental practice, and so on, which may provide a *de facto,* if not *de jure,* authoritative point of reference, reduces – sometimes dramatically – the uncertainty over what constitutes due diligence aimed at preventing or abating transboundary harmful effects." Günther Handl, Trail Smelter *in Contemporary International Environmental Law: Its Relevance in the Nuclear Energy Context*, in TRANSBOUNDARY HARM IN INTERNATIONAL LAW, *supra* note 1, at 125, 132.

8 *See* International Law Commission, *Commentaries, Articles on Prevention of Transboundary Harm, supra* note 6, at 394-95. For a similar point in the context of the due

The United Nations Committee on Economic, Social, and Cultural Rights (CESCR) has touched upon how economic underdevelopment and factual capability interact in an analogous context. In its General Comment Number 3 (Comment), it interprets Article 2(1) of the International Covenant on Economic, Social, and Cultural Rights[9] as meaning that, while recognising the role of progressive achievement, "steps [. . .] must be taken within a reasonably short time after the Covenant's entry into force for the States concerned. Such steps should be deliberate, concrete and targeted as clearly as possible towards meeting the obligations recognized in the Covenant."[10] There exists, furthermore, a "minimum core obligation."[11]

Thus, to use principles developed by the ILC and the CESCR, it is clear that there should be some consideration of economic constraints when assessing factual capability in light of the due diligence principle. However, the focus remains on normative compliance by States with their international legal obligations. As the CESCR states in its Comment, "a State party in which any significant number of individuals is deprived of essential foodstuffs, of essential primary health care, of basic shelter and housing, or of the most basic forms of education is, *prima facie*, failing to discharge its obligations under the Covenant."[12] Likewise, it can be said that a State will be prima facie acting contrary to international law if it does not distribute

---

diligence principle generally, see Stephanie Farrior, *State Responsibility for Human Rights Abuses by Non-State Actors*, 1998 A.S.I.L. PROC. 299, 302-03.

[9] According to that article, "[e]ach State Party to the present Covenant undertakes to take steps, individually and through international assistance and co-operation, especially economic and technical, to the maximum of its available resources, with a view to achieving progressively the full realization of the rights recognized in the present Covenant by all appropriate means, including particularly the adoption of legislative measures." G.A. Res. 2200, Annex, International Covenant on Economic, Social, and Cultural Rights, Art. 2(1) (1966).

[10] COMMITTEE ON ECONOMIC, SOCIAL AND CULTURAL RIGHTS, GENERAL COMMENT NUMBER 3, in COMMITTEE ON ECONOMIC, SOCIAL AND CULTURAL RIGHTS: REPORT ON THE FIFTH SESSION (26 NOVEMBER-14 DECEMBER 1990), U.N. ESCOR, Annex III, 83, 83, U.N. Doc. E/1991/23 E/C.12/1990/8 Supp. No. 3 (1991).

[11] *Ibid.* at 86.

[12] *Ibid.* "By the same token, it must be noted that any assessment as to whether a State has discharged its minimum core obligation must also take account of resource constraints applying within the country concerned. [. . .] In order for a State party to be able to attribute its failure to meet at least its minimum core obligations to a lack of available resources it must demonstrate that every effort has been made to use all resources that are at its disposition in an effort to satisfy, as a matter of priority, those minimum obligations." *Ibid.*

its resources toward counterterrorism, even if this means that it will have to deprioritise, and defund, programmes, however desirable, of lesser international legal importance.[13]

The Security Council has been very clear that it expects States to develop a potent and robust State apparatus to fight terrorism. Resolution 1617, for example, urges them to "allocate sufficient resources, including through international partnership, to meet the ongoing and direct threat posed by Al-Qaida, Usama bin Laden and the Taliban, and individuals, groups, undertakings and entities associated with them."[14] Becker argues that "[f]ormulating a distinct obligation to acquire counter-terrorism capacities is a natural corollary of the due diligence standard, especially in light of the capacity building focus of resolution 1373."[15]

In practice, many States have struggled to secure the factual capability legally required of them and upon which assessment of the due diligence principle in the counterterrorism context depends. According to the *Report by the Chair of the Counter-Terrorism Committee on the Problems Encountered in the Implementation of Security Council Resolution 1373 (2001)*, implementation of Security Council Resolution 1373 has suffered from a "lack of transparency of international financial transactions and the weakness of national legislation to prevent inflows of criminal money,"[16] reluctance by some States to incorporate the extradite or prosecute principle for

---

[13] That the Security Council has adopted so many counterterrorism rules, particularly since 11 September, each rule of which involves discrete and often demanding international legal obligations for States, means that it is now merely rhetorical to ask why the balance has been struck to prioritise, from the point of view of international legal obligation, fighting terrorism over fighting, for example, famine, drought, or AIDS in Africa. *See* Kathryn Sturman, *The AU Plan on Terrorism: Joining the Global War or Leading an African Battle?*, 11(4) AFR. SECURITY REV. 103, 103-04 (2002).

[14] S.C. Res. 1617, U.N. SCOR, at Preamble, U.N. Doc. S/RES/1617 (2005). *Cf.* International Law Commission, *Commentaries, Articles on Prevention of Transboundary Harm, supra* note 6, at 395 (stating that "[t]he operator of the activity is expected to bear the costs of prevention to the extent that he is responsible for the operation. The State of origin is also expected to undertake the necessary expenditure to put in place the administrative, financial and monitoring mechanisms referred to in article 5.").

[15] TAL BECKER, TERRORISM AND THE STATE: RETHINKING THE RULES OF STATE RESPONSIBILITY 145 (2006). According to Becker, "[t]o comply with the duty to prevent, States should be obligated to develop new technologies and tactics for coping with this kind of terrorism in a manner consistent with their legal obligations and commensurate both with their capacity and with the scale of the threat." *Ibid.* at 355.

[16] NOTE BY THE PRESIDENT OF THE SECURITY COUNCIL, U.N. SCOR, Annex, at 5, U.N. Doc. S/2004/70 (2004).

terrorist offences,[17] and the mere cosmetic engagement with international treaty regimes related to terrorism of those States that ratify such treaties but that fail to implement them.[18] Furthermore, according to *Uniting Against Terrorism: Recommendations for a Global Counter-Terrorism Strategy: Report of the Secretary-General,* State capacity to "protect soft targets and respond to attacks on them is highly uneven among Member States, and regrettably may be weakest where it is needed most,"[19] and too many States simply fail to report to the Security Council Committees that deal with terrorism as required by international law.[20]

Scholars and others have highlighted these deficiencies and the role of insufficient resources.[21] Bianchi, for example, asserts that the "decentralized character of the international community, the enormous discrepancies in terms of available resources by states as well as the occasional lack of political will to actually enforce anti-terror measures make the task of ensuring harmonization and effectiveness of regulation a fairly daunting one."[22] In its rawness and candour, however, International Court of Justice (ICJ) Judge Pieter Hendrik Kooijmans' separate opinion in *Armed Activities on the Territory of the Congo* may most persuasively describe the situation of too many States:

---

[17] *See ibid.* at 6.

[18] *See ibid.* at 6-7.

[19] UNITING AGAINST TERRORISM: RECOMMENDATIONS FOR A GLOBAL COUNTER-TERRORISM STRATEGY: REPORT OF THE SECRETARY-GENERAL, U.N. GAOR, at 17, U.N. Doc. A/60/825 (2006).

[20] *See ibid.* at 21-22. *See also UN Anti-Terrorism Committees Stress the Need for Greater Involvement by Member States*, U.N. NEWS SERVICE, 28 September 2006, *available at* http://www.un.org/apps/news/printnewsAr.asp?nid=20073; Andrea Bianchi, *Assessing the Effectiveness of the UN Security Council's Anti-Terrorism Measures: The Quest for Legitimacy and Cohesion,* 17(5) EUR. J. INT'L L. 881, 897-98 (2006).

[21] *See* Daniel Byman, *Passive Sponsors of Terrorism*, 47(4) SURVIVAL 117, 133 (2005-06) (referring to Pakistan and Saudi Arabia); Andrea Bianchi, *Security Council's Anti-Terror Resolutions and Their Implementation by Member States: An Overview,* 4(5) J. INT'L CRIM. JUST. 1044, 1070-71 (2006); Bianchi, *Assessing, supra* note 20, at 898; Statement by His Excellency Mr. Crispin Grey-Johnson, Ambassador and Permanent Representative of the Gambia to the United Nations, Chairman of the Group of the African States, Under Agenda Item 100 of the Sixth Committee, "Measures for the Elimination of International Terrorism," New York 2 (12 October 2006) (on file with author). According to Becker, "[f]or all the efforts of the CTC and other organizations to develop assistance programs and offer financial aid, counter-terrorism capacity is far from being a commodity that can be purchased 'off the shelf' at bargain prices. Lack of capacity may also stem from more widespread and systemic problems, such as civil unrest, poverty, limited territorial control and generally weak institutional structures." BECKER, *supra* note 15, at 145.

[22] Bianchi, *Assessing, supra* note 20, at 903.

> régimes under constant threat from armed movements often operating from the territory of neighbouring States, whose governments sometimes support such movements but often merely tolerate them since they do not have the means to control or repel them. The latter case is one where a government lacks power and consequently fails to exercise effectively its territorial authority; in short, there is a partial failure of State authority and such failure is badly concealed by the formal performance of State functions on the international level. Commitments entered into by governments unable to implement them are unworthy of reliance from the very start and hardly contribute to the creation of more stability.[23]

Clearly, this reveals formidable challenges that arise when attempting to square a demanding legal framework of counterterrorism norms with "failing" or "failed" States.[24]

Some States are more deficient in their factual capability than others, of course, and not all of these deficiencies can be explained away in terms of resource gaps. As Byman notes with specific reference to Saudi Arabia, "[c]apacity and regime priorities are intimately linked."[25] There are potentially-significant domestic political costs for some States if they use their State apparatus to counter terrorism to the extent that international law requires.[26] Becker refers to Saudi Arabia and Pakistan in this regard,[27] classifying these States as "mixed case[s] of compliance and toleration."[28]

Whatever the reasons for the deficiencies in many States' factual capability and the merits of the ways suggested to improve them so as to align them more fully with international legal norms,[29] States remain under an

---

[23] Armed Activities on the Territory of the Congo (*Congo* v. *Uganda*), 2005 I.C.J., at Para. 5 (Kooijmans, J., separate). *See* Noëlle Quénivet, *You Are the Weakest Link and We Will Help You!: The Comprehensive Strategy of the United Nations to Fight Terrorism,* 11(3) J. CONFLICT & SECURITY L. 371, 374 (2006) (asserting that "[t]errorist groups benefit not only from the globalisation and the opening of borders but also from the existence of States that encounter difficulties in assuming full control over their territory. In this context, the jump from a national to an international movement is even easier for such groups.").

[24] On these States, see Daniel Thürer, *The "Failed State" and International Law,* 81(836) INT'L REV. RED CROSS 731 (1999). *See also* JAMES CRAWFORD, THE CREATION OF STATES IN INTERNATIONAL LAW 719-23 (2nd ed. 2006).

[25] Byman, *supra* note 21, at 123.

[26] *See ibid.* at 128-29 (referring to Pakistan in this regard).

[27] *See* BECKER, *supra* note 15, at 247-48.

[28] *Ibid.* at 247.

[29] Byman presents a number of suggestions, such as the provision of military hardware and training, economic measures, and knowledge transfer. *See* Byman, *supra* note 21, at 138-39.

international legal obligation to develop a potent and robust State apparatus to fight terrorism. As Sturman bluntly notes with specific regard to African States, this is so "because the United Nations told them to. UN Security Council Resolution 1373 is mandatory and binding on all member states, whether or not they have the resources to comply."[30]

Given that States have experienced obstacles in meeting their counter-terrorism obligations, what can be concluded about the dynamic interrelationship of theory and practice upon which international law depends? It can be said that the factual incapability of many States effectively disembowels the rules of cohesion, dependability, and balance but that this need not necessarily preclude relevant actors from using legal language as a form of condemnation. Due diligence tests can be tweaked, reformulated and reargued, reconstituted to suit what are asserted to be new facts and circumstances.

Recall, for example, the due diligence test that the ICJ put forward in the *United States Diplomatic and Consular Staff in Tehran* (*Hostages*) case, that Iranian authorities:

> (a) were fully aware of their obligations under the conventions in force to take appropriate steps to protect the premises of the United States Embassy and its diplomatic and consular staff from any attack and from any infringement of their inviolability, and to ensure the security of such other persons as might be present on the said premises;
> (b) were fully aware, as a result of the appeals for help made by the United States Embassy, of the urgent need for action on their part;
> (c) had the means at their disposal to perform their obligations;
> (d) completely failed to comply with these obligations.[31]

A State that finds it difficult to secure the factual capability legally required of it in the counterterrorism context will argue that it cannot properly be held responsible for breaching an international obligation because it fails to satisfy the "means at their disposal to perform their obligations" element of the *Hostages* test. But what is the legal content of "means at their disposal

---

30 Sturman, *supra* note 13, at 104 (continuing by stating that, "[w]hile this is certainly a burden on many African states, it is also an opportunity to secure resources needed to fulfill their obligations.").

31 United States Diplomatic and Consular Staff in Tehran (Hostages) (*U.S.* v. *Iran*), 1980 I.C.J. 3, 32-33.

to perform their obligations"? Depending on who or what answers this question, whether it be a State or States or an international court or courts, "means at their disposal to perform their obligations" can be legally construed any which way, as being absent or actually or constructively shown, regardless of what contrarians think about the particular facts and circumstances.

In rendering judgment on these matters, there are grey areas and fine lines, negotiations to be had and horse-trading to be done. "The question of imputability," Dupuy and Hoss argue, "is sometimes difficult to distinguish from that of due diligence in the context of terrorism."[32] Cases of continuing terrorism can eventually tip the balance of State responsibility from mere breach of a due diligence obligation to attribution to the State of the terrorist acts themselves,[33] but there is ample fluidity and room for debate on particular facts and circumstances.[34]

This analysis need not necessarily, although it may, lead one to conclude that international law is a mere shibboleth or conspiracy of a mandarin class or cadre of philosopher kings adept at legal linguistics or, to quote former United States Ambassador to the United Nations John R. Bolton, that "[i]nternational law is not law; it is a series of political and moral arrangements that stand or fall on their own merits, and anything else is simply theology and superstition masquerading as law."[35] Ultimately, this depends on one's "perceptions," and these, in turn, depend on one's preferred hegemonic frame of reference, how one views, or chooses to view, the complex world in which we live.

---

[32] Dupuy & Hoss, *supra* note 1, at 236 (continuing by stating that, "as a general rule, one can assume that a certain degree of failure of compliance with due diligence obligations will lead to the attribution of terrorist acts to the state itself, and will then be treated as 'state terrorism' by other states."). Compare this with the distinction that the ICJ draws between the "obligation to prevent" and "complicity" within the context of the Genocide Convention. *See* Application of the Convention on the Prevention and Punishment of the Crime of Genocide, *supra* note 4, at Para. 432.

[33] *See* BECKER, *supra* note 15, at 335. Becker makes this assertion under his causation-based framework, but it is also applicable within a more conventional understanding of the law of State responsibility.

[34] "Justice may be blind, but the latitude given to States in the political arena, whether in the role of accuser or accused, is regularly tainted by non-legal considerations." *Ibid.* at 340. "Presumptions and burdens of proof can always be manipulated so as to make a claim's prospects of success rise or fall." *Ibid.* at 341.

[35] John R. Bolton, *Is There Really "Law" in International Affairs?,* 10(1) TRANSNAT'L L. & CONTEMP. PROBS. 1, 48 (2000).

BIBLIOGRAPHY

BIBLIOGRAPHY

I. Books (arranged alphabetically by author's/editor's surname)

Federico Andreu-Guzmán, International Commission of Jurists, Terrorism and Human Rights No. 2: New Challenges and Old Dangers (2003)
Hannah Arendt, The Origins of Totalitarianism (1966)
M. Cherif Bassiouni (ed.), 1-2 International Terrorism: A Compilation of U.N. Documents (1972-2001) (2002)
Tal Becker, Terrorism and the State: Rethinking the Rules of State Responsibility (2006)
P. W. Birnie & A. E. Boyle, International Law and the Environment (2nd ed. 2002)
Robert H. Bork, The Tempting of America: The Political Seduction of the Law (1990)
Ian Brownlie, Principles of Public International Law (6th ed. 2003)
Ian Brownlie, System of the Law of Nations: State Responsibility (Part I) (1983)
Clayborne Carson (ed.), The Autobiography of Martin Luther King, Jr. (1998)
Antonio Cassese, International Criminal Law (2003)
Antonio Cassese, International Law (2003)
Antonio Cassese, International Law (2nd ed. 2005)
James Crawford, The Creation of States in International Law (2nd ed. 2006)
Jacobus Gijsbertus de Beus, The Jurisprudence of the General Claims Commission, United States and Mexico Under the Convention of September 8, 1923 (1938)
Alan M. Dershowitz, Why Terrorism Works: Understanding the Threat, Responding to the Challenge (2002)
Yoram Dinstein, The Conduct of Hostilities under the Law of International Armed Conflict (2004)
Helen Duffy, The "War on Terror" and the Framework of International Law (2005)
Oriana Fallaci, The Force of Reason (2006)
Frantz Fanon, Toward the African Revolution (Haakon Chevalier trans., Pelican Bks. 1970)
Milton Friedman, Capitalism and Freedom (1967)
H.L.A. Hart, The Concept of Law (2nd ed. 1994)
Jean-Marie Henckaerts & Louise Doswald-Beck (eds.), International Committee of the Red Cross, Customary International Humanitarian Law: Volume 1: Rules (2005)
Tim Hillier, Sourcebook on Public International Law (1998)
Ayaan Hirsi Ali, The Caged Virgin: An Emancipation Proclamation for Women and Islam (2006)
Samuel P. Huntington, The Clash of Civilizations and the Remaking of World Order (2002)
Mark Kelly, Northern Ireland Human Rights Commission, A Practical Guide to the European Convention on Human Rights: The Right to Life (2005)
David Kennedy, Of War and Law (2006)
Henry Kissinger, Does America Need a Foreign Policy?: Toward a Diplomacy for the 21st Century (2001)

René Lefeber, Transboundary Environmental Interference and the Origin of State Liability (1996)
Tim May, Social Research: Issues, Methods and Process (3rd ed. 2001)
Guénaël Mettraux, International Crimes and the *Ad Hoc* Tribunals (2006)
H. B. Mishra, Terrorism: Threat to Peace and Harmony (1999)
Daniel Pipes, Militant Islam Reaches America (2002)
Sayyid Qutb, Milestones (2005)
Edward W. Said, Orientalism (2003)
William A. Schabas, An Introduction to the International Criminal Court (2001)
Alex P. Schmid & Janny de Graaf, Violence As Communication: Insurgent Terrorism and the Western News Media (1982)
Haile Sellassie I, My Life and Ethiopia's Progress: Volume One (Edward Ullendorff trans., Frontline Dist. Int'l, Inc. 2003)
Malcolm N. Shaw, International Law (5th ed. 2004)
Christian Tomuschat, Human Rights: Between Idealism and Realism (2003)
Max Weber, The Profession of Politics (Simona Draghici ed., 2000)
Paul Wilkinson, Terrorism and the Liberal State (2nd ed. 1986)
Liesbeth Zegveld, Accountability of Armed Opposition Groups in International Law (2002)
Howard Zinn, A People's History of the United States: 1492-Present (2003)

II. Articles (arranged alphabetically by author's surname)

Georges Abi-Saab, *The Proper Role of International Law in Combating Terrorism,* 1(1) Chin. J. Int'l L. 305 (2002)
Jean Allain, *The Legacy of Lockerbie: Judicial Review of Security Council Actions or the First Manifestation of "Terrorism" as a Threat to International Peace?,* 44(1) Indian J. Int'l L. 74 (2004)
Abdullahi Ahmed An-Na'im, *Islamic Ambivalence to Political Violence: Islamic Law and International Terrorism,* 31 Germ. Y.B. Int'l L. 307 (1988)
Aharon Barak, *A Judge on Judging: The Role of a Supreme Court in a Democracy,* 116(1) Harv. L. Rev. 16 (2002)
Robert P. Barnidge, Jr., *States' Due Diligence Obligations with Regard to International Non-State Terrorist Organizations Post-11 September 2001: The Heavy Burden That States Must Bear,* 16 Ir. Stud. Int'l Aff. 103 (2005)
M. Cherif Bassiouni, *A Functional Approach to "General Principles of International Law,"* 11(3) Mich. J. Int'l L. 768 (1990)
M. Cherif Bassiouni, *Legal Control of International Terrorism: A Policy-Oriented Assessment,* 43(1) Harv. Int'l L.J. 83 (2002)
M. Cherif Bassiouni, *The Regression of the Rule of Law Under the Guise of Combating Terrorism,* 76(1-2) Rev. Int'l Droit Pénal 17 (2005)
Andrea Bianchi, *Assessing the Effectiveness of the UN Security Council's Anti-Terrorism Measures: The Quest for Legitimacy and Cohesion,* 17(5) Eur. J. Int'l L. 881 (2006)
Andrea Bianchi, *Security Council's Anti-Terror Resolutions and Their Implementation by Member States: An Overview,* 4(5) J. Int'l Crim. Just. 1044 (2006)
Daniel Bodansky & John R. Crook, *Introduction and Overview,* 96(4) Am. J. Int'l L. 773 (2002)
John R. Bolton, *Is There Really "Law" in International Affairs?,* 10(1) Transnat'l L. & Contemp. Probs. 1 (2000)

Daniel Byman, *Passive Sponsors of Terrorism*, 47(4) SURVIVAL 117 (2005-06)
Colm Campbell, *Extradition to Northern Ireland: Prospects and Problems,* 52(5) MOD. L. REV. 585 (1989)
Andrea Carcano, *End of the Occupation in 2004?: The Status of the Multinational Force in Iraq After the Transfer of Sovereignty to the Interim Iraqi Government,* 11(1) J. CONFLICT & SECURITY L. 41 (2006)
Antonio Cassese, *Terrorism Is Also Disrupting Some Crucial Legal Categories of International Law,* 12(5) EUR. J. INT'L L. 993 (2001)
Hilary Charlesworth, *International Law: A Discipline of Crisis*, 65(3) MOD. L. REV. 377 (2002)
Christine Chinkin, *A Critique of the Public/Private Dimension,* 10(2) EUR. J. INT'L L. 387 (1999)
Luigi Condorelli, *The Imputability to States of Acts of International Terrorism,* 19 ISR. Y.B. H.R. 233 (1989)
Carsten Corino, *Environmental Due Diligence,* 9(4) EUR. ENVTL. L. REV. 120 (2000)
James Crawford, *Revising the Draft Articles on State Responsibility,* 10(2) EUR. J. INT'L L. 435 (1999)
James Crawford & Simon Olleson, *The Continuing Debate on a UN Convention on State Responsibility,* 54(4) INT'L & COMP. L.Q. 959 (2005)
John R. Crook, *Contemporary Practice of the United States Relating to International Law*, 100(4) AM. J. INT'L L. 918 (2006)
Anthony D'Amato, *On Consensus*, 8 CAN. Y.B. INT'L L. 104 (1970)
Anthony D'Amato, *Trashing Customary International Law*, 81 AM. J. INT'L L. 101 (1987)
Jayantha Dhanapala, *The United Nations' Response to 9/11*, 17(1-2) TERRORISM & POL. VIOLENCE 17 (2005)
Yoram Dinstein, *Terrorism as an International Crime,* 19 ISR. Y.B. H.R. 55 (1989)
Bertil Dunér, *Disregard for Security: The Human Rights Movement and 9/11,* 17(1-2) TERRORISM & POL. VIOLENCE 89 (2005)
Pierre-Marie Dupuy, *Reviewing the Difficulties of Codification: On Ago's Classification of Obligations of Means and Obligations of Result in Relation to State Responsibility,* 10(2) EUR. J. INT'L L. 371 (1999)
K. D. Ewing, *The Futility of the Human Rights Act*, PUB. L. 829 (Winter 2004)
Stephanie Farrior, *State Responsibility for Human Rights Abuses by Non-State Actors*, 1998 A.S.I.L. PROC. 299
Lee Feinstein & Anne-Marie Slaughter, *A Duty to Prevent*, 83(1) FOREIGN AFF. 136 (2004)
Joan Fitzpatrick, *Speaking Law to Power: The War Against Terrorism and Human Rights,* 14(2) EUR. J. INT'L L. 241 (2003)
Edward J. Flynn, *Counter-Terrorism and Human Rights: The View from the United Nations,* 1 EUR. HUM. RTS. L. REV. 29 (2005)
Thomas M. Franck, *The Power of Legitimacy and the Legitimacy of Power: International Law in an Age of Power Disequilibrium*, 100(1) AM. J. INT'L L. 88 (2006)
Barbara A. Frey, *Small Arms and Light Weapons: The Tools Used to Violate Human Rights*, (3) DISARMAMENT FORUM: HUMAN RIGHTS, HUMAN SECURITY AND DISARMAMENT 37 (2004)
Jörg Friedrichs, *Defining the International Public Enemy: The Political Struggle Behind the Legal Debate on International Terrorism*, 19(1) LEIDEN J. INT'L L. 69 (2006)
Hans-Peter Gasser, *Acts of Terror, "Terrorism" and International Humanitarian Law,* 84(847) INT'L REV. RED CROSS 547 (2002)
Andrea Gattini, *Smoking/No Smoking: Some Remarks on the Current Place of Fault in the ILC Draft Articles on State Responsibility,* 10(2) EUR. J. INT'L L. 397 (1999)

C.A. Gearty, *Terrorism and Human Rights,* 1 EUR. HUM. RTS. L. REV. 1 (2005)
Michael Glennon, *Does International Law Matter?*, 2004 A.S.I.L. PROC. 315
Michael J. Glennon, *How International Rules Die*, 93(3) GEO. L.J. 939 (2005)
Kennedy Graham, *The Security Council and Counterterrorism: Global and Regional Approaches to an Elusive Public Good,* 17(1-2) TERRORISM & POL. VIOLENCE 37 (2005)
Christopher Greenwood, *International Law and the "War Against Terrorism,"* 78(2) INT'L AFF. 301 (2002)
Gilbert Guillaume, *Terrorism and International Law,* 53(3) INT'L & COMP. L.Q. 537 (2004)
Günther Handl, *State Liability for Accidental Transnational Environmental Damage by Private Persons,* 74(3) AM. J. INT'L L. 525 (1980)
Hans-Joachim Heintze, *On the Relationship Between Human Rights Law Protection and International Humanitarian Law*, 86(856) INT'L REV. RED CROSS 789 (2004)
Jan Arno Hessbruegge, *The Historical Development of the Doctrines of Attribution and Due Diligence in International Law,* 36(2-3) N.Y.U. J. INT'L L. & POL. 265 (2004)
Yuji Iwasawa & Yumi Nishimura, *A Review of Japanese Legal Literature on State Responsibility, available at* http://www.lcil.cam.ac.uk/Media/ILCSR/rft/JapanRev.rtf (1999)
R.Y. Jennings, *The* Caroline *and McLeod Cases,* 32 AM. J. INT'L L. 82 (1938)
Jan Klabbers, *The Right to Be Taken Seriously: Self-Determination in International Law*, 28(1) HUM. RTS. Q. 186 (2006)
Martti Koskenniemi, *The Politics of International Law,* 1(1-2) EUR. J. INT'L L. 4 (1990)
Martti Koskenniemi, *The Fate of Public International Law: Between Technique and Politics,* 70(1) MOD. L. REV. 1 (2007)
Nico Krisch, *International Law in Times of Hegemony: Unequal Power and the Shaping of the International Legal Order*, 16(3) EUR. J. INT'L L. 369 (2005)
Luke T. Lee, *The Right to Compensation: Refugees and Countries of Asylum,* 80(3) AM. J. INT'L L. 532 (1986)
Ulf Linderfalk, *Is the Hierarchical Structure of Articles 31 and 32 of the Vienna Convention Real or Not?: Interpreting the Rules of Interpretation*, 54(1) NETH. INT'L L. REV. 133 (2007)
Noam Lubell, *Challenges in Applying Human Rights Law to Armed Conflict,* 87(860) INT'L REV. RED CROSS 737 (2005)
V.S. Mani, *Future Strategies in the War Against Terrorism and Proliferation of Weapons of Mass Destruction: An Indian Perception,* 44(2) INDIAN J. INT'L L. 221 (2004)
Thomas W. Merrill, *Golden Rules for Transboundary Pollution*, 46(5) DUKE L.J. 931 (1997)
David S. Mitchell, *The Prohibition of Rape in International Humanitarian Law as a Norm of* Jus Cogens: *Clarifying the Doctrine,* 15(2) DUKE J. COMP. & INT'L L. 219 (2005)
Gerald L. Neuman, *Humanitarian Law and Counterterrorist Force*, 14(2) EUR. J. INT'L L. 283 (2003)
André Nollkaemper, *Concurrence Between Individual Responsibility and State Responsibility in International Law,* 52(3) INT'L & COMP. L.Q. 615 (2003)
Jordan J. Paust, *Post-9/11 Overreaction and Fallacies Regarding War and Defense, Guantanamo, the Status of Persons, Treatment, Judicial Review of Detention, and Due Process in Military Commissions*, 79(4) NOTRE DAME L. REV. 1335 (2004)
Jelena Pejic, *Terrorist Acts and Groups: A Role for International Law?*, 75 BRIT. Y.B. INT'L L. 71 (2004)
Jarna Petman, *Evil and International Law*, 5(4) INT'L L. FORUM DROIT INT'L 236 (2003)
Toni Pfanner, *Asymmetrical Warfare from the Perspective of Humanitarian Law and Humanitarian Action*, 87(857) INT'L REV. RED CROSS 149 (2005)

Riccardo Pisillo Mazzeschi, *The Due Diligence Rule and the Nature of the International Responsibility of States,* 35 GERM. Y.B. INT'L L. 9 (1992)
Riccardo Pisillo Mazzeschi, *Reparation Claims by Individuals for State Breaches of Humanitarian Law and Human Rights: An Overview,* 1(2) J. INT'L CRIM. JUST. 339 (2003)
Eric A. Posner, *Terrorism and the Laws of War*, 5(2) CHI. J. INT'L L. 423 (2005)
Vincent-Joel Proulx, *Babysitting Terrorists: Should States Be Strictly Liable for Failing to Prevent Transborder Attacks?,* 23(3) BERKELEY J. INT'L L. 615 (2005)
Noëlle Quénivet, *You Are the Weakest Link and We Will Help You!: The Comprehensive Strategy of the United Nations to Fight Terrorism,* 11(3) J. CONFLICT & SECURITY L. 371 (2006)
Anthea Roberts, *Righting Wrongs or Wronging Rights?: The United States and Human Rights Post-September 11*, 15(4) EUR. J. INT'L L. 721 (2004)
Davis R. Robinson, *The Role of Politics in the Election and the Work of Judges of the International Court of Justice*, 2003 A.S.I.L. PROC. 277
Gabor Rona, *Interesting Times for International Humanitarian Law: Challenges from the "War on Terror,"* 27(2) FLETCHER FORUM WORLD AFF. 55 (2003)
Shabtai Rosenne, *State Responsibility:* Festina Lente, 75 BRIT. Y.B. INT'L L. 363 (2004)
Ben Saul, *Attempts to Define "Terrorism" in International Law*, 52(1) NETH. INT'L L. REV. 57 (2005)
Ben Saul, *Crimes and Prohibitions of "Terror" and "Terrorism" in Armed Conflict: 1919-2005*, 18(4) HUMANITÄRES VÖLKERRECHT 264 (2005)
Ben Saul, *Definition of "Terrorism" in the UN Security Council: 1985-2004,* 4(1) CHIN. J. INT'L L. 141 (2005)
Ben Saul, *The Legal Response of the League of Nations to Terrorism*, 4(1) J. INT'L CRIM. JUST. 78 (2006)
Michael P. Scharf, *Defining Terrorism as the Peace Time Equivalent of War Crimes: A Case of Too Much Convergence Between International Humanitarian Law and International Criminal Law?*, 7(2) ILSA J. INT'L & COMP. L. 391 (2001)
Alex P. Schmid, *Terrorism and Human Rights: A Perspective from the United Nations,* 17(1-2) TERRORISM & POL. VIOLENCE 25 (2005)
Jean-Marc Sorel, *Some Questions About the Definition of Terrorism and the Fight Against Its Financing,* 14(2) EUR. J. INT'L L. 365 (2003)
Gerald M. Steinberg, *The UN, the ICJ and the Separation Barrier: War by Other Means,* 38(1-2) ISR. L. REV. 331 (2005)
Kathryn Sturman, *The AU Plan on Terrorism: Joining the Global War or Leading an African Battle?,* 11(4) AFR. SECURITY REV. 103 (2002)
Surya P. Subedi, *The UN Response to International Terrorism in the Aftermath of the Terrorist Attacks in America and the Problem of the Definition of Terrorism in International Law,* 4(3) INT'L L. FORUM DROIT INT'L 159 (2002)
William H. Taft, Keynote Address, 21(2) AM. U. INT'L L. REV. 149 (2005)
Daniel Thürer, *The "Failed State" and International Law,* 81(836) INT'L REV. RED CROSS 731 (1999)
Stephen C. Vasciannie, *Bilateral Investment Treaties and Civil Strife: The AAPL/Sri Lanka Arbitration,* 39(3) NETH. INT'L L. REV. 332 (1992)
Colin Warbrick, *The European Response to Terrorism in an Age of Human Rights,* 15(5) EUR. J. INT'L L. 989 (2004)
Ruth Wedgwood, *Al Qaeda, Terrorism, and Military Commissions*, 96(2) AM. J. INT'L L. 328 (2002)

Edwin D. Williamson, *Realism and Legalism: Realism Versus Legalism in International Relations*, 2002 A.S.I.L. PROC. 262

Onuma Yasuaki, *A Transcivilizational Perspective on Global Legal Order in the Twenty-First Century: A Way to Overcome West-Centric and Judiciary-Centric Deficits in International Legal Thoughts,* 8(1) INT'L CMTY. L. REV. 29 (2006)

III. WORKS IN COLLECTIONS (arranged alphabetically by author's surname)

Philip Alston, *The "Not-a-Cat" Syndrome: Can the International Human Rights Regime Accommodate Non-State Actors,* in NON-STATE ACTORS AND HUMAN RIGHTS 3 (Philip Alston ed., 2005)

Susan Anderson, *When the Law Breaker Becomes the Law Maker*, in THE CHALLENGE OF CONFLICT: INTERNATIONAL LAW RESPONDS 413 (Ustinia Dolgopol & Judith Gardam eds., 2006)

Abdullahi Ahmed An-Na'im, *Upholding International Legality Against Islamic and American Jihad,* in WORLDS IN COLLISION: TERROR AND THE FUTURE OF GLOBAL ORDER 162 (Ken Booth & Tim Dunne eds., 2002)

Gaetano Arangio-Ruiz, *State Fault and the Forms and Degrees of International Responsibility: Questions of Attribution and Relevance,* in LE DROIT INTERNATIONAL AU SERVICE DE LA PAIX, DE LA JUSTICE ET DU DÉVELOPPEMENT 25 (Mélanges Michel Virally ed., 1991)

Benjamin R. Barber, *Democracy and Terror in the Era of Jihad vs. McWorld,* in WORLDS IN COLLISION: TERROR AND THE FUTURE OF GLOBAL ORDER 245 (Ken Booth & Tim Dunne eds., 2002)

M. Cherif Bassiouni, *Great Nations and Torture*, in THE TORTURE DEBATE IN AMERICA 256 (Karen J. Greenberg ed., 2006)

Andrea Bianchi, *Enforcing International Law Norms Against Terrorism: Achievements and Prospects,* in ENFORCING INTERNATIONAL LAW NORMS AGAINST TERRORISM 491 (Andrea Bianchi ed., 2004)

Tore Bjørgo, *Introduction*, in ROOT CAUSES OF TERRORISM: MYTHS, REALITY AND WAYS FORWARD 1 (Tore Bjørgo ed., 2005)

Ladan Boroumand & Roya Boroumand, *Terror, Islam, and Democracy*, in UNDERSTANDING THE WAR ON TERROR 134 (James F. Hoge, Jr., & Gideon Rose eds., 2005)

Ian Brownlie, *State Responsibility and the International Court of Justice,* in ISSUES OF STATE RESPONSIBILITY BEFORE INTERNATIONAL JUDICIAL INSTITUTIONS 11 (Malgosia Fitzmaurice & Dan Sarooshi eds., 2004)

Antônio Augusto Cançado Trindade, *Complementarity Between State Responsibility and Individual Responsibility for Grave Violations of Human Rights: The Crime of State Revisited,* in INTERNATIONAL RESPONSIBILITY TODAY 253 (Maurizio Ragazzi ed., 2005)

E. H. CARR, *The Historian and His Facts,* in WHAT IS HISTORY?: THE GEORGE MACAULAY TREVELYAN LECTURES DELIVERED IN THE UNIVERSITY OF CAMBRIDGE JANUARY-MARCH 1961 7 (1970)

Lee A. Casey & David B. Rivkin, Jr., *Rethinking the Geneva Conventions*, in THE TORTURE DEBATE IN AMERICA 203 (Karen J. Greenberg ed., 2006)

Antonio Cassese, *International Criminal Law*, in INTERNATIONAL LAW 721 (Malcolm D. Evans ed., 2003)

Noam Chomsky, *International Terrorism: Image and Reality,* in WESTERN STATE TERRORISM 12 (Alexander George ed., 1991)

Noam Chomsky, *Is the War on Terrorism Winnable?*, in 9-11 23 (2002)

Noam Chomsky, *Civilizations East and West*, in 9-11 71 (2002)

Council of Europe, *Guidelines of the Committee of Ministers of the Council of Europe on Human Rights and the Fight Against Terrorism,* adopted 11 July 2002, in COUNCIL OF EUROPE, HUMAN RIGHTS AND THE FIGHT AGAINST TERRORISM: THE COUNCIL OF EUROPE GUIDELINES 7 (2005)

James Crawford, *Introduction*, in JAMES CRAWFORD, THE INTERNATIONAL LAW COMMISSION'S ARTICLES ON STATE RESPONSIBILITY: INTRODUCTION, TEXT AND COMMENTARIES 1 (2003)

James Crawford & Simon Olleson, *The Nature and Forms of International Responsibility,* in INTERNATIONAL LAW 445 (Malcolm D. Evans ed., 2003)

Terry Davis, *Preface*, in COUNCIL OF EUROPE, HUMAN RIGHTS AND THE FIGHT AGAINST TERRORISM: THE COUNCIL OF EUROPE GUIDELINES 5 (2005)

Olivier de Schutter, *The Accountability of Multinationals for Human Rights Violations in European Law,* in NON-STATE ACTORS AND HUMAN RIGHTS 227 (Philip Alston ed., 2005)

Mireille Delmas-Marty, *The ICC and the Interaction of International and National Legal Systems*, in 2 THE ROME STATUTE OF THE INTERNATIONAL CRIMINAL COURT: A COMMENTARY 1915 (Antonio Cassese et al. eds., 2002)

Yoram Dinstein, *Ius Ad Bellum Aspects of the "War on Terrorism,"* in TERRORISM AND THE MILITARY: INTERNATIONAL LEGAL IMPLICATIONS 13 (Wybo P. Heere ed., 2003)

Yoram Dinstein, *Collateral Damage and the Principle of Proportionality*, in NEW WARS, NEW LAWS?: APPLYING THE LAWS OF WAR IN 21ST CENTURY CONFLICTS 211 (David Wippman & Matthew Evangelista eds., 2005)

John Dugard, *The Problem of the Definition of Terrorism in International Law,* in SEPTEMBER 11, 2001: A TURNING POINT IN INTERNATIONAL AND DOMESTIC LAW? 187 (Paul Eden & Thérèse O'Donnell eds., 2005)

Pierre Dupuy, *Due Diligence in the International Law of Liability*, in LEGAL ASPECTS OF TRANSFRONTIER POLLUTION 369 (Organisation for Economic Co-operation and Development ed., 1977)

Pierre Dupuy, *International Liability of States for Damage Caused by Transfrontier Pollution,* in LEGAL ASPECTS OF TRANSFRONTIER POLLUTION 345 (Organisation for Economic Co-operation and Development ed., 1977)

Pierre-Marie Dupuy, *State Sponsors of Terrorism: Issues of International Responsibility,* in ENFORCING INTERNATIONAL LAW NORMS AGAINST TERRORISM 3 (Andrea Bianchi ed., 2004)

Pierre-Marie Dupuy & Cristina Hoss, Trail Smelter *and Terrorism: International Mechanisms to Combat Transboundary Harm*, in TRANSBOUNDARY HARM IN INTERNATIONAL LAW: LESSONS FROM THE *TRAIL SMELTER* ARBITRATION 225 (Rebecca M. Bratspies & Russell A. Miller eds., 2006)

Richard Falk, *Human Rights: A Descending Spiral,* in HUMAN RIGHTS IN THE "WAR ON TERROR" 225 (Richard Ashby Wilson ed., 2005)

Bardo Fassbender, *The UN Security Council and International Terrorism,* in ENFORCING INTERNATIONAL LAW NORMS AGAINST TERRORISM 83 (Andrea Bianchi ed., 2004)

Gerald G. Fitzmaurice, *Some Problems Regarding the Formal Sources of International Law,* in SYMBOLAE VERZIJL: PRÉSENTÉES AU PROFESSEUR J. H. W. VERZIJL À L'OCCASION DE SON LXX-IÈME ANNIVERSAIRE 153 (1958)

Maurice Flory, *International Law: An Instrument to Combat Terrorism,* in TERRORISM AND INTERNATIONAL LAW 30 (Rosalyn Higgins & Maurice Flory eds., 1997)

F.V. García Amador, *State Responsibility: Some New Problems,* in 94(2) ACADÉMIE DE DROIT INTERNATIONAL DE LA HAYE: RECUEIL DES COURS 365 (1958)

Richard Goldstone, *The Tension Between Combating Terrorism and Protecting Civil Liberties,* in HUMAN RIGHTS IN THE "WAR ON TERROR" 157 (Richard Ashby Wilson ed., 2005)

Guy S. Goodwin-Gill, *State Responsibility and the "Good Faith" Obligation in International Law,* in ISSUES OF STATE RESPONSIBILITY BEFORE INTERNATIONAL JUDICIAL INSTITUTIONS 75 (Malgosia Fitzmaurice & Dan Sarooshi eds., 2004)

Konstanz Hailbronner & Eckart Klein, *The General Assembly: Functions and Powers: Articles 10-12*, in 1 THE CHARTER OF THE UNITED NATIONS: A COMMENTARY 257 (Bruno Simma et al. eds., 2nd ed. 2002)

Günther Handl, Trail Smelter *in Contemporary International Environmental Law: Its Relevance in the Nuclear Energy Context*, in TRANSBOUNDARY HARM IN INTERNATIONAL LAW: LESSONS FROM THE *TRAIL SMELTER* ARBITRATION 125 (Rebecca M. Bratspies & Russell A. Miller eds., 2006)

Rosalyn Higgins, *Oiling the Wheels of International Law: Equity and Proportionality*, in PROBLEMS AND PROCESS: INTERNATIONAL LAW AND HOW WE USE IT 219 (1994)

Rosalyn Higgins, *Sources of International Law: Provenance and Problems*, in PROBLEMS AND PROCESS: INTERNATIONAL LAW AND HOW WE USE IT 17 (1994)

Rosalyn Higgins, *The General International Law of Terrorism,* in TERRORISM AND INTERNATIONAL LAW 13 (Rosalyn Higgins & Maurice Flory eds., 1997)

Rosalyn Higgins, *Issues of State Responsibility Before the International Court of Justice,* in ISSUES OF STATE RESPONSIBILITY BEFORE INTERNATIONAL JUDICIAL INSTITUTIONS 1 (Malgosia Fitzmaurice & Dan Sarooshi eds., 2004)

Patrice Jean, *The Jurisprudence of the European Commission and Court of Human Rights with Regard to Terrorism,* in TERRORISM AND INTERNATIONAL LAW 217 (Rosalyn Higgins & Maurice Flory eds., 1997)

Shri D.R. Kaarthikeyan, *Root Causes of Terrorism?: A Case Study of the Tamil Insurgency and the LTTE*, in ROOT CAUSES OF TERRORISM: MYTHS, REALITY AND WAYS FORWARD 131 (Tore Bjørgo ed., 2005)

David Kairys, *Legal Reasoning*, in THE POLITICS OF LAW: A PROGRESSIVE CRITIQUE 11 (David Kairys ed., 1982)

Duncan Kennedy, *Legal Education as Training for Hierarchy*, in THE POLITICS OF LAW: A PROGRESSIVE CRITIQUE 40 (David Kairys ed., 1982)

Jan Klabbers, *Straddling Law and Politics: Judicial Review in International Law,* in TOWARDS WORLD CONSTITUTIONALISM: ISSUES IN THE LEGAL ORDERING OF THE WORLD COMMUNITY 809 (Ronald St. John Macdonald & Douglas M. Johnston eds., 2005)

Robert Kolb, *The Exercise of Criminal Jurisdiction Over International Terrorists,* in ENFORCING INTERNATIONAL LAW NORMS AGAINST TERRORISM 227 (Andrea Bianchi ed., 2004)

Martti Koskenniemi, *What Is International Law For?,* in INTERNATIONAL LAW 89 (Malcolm D. Evans ed., 2003)

Walter Laqueur, *Left, Right, and Beyond – The Changing Face of Terror,* in UNDERSTANDING THE WAR ON TERROR 154 (James F. Hoge, Jr., & Gideon Rose eds., 2005)

C.L. Lim, *The Question of a Generic Definition of Terrorism Under General International Law,* in GLOBAL ANTI-TERRORISM LAW AND POLICY 37 (Victor V. Ramraj et al. eds., 2005)

Jitka Malečková, *Impoverished Terrorists: Stereotype or Reality?*, in ROOT CAUSES OF TERRORISM: MYTHS, REALITY AND WAYS FORWARD 33 (Tore Bjørgo ed., 2005)

Rama Mani, *The Root Causes of Terrorism and Conflict Prevention,* in TERRORISM AND THE UN: BEFORE AND AFTER SEPTEMBER 11 219 (Jane Boulden & Thomas G. Weiss eds., 2004)

V.S. Mani, *Centrifugal and Centripetal Tendencies in the International System: Some Reflections,* in TOWARDS WORLD CONSTITUTIONALISM: ISSUES IN THE LEGAL ORDERING OF THE WORLD COMMUNITY 241 (Ronald St. John Macdonald & Douglas M. Johnston eds., 2005)

David Meltzer, *Al Qa'ida: Terrorists or Irregulars?,* in LAW AFTER GROUND ZERO 71 (John Strawson ed., 2002)
Hermann Mosler & Karin Oellers-Frahm, *The International Court of Justice*, in 2 THE CHARTER OF THE UNITED NATIONS: A COMMENTARY 1139 (Bruno Simma et al. eds., 2nd ed. 2002)
Benjamin Netanyahu, *Defining Terrorism,* in TERRORISM: HOW THE WEST CAN WIN 7 (Benjamin Netanyahu ed., 1986)
Benzion Netanyahu, *Terrorists and Freedom Fighters,* in TERRORISM: HOW THE WEST CAN WIN 25 (Benjamin Netanyahu ed., 1986)
Math Noortmann, *Non-State Actors in International Law,* in NON-STATE ACTORS IN INTERNATIONAL RELATIONS 59 (Bas Arts et al. eds., 2001)
Organisation for Economic Co-operation and Development Secretariat, *Observations on the Concept of the International Responsibility of States in Relation to the Protection of the Environment,* in LEGAL ASPECTS OF TRANSFRONTIER POLLUTION 380 (Organisation for Economic Co-operation and Development ed., 1977)
George Orwell, *The Lion and the Unicorn,* in WHY I WRITE 11 (2004)
George Orwell, *Why I Write,* in WHY I WRITE 1 (2004)
Riccardo Pisillo Mazzeschi, *Forms of International Responsibility for Environmental Harm*, in INTERNATIONAL RESPONSIBILITY FOR ENVIRONMENTAL HARM 15 (Francesco Francioni & Tullio Scovazzi eds., 1991)
Riccardo Pisillo Mazzeschi, *International Obligations to Provide for Reparation Claims?,* in STATE RESPONSIBILITY AND THE INDIVIDUAL: REPARATION IN INSTANCES OF GRAVE VIOLATIONS OF HUMAN RIGHTS 149 (Albrecht Randelzhofer & Christian Tomuschat eds., 1999)
Bertrand G. Ramcharan, *Terrorism and Non-State Organizations,* in TOWARDS WORLD CONSTITUTIONALISM: ISSUES IN THE LEGAL ORDERING OF THE WORLD COMMUNITY 681 (Ronald St. John Macdonald & Douglas M. Johnston eds., 2005)
Bertrand G. Ramcharan, *The United Nations and New Threats, Challenges and Change: The Report of the High-Level Panel,* in TOWARDS WORLD CONSTITUTIONALISM: ISSUES IN THE LEGAL ORDERING OF THE WORLD COMMUNITY 911 (Ronald St. John Macdonald & Douglas M. Johnston eds., 2005)
August Reinisch, *The Changing International Legal Framework for Dealing with Non-State Actors,* in NON-STATE ACTORS AND HUMAN RIGHTS 37 (Philip Alston ed., 2005)
Christian Reus-Smit, *Introduction*, in THE POLITICS OF INTERNATIONAL LAW 1 (Christian Reus-Smit ed., 2004)
Condoleezza Rice, *The President's National Security Strategy,* in THE NEOCON READER 79 (Irwin Stelzer ed., 2004)
Mary Robinson, *Connecting Human Rights, Human Development, and Human Security,* in HUMAN RIGHTS IN THE "WAR ON TERROR" 308 (Richard Ashby Wilson ed., 2005)
Patrick Robinson, *Jurisdiction* Ratione Materiae: *The Missing Crimes*, in 1 THE ROME STATUTE OF THE INTERNATIONAL CRIMINAL COURT: A COMMENTARY 497 (Antonio Cassese et al. eds., 2002)
EDWARD W. SAID, *Representations of the Intellectual*, in REPRESENTATIONS OF THE INTELLECTUAL: THE 1993 REITH LECTURES 3 (1996)
Oscar Schachter, *The Lawful Use of Force by a State Against Terrorists in Another Country,* in TERRORISM & POLITICAL VIOLENCE: LIMITS & POSSIBILITIES OF LEGAL CONTROL 243 (Henry H. Han ed., 1993)
Rudi Troosters, *The European Union Framework Decision of 13th June 2002 on Combating Terrorism,* in EUROPEAN COOPERATION AGAINST TERRORISM: CONFERENCE PROCEEDINGS 67 (2004)

V. Vijayakumar, *Legal and Institutional Responses to Terrorism in India,* in GLOBAL ANTI-TERRORISM LAW AND POLICY 351 (Victor V. Ramraj et al. eds., 2005)

Ruth Wedgwood, *Countering Catastrophic Terrorism: An American View,* in ENFORCING INTERNATIONAL LAW NORMS AGAINST TERRORISM 103 (Andrea Bianchi ed., 2004)

Ruth Wedgwood, *The Multinational Action in Iraq and International Law,* in THE IRAQ CRISIS AND WORLD ORDER: STRUCTURAL, INSTITUTIONAL AND NORMATIVE CHALLENGES 413 (Ramesh Thakur & Waheguru Pal Singh Sidhu eds., 2006)

IV. REPORTS (arranged alphabetically by title)

A MORE SECURE WORLD: OUR SHARED RESPONSIBILITY: REPORT OF THE SECRETARY-GENERAL'S HIGH-LEVEL PANEL ON THREATS, CHALLENGES, AND CHANGE (2004)

DIGEST OF JURISPRUDENCE OF THE UNITED NATIONS AND REGIONAL ORGANIZATIONS ON THE PROTECTION OF HUMAN RIGHTS WHILE COUNTERING TERRORISM, OFFICE OF THE UNITED NATIONS HIGH COMMISSIONER FOR HUMAN RIGHTS, U.N. Sales No. HR/PUB/03/1 (2003)

DIGEST OF THE DECISIONS OF INTERNATIONAL TRIBUNALS RELATING TO STATE RESPONSIBILITY, PREPARED BY THE SECRETARIAT, U.N. Doc. A/CN.4/169 (1964), in 2 Y.B. Int'l L. Comm'n 132, U.N. Doc. A/CN.4/SER.A/1964/ADD.1 (1964)

EXCERPT OF THE REPORT PREPARED BY THE INTERNATIONAL COMMITTEE OF THE RED CROSS FOR THE 28TH INTERNATIONAL CONFERENCE OF THE RED CROSS AND RED CRESCENT, INTERNATIONAL HUMANITARIAN LAW AND THE CHALLENGES OF CONTEMPORARY ARMED CONFLICTS, Geneva, December 2003, 86(853) INT'L REV. RED CROSS 213 (2004)

EXTRACT FROM THE REPORT OF THE SECRETARY-GENERAL ON MEASURES TO ELIMINATE INTERNATIONAL TERRORISM (DOC. A/58/116), AS UPDATED ON 31 DECEMBER 2003

FRAGMENTATION OF INTERNATIONAL LAW: DIFFICULTIES ARISING FROM THE DIVERSIFICATION AND EXPANSION OF INTERNATIONAL LAW: REPORT OF THE STUDY GROUP OF THE INTERNATIONAL LAW COMMISSION, FINALIZED BY MARTTI KOSKENNIEMI, U.N. GAOR, U.N. Doc. A/CN.4/L.682 (2006)

GENERAL COMMENT NUMBER 3, in COMMITTEE ON ECONOMIC, SOCIAL AND CULTURAL RIGHTS: REPORT ON THE FIFTH SESSION, COMMITTEE ON ECONOMIC, SOCIAL AND CULTURAL RIGHTS (26 NOVEMBER-14 DECEMBER 1990), U.N. ESCOR, Annex III, 83 U.N. Doc. E/1991/23 E/C.12/1990/8 Supp. No. 3 (1991)

IN LARGER FREEDOM: TOWARDS DEVELOPMENT, SECURITY AND HUMAN RIGHTS FOR ALL: REPORT OF THE SECRETARY-GENERAL, U.N. GAOR, U.N. Doc. A/59/2005 (2005)

LETTER DATED 3 MARCH 2003 FROM THE CHAIRMAN OF THE SECURITY COUNCIL COMMITTEE ESTABLISHED PURSUANT TO RESOLUTION 1373 (2001) CONCERNING COUNTER-TERRORISM ADDRESSED TO THE PRESIDENT OF THE SECURITY COUNCIL, U.N. SCOR, U.N. Doc. S/2003/266 (2003)

LETTER DATED 3 FEBRUARY 2005 FROM THE CHAIRMAN OF THE SECURITY COUNCIL COMMITTEE ESTABLISHED PURSUANT TO RESOLUTION 1373 (2001) CONCERNING COUNTER-TERRORISM ADDRESSED TO THE PRESIDENT OF THE SECURITY COUNCIL, U.N. SCOR, U.N. Doc. S/2005/87 (2005)

LETTER DATED 3 AUGUST 2005 FROM THE CHAIRMAN OF THE SIXTH COMMITTEE ADDRESSED TO THE PRESIDENT OF THE GENERAL ASSEMBLY, U.N. GAOR, U.N. Doc. A/59/894 (2005)

NOTE BY THE PRESIDENT OF THE SECURITY COUNCIL, U.N. SCOR, U.N. Doc. S/2004/70 (2004)

NOTE VENABLE DATED 14 AUGUST 2002 FROM THE CHAIRMAN OF THE SECURITY COUNCIL COMMITTEE ESTABLISHED PURSUANT TO RESOLUTION 1373 (2001) CONCERNING COUNTER-TERRORISM ADDRESSED TO THE PRESIDENT OF THE SECURITY COUNCIL, U.N. SCOR, U.N. Doc. S/2002/943 (2002)

PALESTINIAN CENTRE FOR HUMAN RIGHTS, SECURING THE WALL FROM INTERNATIONAL LAW: AN INITIAL RESPONSE TO THE ISRAELI STATE AUTHORITY, *available at* http://www.pchrgaza.org/Interventions/Securing%20the%20Wall.pdf (2005)

PROMOTION AND PROTECTION OF HUMAN RIGHTS: PROTECTION OF HUMAN RIGHTS AND FUNDAMENTAL FREEDOMS WHILE COUNTERING TERRORISM: REPORT OF THE HIGH COMMISSIONER FOR HUMAN RIGHTS, U.N. ESCOR, U.N. Doc. E/CN.4/2005/100 (2004)

PROTECTING HUMAN RIGHTS AND FUNDAMENTAL FREEDOMS WHILE COUNTERING TERRORISM: REPORT OF THE SECRETARY-GENERAL, U.N. GAOR, U.N. Doc. A/60/374 (2005)

REPLY OF THE GOVERNMENT OF THE UNITED STATES OF AMERICA TO THE REPORT OF THE FIVE UNCHR SPECIAL RAPPORTEURS ON DETAINEES IN GUANTANAMO BAY, CUBA, 45(3) I.L.M. 742 (2006)

REPORT OF THE AD HOC COMMITTEE ESTABLISHED BY GENERAL ASSEMBLY RESOLUTION 51/210 OF 17 DECEMBER 1996: EIGHTH SESSION (28 JUNE-2 JULY 2004), U.N. GAOR, U.N. Doc. A/59/37 (2004)

REPORT OF THE AD HOC COMMITTEE ESTABLISHED BY GENERAL ASSEMBLY RESOLUTION 51/210 OF 17 DECEMBER 1996: NINTH SESSION (28 MARCH-1 APRIL 2005), U.N. GAOR, U.N. Doc. A/60/37 (2005)

REPORT OF THE AD HOC COMMITTEE ESTABLISHED BY GENERAL ASSEMBLY RESOLUTION 51/210 OF 17 DECEMBER 1996: TENTH SESSION (27 FEBRUARY-3 MARCH 2006), U.N. GAOR, U.N. Doc. A/61/37 (2006)

REPORT OF THE SPECIAL RAPPORTEUR ON THE SITUATION OF HUMAN RIGHTS IN THE PALESTINIAN TERRITORIES OCCUPIED SINCE 1967, U.N. GAOR, U.N. Doc. A/HRC/2/5 (2006)

SITUATION OF DETAINEES AT GUANTÁNAMO BAY, U.N. ESCOR, U.N. Doc. Future E/CN.4/2006/120 (2006)

SPECIFIC HUMAN RIGHTS ISSUES: NEW PRIORITIES, IN PARTICULAR TERRORISM AND COUNTER-TERRORISM: TERRORISM AND HUMAN RIGHTS: FINAL REPORT OF THE SPECIAL RAPPORTEUR, KALLIOPI K. KOUFA, U.N. ESCOR, U.N. Doc. E/CN.4/Sub.2/2004/40 (2004)

THE IRAQ STUDY GROUP REPORT, *available at* http://www.usip.org/isg/iraq_study_group_report/report/1206/iraq_study_group_report.pdf (2006)

THE WHITE HOUSE, THE NATIONAL SECURITY STRATEGY OF THE UNITED STATES OF AMERICA (2002)

THE RESPONSIBILITY TO PROTECT: REPORT OF THE INTERNATIONAL COMMISSION ON INTERVENTION AND STATE SOVEREIGNTY, INTERNATIONAL COMMISSION ON INTERVENTION AND STATE SOVEREIGNTY, *available at* http://www.iciss.ca/pdf/Commission-Report.pdf (2001)

TRUTH AND RECONCILIATION COMMISSION OF SOUTH AFRICA REPORT, *available at* http://www.info.gov.za/otherdocs/2003/trc/rep.pdf (released 21 March 2003)

UNDER THE GUISE OF SECURITY: ROUTING THE SEPARATION BARRIER TO ENABLE THE EXPANSION OF ISRAELI SETTLEMENTS IN THE WEST BANK, BIMKOM & B'TSELEM, *available at* http://www.btselem.org/Download/200512_Under_the_Guise_of_Security_eng.pdf (2005)

UNITING AGAINST TERRORISM: RECOMMENDATIONS FOR A GLOBAL COUNTER-TERRORISM STRATEGY: REPORT OF THE SECRETARY-GENERAL, U.N. GAOR, U.N. Doc. A/60/825 (2006)

V. ENTRIES IN ENCYCLOPEDIA (arranged alphabetically by author's surname)

Mohammed Bedjaoui, *Responsibility of States: Fault and Strict Liability,* in 10 ENCYCLOPEDIA OF PUBLIC INTERNATIONAL LAW 358 (1987)

Horst Blomeyer-Bartenstein, *Due Diligence,* in 10 ENCYCLOPEDIA OF PUBLIC INTERNATIONAL LAW 138 (1987)

Kevin J. Madders, *Trail Smelter Arbitration,* in 2 ENCYCLOPEDIA OF PUBLIC INTERNATIONAL LAW 276 (1981)

Giuseppe Sperduti, *Responsibility of States for Activities of Private Law Persons,* in 10 ENCYCLOPEDIA OF PUBLIC INTERNATIONAL LAW 373 (1987)

Henn-Jüri Uibopuu, *Wars of National Liberation,* in 4 ENCYCLOPEDIA OF PUBLIC INTERNATIONAL LAW 343 (1982)

Rüdiger Wolfrum, *Internationally Wrongful Acts,* in 10 ENCYCLOPEDIA OF PUBLIC INTERNATIONAL LAW 271 (1987)

VI. NEWSPAPER ARTICLES AND MISCELLANEOUS (arranged alphabetically by author's surname)

How Zarqawi Was Found and Killed, BBC NEWS, *available at* http://news.bbc.co.uk/2/hi/middle_east/5060468.stm (last updated 9 June 2006)

Human Rights, BBC SUNDAY AM, BBC NEWS, *available at* http://news.bbc.co.uk/2/hi/programmes/how_euro_are_you/4769979.stm (last updated 14 May 2006)

Uproar at Syrian Cartoon Protests, BBC NEWS, 5 February 2006, *available at* http://news.bbc.co.uk/go/pr/fr/-/1/hi/world/middle_east/4682388.stm

David Brooks, *Savagery's Stranglehold*, N.Y. TIMES, 8 June 2006

David Brooks, *Trading Cricket for Jihad,* N.Y. TIMES, 4 August 2005

Traci Carl, *Iran Leader Courts Latin American Allies*, N.Y. SUN, 15 January 2007, *available at* http://hosted.ap.org/dynamic/stories/N/NICARAGUA_IRAN?SITE=NYNSN&SECTION=HOME&TEMPLATE=DEFAULT

Sara A. Carter, *Of Special Interest: Links Between Illegal Immigration, Terrorism, Drug Trade Worry U.S. Officials*, SAN BERNARDINO SUN, 29 December 2006, *available at* http://www.sbsun.com/portlet/article/html/fragments/print_article.jsp?articleId=4917114&siteId=208

China Rejects Japan's Demand for Apology, CBC NEWS, 17 April 2005, *available at* http://www.cbc.ca/storyview/MSN/world/national/2005/04/17/china-japan050417.html

Alan M. Dershowitz, *The Abuse Excuse: Zacarias Moussaoui's Lawyers Float the "Impoverished French Muslim Syndrome,"* SLATE, 20 April 2006, *available at* http://www.slate.com/id/2140262

Distinctions Between Security Council Committees Dealing with Terrorism (1267 Committee and Counter-Terrorism Committee), Press Release SC/7827, 28 July 2003, *available at* http://www.un.org/News/Press/docs/2003/sc7827.doc.htm

Thomas L. Friedman, *Muslims in Danger,* N.Y. TIMES, 9 July 2005

Conor Gearty, *What is Terror?,* THE TIMES, 9 March 1991

HUMAN RIGHTS WATCH, *Human Rights Watch World Report 2006: U.S. Policy of Abuse Undermines Rights Worldwide,* 18 January 2006, *available at* http://hrw.org/english/docs/2006/01/13/global12428_txt.htm

Iranian Envoy Criticizes Ineffective Attitude of SC, ISLAMIC REPUBLIC NEWS AGENCY, 13 December 2006, *available at* http://www.irna.com/index2.php?option=com_news&task=print&code=0612130850140221&Itemid=&lang=en

Israel Ministry of Foreign Affairs, *Israel's Anti-Terrorist Fence: The Anti-Terrorist Fence – An Overview*, *available at* http://securityfence.mfa.gov.il/mfm/Data/48152.doc (last visited 12 April 2007)

Israel Ministry of Foreign Affairs, *Saving Lives: Israel's Anti-Terrorist Fence – Answers to Questions*, *available at* http://www.mfa.gov.il/mfa/mfaarchive/2000_2009/2003/11/saving%20lives-%20israel-s%20anti-terrorist%20fence%20-%20answ (1 January 2004)

Israel Ministry of Foreign Affairs, *2005 Terrorism Review*, *available at* http://www.mfa.gov.il/MFA/Terrorism-+Obstacle+to+Peace/Terrorism+and+Islamic+Fundamentalism-/2005+Terrorism+Review.htm (2 January 2006)

Tarik Kafala & Martin Asser, *Analysis: Palestinian Suicide Attacks,* BBC NEWS, *available at* http://news.bbc.co.uk/2/hi/middle_east/3256858.stm (last updated 17 April 2006)

Irene Khan, AMNESTY INTERNATIONAL, *Foreword, available at* http://web.amnesty.org/web/web.nsf/print/4C6D9C974BE73CA880256FE7005A49C7 (last visited 12 April 2007)

Charles Krauthammer, *The Legacy of Ariel Sharon: What's Ahead for the State of Israel?: Sharon Put Israel on a Strategic Path out of the Wreckage of the Post-Oslo World,* CHI. TRIB., 9 January 2006

Alix Kroeger, *New Challenges Strain EU-US Ties*, BBC NEWS, 1 June 2006, *available at* http://news.bbc.co.uk/go/pr/fr/-/1/hi/world/europe/5036282.stm

Lateline: Bush Criticised for "Confused" Middle East Goals: Noam Chomsky Interviewed by Tony Jones, 8 April 2002, *available at* http://www.chomsky.info/interviews/20020408.htm

Julian Lindley-French, *The Use of Force: Western Military Power Is in Crisis*, INT'L HERALD TRIB., 26-27 August 2006

Irshad Manji, *How I Learned to Love the Wall*, N.Y. TIMES, 18 March 2006

Ministry of Defence, *Israel's Security Fence: Questions and Answers*, *available at* http://www.securityfence.mod.gov.il/Pages/ENG/questions.htm (last updated 22 February 2004)

Bhikhu Parekh, *Why Terror?*, PROSPECT, April 2004

Daniel Pipes, *They're Terrorists – Not Activists,* N.Y. SUN, 7 September 2004

Steven Plaut, *The Anti-Terror Campaign That Succeeded*, JEWISH PRESS, 27 June 2007, *available at* http://www.jewishpress.com/page.do/21967/The_Anti%2DTerror_Campaign_That_Succeeded.html

David B. Rivkin, Jr., & Lee A. Casey, *Hamdan: What the Ruling Says – And What It Doesn't Say*, WALL ST. J., 3 July 2006, *available at* http://www.opinionjournal.com/extra/?id=110008599

Ari Shavit, *Survival of the Fittest,* HAARETZ, *available at* http://www.haaretz.com/hasen/objects/pages/PrintArticleEn.jhtml?itemNo=380984 (last updated 1 September 2004)

Philip Sherwell, *US Forces Turn on Iranians*, SUN. TELEGRAPH, 15 January 2007, *available at* http://www.telegraph.co.uk/core/Content/displayPrintable.jhtml;jsessionid=RIB4UNO4N0IBHQFIQMGSFFWAVCBQWIV0?xml=/news/2007/01/14/wirq114.xml&site=5&page=0

Thomas Sowell, *Pacifists Versus Peace*, JEWISH WORLD REV., 21 July 2006, *available at* http://jewishworldreview.com/cols/sowell072106.asp

Status of Participation by States in the 13 Universal Instruments Related to the Prevention and Suppression of Terrorism, available at http://www.un.org/sc/ctc/documents/treatytable.pdf (last visited 25 January 2007)

UN Action to Counter Terrorism, available at http://www.un.org/terrorism/ (last visited 12 April 2007)

UN Anti-Terrorism Committees Stress the Need for Greater Involvement by Member States, U.N. NEWS SERVICE, 28 September 2006, *available at* http://www.un.org/apps/news/printnewsAr.asp?nid=20073

VII. SPEECHES AND STATEMENTS (arranged alphabetically by surname)

Interview on Al-Alam TV with Ziyad Abu'Ein, *If Not for the Oslo Accords, There Would Have Been No Intifada*, MEMRI (4 July 2006), *available at* http://www.memritv.org/Transcript.asp?P1=1205

Dermot Ahern, Address by the Minister for Foreign Affairs to the Royal Irish Academy Marking 50 Years of UN Participation (18 November 2005), *available at* http://foreignaffairs.gov.ie/Press_Releases/20051118/1915.htm

Kofi Annan, A Global Strategy for Fighting Terrorism: Keynote Address to the Closing Plenary of the International Summit on Democracy, Terrorism, and Security (10 March 2005), *available at* http://www.un.org/apps/sg/printsgstats.asp?nid=1345

Louise Arbour, Address by Louise Arbour, UN High Commissioner for Human Rights at Chatham House and the British Institute of International and Comparative Law (16 February 2006), *available at* http://www.unhchr.ch/huricane/huricane.nsf/view01/E60AF3995B87D7EDC125711700571 1E8?opendocument

Louise Arbour, Security Under the Rule of Law, Address of Louise Arbour UN High Commissioner for Human Rights to the Biennial Conference of the International Commission of Jurists (Berlin) (27 August 2004), *available at* http://www.unhchr.ch/huricane/huricane.nsf/view01/3485B28EDDA173F0C1256EFD0035373C?opendocument

Osama Bin Laden, *"Letter to America,"* OBSERVER (24 November 2002), *available at* http://observer.guardian.co.uk/worldview/story/0,11581,845725,00.html

Shaykh Usamah Bin-Muhammad Bin-Ladin et al., *Jihad Against Jews and Crusaders: World Islamic Front Statement*, WASH. POST (23 February 1998), *available at* http://www.washingtonpost.com/ac2/wp-dyn/A4993-2001Sep21?language=printer (2001)

George W. Bush, State of the Union Address by the President (31 January 2006), *available at* http://www.whitehouse.gov/stateoftheunion/2006

Noam Chomsky, Amnesty International Annual Lecture, Hosted by Trinity College: "War on Terror" (18 January 2006), *available at* http://www.amnesty.ie/user/content/download/3898/20352/file/chomskylecture06.pdf

Statement by Prof. John Dugard, Special Rapporteur on the Situation of Human Rights in the Occupied Palestinian Territory, Third Committee of the General Assembly (19 October 2006) (on file with author)

Statement by His Excellency Mr. Crispin Grey-Johnson, Ambassador and Permanent Representative of the Gambia to the United Nations, Chairman of the Group of the African States, Under Agenda Item 100 of the Sixth Committee, "Measures for the Elimination of International Terrorism," New York (12 October 2006) (on file with author)

Statement of His Excellency Prof. Ekmeleddin Ihsanoglu, Secretary-General of the Organization of the Islamic Conference, at the High-Level Plenary Meeting of the United Nations General Assembly (16 September 2005), *available at* http://www.un.org/webcast/summit2005/statements16/islamic050916eng.pdf

David Kennedy, Keynote Address, The TWAIL Conference, Albany, New York (April 2007), *available at* http://www.law.harvard.edu/faculty/dkennedy/speeches/TwailKeynote.htm

Chandrika Bandaranaike Kumaratunga, Address by Her Excellency Chandrika Bandaranaike Kumaratunga, President of the Democratic Socialist Republic of Sri Lanka, at the High-Level Plenary Meeting of the General Assembly of the United Nations (15 September 2005), *available at* http://www.un.org/webcast/summit2005/statements15/sri050915l5eng.pdf

Vladimir V. Putin, Statement by His Excellency Mr. Vladimir V. Putin, President of the Russian Federation, at the High-Level Plenary Meeting of the United Nations General Assembly (15 September 2005), *available at* http://www.un.org/webcast/summit2005/statements15/rfe050915eng.pdf

A Conversation with Secretary of State Condoleezza Rice, Centennial Annual Meeting of the American Society of International Law (29 March 2006), *available at* http://www.state.gov/secretary/rm/2006/63855.htm

Statement by Mr. Hassan Saleh, Counsellor, at the Sixth Committee, 61st Session of the United Nations General Assembly on Agenda Item 100, "Measures to Eliminate International Terrorism" (12 October 2006) (on file with author)

William A. Schabas, *Statement of 17 September 2001*, *available at* http://www.nuigalway.ie/human_rights/Docs/Press%20Releases/170901%20PR.doc

The White House, *President Commemorates Veterans Day, Discusses War on Terror* (11 November 2005), *available at* http://www.whitehouse.gov/news/releases/2005/11/20051111-1.html

The White House, *President's Address to the Nation* (10 January 2007), *available at* http://www.whitehouse.gov/news/releases/2007/01/print/20070110-7.html

United Nations Committee Against Torture, the United Nations Special Rapporteur on Torture and Other Cruel, Inhuman or Degrading Treatment, the Board of Trustees of the United Nations Voluntary Fund for Victims of Torture, and the United Nations High Commissioner for Human Rights, Joint Statement on the Occasion of the United Nations International Day in Support of Victims of Torture (26 June 2006), *available at* http://www.ohchr.org/english/about/funds/torture/docs/JointStatement26.06.06.pdf

VIII. Jurisprudence (arranged chronologically)

A. International Court of Justice

Conditions of Admission of a State to Membership in the United Nations (Advisory Opinion), 1948 I.C.J. 57

Conditions of Admission of a State to Membership in the United Nations (Advisory Opinion), 1948 I.C.J. 57 (Azevedo, J., separate)

Corfu Channel (*U.K.* v. *Alb.*), 1949 I.C.J. 4

Corfu Channel (*U.K.* v. *Alb.*), 1949 I.C.J. 4 (Alvarez, J., separate)

United States Diplomatic and Consular Staff in Tehran (Hostages) (*U.S.* v. *Iran*), 1980 I.C.J. 3

Military and Paramilitary Activities in and Against Nicaragua (*Nicar.* v. *U.S.*), 1986 I.C.J. 14

Military and Paramilitary Activities in and Against Nicaragua (*Nicar.* v. *U.S.*), 1986 I.C.J. 14 (Lachs, J., separate)

Military and Paramilitary Activities in and Against Nicaragua (*Nicar.* v. *U.S.*), 1986 I.C.J. 14 (Nagendra Singh, J., separate)

Military and Paramilitary Activities in and Against Nicaragua (*Nicar.* v. *U.S.*), 1986 I.C.J. 14 (Ni, J., separate)

Military and Paramilitary Activities in and Against Nicaragua (*Nicar.* v. *U.S.*), 1986 I.C.J. 14 (Sette-Camara, J., separate)

Elettronica Sicula S.p.A. (*U.S.* v. *Italy*), 1989 I.C.J. 15

Request for an Examination of the Situation in Accordance with Paragraph 63 of the Court's Judgment of 20 December 1974 in the Nuclear Tests (*N.Z.* v. *Fr.*) Case, 1995 I.C.J. 288 (Koroma, J., dissenting)

Request for an Examination of the Situation in Accordance with Paragraph 63 of the Court's Judgment of 20 December 1974 in the Nuclear Tests Case (*N.Z.* v. *Fr.*), 1995 I.C.J. 288 (Weeramantry, J., dissenting)

Legality of the Threat or Use of Nuclear Weapons (Advisory Opinion), 1996 I.C.J. 226

Legality of the Threat or Use of Nuclear Weapons (Advisory Opinion), 1996 I.C.J. 226 (Schwebel, J., dissenting)

Legality of the Threat or Use of Nuclear Weapons (Advisory Opinion), 1996 I.C.J. 226 (Weeramantry, J., dissenting)

Gabčíkovo-Nagymaros (*Hung.* v. *Slovk.*), 1997 I.C.J. 7
Land and Maritime Boundary Between Cameroon and Nigeria, Preliminary Objections (*Cameroon* v. *Nig.*), 1998 I.C.J. 275
Oil Platforms (*Iran* v. *U.S.*), 2003 I.C.J. 161 (Simma, J., separate)
Written Statement of the Government of Israel on Jurisdiction and Propriety, Legal Consequences of the Construction of a Wall in the Occupied Palestinian Territory (Advisory Opinion), 2004 I.C.J.
Written Statement Submitted by Palestine, Legal Consequences of the Construction of a Wall in the Occupied Palestinian Territory (Advisory Opinion), 2004 I.C.J.
Legal Consequences of the Construction of a Wall in the Occupied Palestinian Territory (Advisory Opinion), 2004 I.C.J.
Legal Consequences of the Construction of a Wall in the Occupied Palestinian Territory (Advisory Opinion), 2004 I.C.J. (Elaraby, J., separate)
Legal Consequences of the Construction of a Wall in the Occupied Palestinian Territory (Advisory Opinion), 2004 I.C.J. (Higgins, J., separate)
Legal Consequences of the Construction of a Wall in the Occupied Palestinian Territory (Advisory Opinion), 2004 I.C.J. (Kooijmans, J., separate)
Legal Consequences of the Construction of a Wall in the Occupied Palestinian Territory (Advisory Opinion), 2004 I.C.J. (Owada, J., separate)
Armed Activities on the Territory of the Congo (*Congo* v. *Uganda*), 2005 I.C.J.
Armed Activities on the Territory of the Congo (*Congo* v. *Uganda*), 2005 I.C.J. (Kooijmans, J., separate)
Application of the Convention on the Prevention and Punishment of the Crime of Genocide (*Bosn. & Herz.* v. *Serb. & Mont.*), 2007 I.C.J.

B. **International Criminal Tribunal for the Former Yugoslavia**

Prosecutor v. *Furundzija* (IT-95-17/1-T), Trial Chamber, 1998 I.C.T.Y.
Prosecutor v. *Tadić* (IT-94-1-A), Appeals Chamber, 1999 I.C.T.Y.
Prosecutor v. *Galić* (IT-98-29-T), Trial Chamber I, 2003 I.C.T.Y.

C. **Inter-American Court of Human Rights**

Velásquez Rodríguez, Ser. C, Case No. 4, Inter-Am. Ct. H.R. 1988

D. **Arbitral Awards**

Sambiaggio (*Italy* v. *Venez.*), 10 R.I.A.A. 499 (1903)
Janes (*U.S.* v. *Mex.*), 4 R.I.A.A. 82 (1926)
Youmans (*U.S.* v. *Mex.*), 4 R.I.A.A. 110 (1926)
Massey (*U.S.* v. *Mex.*), 4 R.I.A.A. 155 (1927)
Island of Palmas, 2 R.I.A.A. 829 (1928)
Trail Smelter Arbitral Tribunal, Decision, Reported on March 11, 1941, to the Government of the United States of America and to the Government of the Dominion of Canada, Under the Convention Signed April 15, 1935, 35 AM. J. INT'L L. 684 (1941)
Lake Lanoux (*Spain* v. *Fr.*), I.L.R. 100 (1961) (1957)
Asian Agricultural Products Ltd. v. *Sri Lanka*, ICSID Case No. ARB/87/3, 30(3) I.L.M. 577 (1991)
Mondev International Ltd. v. *U.S.*, ICSID (Additional Facility) Case No. ARB(AF)/99/2 (2002)

Noble Ventures, Inc. v. *Rom.*, ICSID Case No. ARB/01/11 (2005)
9 R.I.A.A. 99-110 (1960)
10 R.I.A.A. 477-84 (1962)

E. **House of Lords**

A. & Others v. *Secretary of State for the Home Department*, U.K.H.L. 56 (2004)

F. **United States Supreme Court**

Dred Scott v. *Sandford*, 60 U.S. 393 (1857)
Hamdan v. *Rumsfeld*, No. 05-184, slip op. (U.S. S. Ct. 29 June 2006)

G. **Amnesty Committee, Truth and Reconciliation Commission of South Africa**

Amnesty Committee, Truth and Reconciliation Commission of South Africa, December No. AC/2001/147, *available at* http://www.doj.gov.za/trc/decisions/2001/ac21147.htm (2001)

IX. SECURITY COUNCIL RESOLUTIONS (arranged chronologically)

S.C. Res. 748, U.N. SCOR, U.N. Doc. S/RES/748 (1992)
S.C. Res. 1044, U.N. SCOR, U.N. Doc. S/RES/1044 (1996)
S.C. Res. 1189, U.N. SCOR, U.N. Doc. S/RES/1189 (1998)
S.C. Res. 1214, U.N. SCOR, U.N. Doc. S/RES/1214 (1998)
S.C. Res. 1267, U.N. SCOR, U.N. Doc. S/RES/1267 (1999)
S.C. Res. 1333, U.N. SCOR, U.N. Doc. S/RES/1333 (2000)
S.C. Res. 1368, U.N. SCOR, U.N. Doc. S/RES/1368 (2001)
S.C. Res. 1373, U.N. SCOR, U.N. Doc. S/RES/1373 (2001)
S.C. Res. 1438, U.N. SCOR, U.N. Doc. S/RES/1438 (2002)
S.C. Res. 1440, U.N. SCOR, U.N. Doc. S/RES/1440 (2002)
S.C. Res. 1450, U.N. SCOR, U.N. Doc. S/RES/1450 (2002)
S.C. Res. 1456, U.N. SCOR, U.N. Doc. S/RES/1456 (2003)
S.C. Res. 1465, U.N. SCOR, U.N. Doc. S/RES/1465 (2003)
S.C. Res. 1516, U.N. SCOR, U.N. Doc. S/RES/1516 (2003)
S.C. Res. 1530, U.N. SCOR, U.N. Doc. S/RES/1530 (2004)
S.C. Res. 1540, U.N. SCOR, U.N. Doc. S/RES/1540 (2004)
S.C. Res. 1546, U.N. SCOR, U.N. Doc. S/RES/1546 (2004)
S.C. Res. 1566, U.N. SCOR, U.N. Doc. S/RES/1566 (2004)
S.C. Res. 1611, U.N. SCOR, U.N. Doc. S/RES/1611 (2005)
S.C. Res. 1617, U.N. SCOR, U.N. Doc. S/RES/1617 (2005)
S.C. Res. 1618, U.N. SCOR, U.N. Doc. S/RES/1618 (2005)
S.C. Res. 1624, U.N. SCOR, U.N. Doc. S/RES/1624 (2005)
S.C. Res. 1625, U.N. SCOR, U.N. Doc. S/RES/1625 (2005)
S.C. Res. 1637, U.N. SCOR, U.N. Doc. S/RES/1637 (2005)
S.C. Res. 1723, U.N. SCOR, U.N. Doc. S/RES/1723 (2006)

X. GENERAL ASSEMBLY RESOLUTIONS AND SPEECHES (arranged chronologically)

G.A. Res. 2625, U.N. GAOR, U.N. Doc. A/RES/2625 (1970)
G.A. Res. 34/145, U.N. GAOR, U.N. Doc. A/RES/34/145 (1979)

G.A. Res. 39/159, U.N. GAOR, U.N. Doc. A/RES/39/159 (1984)
G.A. Res. 40/61, U.N. GAOR, U.N. Doc. A/RES/40/61 (1985)
G.A. Res. 49/60, U.N. GAOR, U.N. Doc. A/RES/49/60 (1994)
U.N. GAOR, U.N. Doc. A/54/PV.76 (1999) (speech by Cuba)
G.A. Res. 56/83, U.N. GAOR, U.N. Doc. A/RES/56/83 (2001)
G.A. Res. 57/219, U.N. GAOR, U.N. Doc. A/RES/57/219 (2002)
G.A. Res. ES-10/14, U.N. GAOR, U.N. Doc. A/RES/ES-10/14 (2003)
U.N. GAOR, U.N. Doc. A/59/PV.91 (2005) (speech by Russia)
U.N. GAOR, U.N. Doc. A/59/PV.91 (2005) (speech by Pakistan)
G.A. Res. 60/1, U.N. GAOR, U.N. Doc. A/RES/60/1 (2005)
G.A. Res. 60/43, U.N. GAOR, U.N. Doc. A/RES/60/43 (2005)
G.A. Res. 60/147, U.N. GAOR, U.N. Doc. A/RES/60/147 (2005)

XI. International Law Commission Materials (arranged alphabetically by title)

International Law Commission, *Articles on Prevention of Transboundary Harm from Hazardous Activities*, in Report of the International Law Commission on the Work of Its Fifty-Third Session 370, U.N. Doc. A/56/10 Supp. No. 10 (2001)
International Law Commission, *Articles on Responsibility of States for Internationally Wrongful Acts,* in James Crawford, The International Law Commission's Articles on State Responsibility: Introduction, Text and Commentaries 61 (2003) (2001)
International Law Commission, *Commentaries*, *Articles on Prevention of Transboundary Harm from Hazardous Activities*, in Report of the International Law Commission on the Work of Its Fifty-Third Session 377, U.N. Doc. A/56/10 Supp. No. 10 (2001)
International Law Commission, *Commentaries, Articles on Responsibility of States for Internationally Wrongful Acts,* in James Crawford, The International Law Commission's Articles on State Responsibility: Introduction, Text and Commentaries 74 (2003) (2001)
International Law Commission, *Draft Articles on State Responsibility Provisionally Adopted by the International Law Commission on First Reading (1996)*, in James Crawford, The International Law Commission's Articles on State Responsibility: Introduction, Text and Commentaries 348 app. (2003) (1996)
First Report on State Responsibility by Mr. James Crawford, Special Rapporteur, U.N. GAOR, U.N. Doc. A/CN.4/490/Add.5 (1998)

XII. United Nations Basic Documents (arranged alphabetically by title)

I.C.J. Stat.
U.N. Charter

XIII. Treaty Materials (arranged chronologically)

G.A. Res. 260, U.N. GAOR, Annex, Convention on the Prevention and Punishment of the Crime of Genocide (1948)
Convention Relative to the Protection of Civilian Persons in Time of War, Geneva, 12 August 1949
Convention on Offences and Certain Other Acts Committed on Board Aircraft, Tokyo, 14 September 1963
G.A. Res. 2200, Annex, International Covenant on Economic, Social, and Cultural Rights (1966)

Vienna Convention on the Law of Treaties, Vienna, 23 May 1969

Convention for the Suppression of Unlawful Seizure of Aircraft, The Hague, 16 December 1970

Convention for the Suppression of Unlawful Acts Against the Safety of Civil Aviation, Montreal, 23 September 1971

G.A. Res. 3166, U.N. GAOR, Annex, Convention on the Prevention and Punishment of Crimes Against Internationally Protected Persons, Including Diplomatic Agents, U.N. Doc. A/RES/3166 (1973)

Protocol Additional to the Geneva Conventions of 12 August 1949, and Relating to the Protection of Victims of International Armed Conflicts, Geneva, 8 June 1977

G.A. Res. 34/146, U.N. GAOR, Annex, International Convention Against the Taking of Hostages, U.N. Doc. A/RES/34/146 (1979)

South Asian Association for Regional Cooperation Regional Convention on Suppression of Terrorism, Kathmandu, 4 November 1987

Protocol for the Suppression of Unlawful Acts of Violence at Airports Serving International Civil Aviation, Supplementary to the Convention for the Suppression of Unlawful Acts Against the Safety of Civil Aviation, Montreal, 24 February 1988

Convention for the Suppression of Unlawful Acts Against the Safety of Maritime Navigation, Rome, 10 March 1988

Protocol for the Suppression of Unlawful Acts Against the Safety of Fixed Platforms Located on the Continental Shelf, Rome, 10 March 1988

Convention on the Marking of Plastic Explosives for the Purpose of Detection, Montreal, 1 March 1991

G.A. Res. 52/164, U.N. GAOR, Annex, International Convention for the Suppression of Terrorist Bombings, U.N. Doc. A/RES/52/164 (1998)

Arab Convention for the Suppression of Terrorism, Cairo, 22 April 1998

Rome Statute of the International Criminal Court, Rome, 17 July 1998

Treaty on Cooperation Among the States Members of the Commonwealth of Independent States in Combating Terrorism, Minsk, 4 June 1999

Convention of the Organisation of the Islamic Conference on Combating International Terrorism, Ouagadougou, 1 July 1999

Organisation of African Unity Convention on the Prevention and Combating of Terrorism, Algiers, 14 July 1999

G.A. Res. 54/109, U.N. GAOR, Annex, International Convention for the Suppression of the Financing of Terrorism, U.N. Doc. A/RES/54/109 (2000)

Shanghai Convention on Combating Terrorism, Separatism, and Extremism, Shanghai, 15 June 2001

Inter-American Convention Against Terrorism, Bridgetown, 3 June 2002

Jordan, Declaration, International Convention for the Suppression of the Financing of Terrorism, New York, 9 December 1999, Ref. No. C.N.910.2003.TREATIES-32, 28 August 2003

Additional Protocol to the South Asian Association for Regional Cooperation Regional Convention on the Suppression of Terrorism, Islamabad, 6 January 2004

Protocol to the Organisation of African Unity Convention on the Prevention and Combating of Terrorism, Addis Ababa, 8 July 2004

Egypt, Reservation and Declaration, International Convention for the Suppression of the Financing of Terrorism, New York, 9 December 1999, Ref. No. C.N.176.2005.TREATIES-3, 1 March 2005

G.A. Res. 59/290, U.N. GAOR, Annex, International Convention for the Suppression of Acts of Nuclear Terrorism, U.N. Doc. A/RES/59/290 (2005)

Syrian Arab Republic, Reservation and Declaration, International Convention for the Suppression of the Financing of Terrorism, New York, 9 December 1999, Ref. No. C.N.326.2005.TREATIES-6, 24 April 2005

Convention on the Physical Protection of Nuclear Material and Nuclear Facilities/Amendment to the Convention on the Physical Protection of Nuclear Material, Vienna, 8 July 2005

XIV. European Union Instruments (arranged chronologically)

Council Framework Decision of 13 June 2002 on Combating Terrorism, 2002/475/JHA, 2002 O.J. (L 164) 3

Council Framework Decision of 13 June 2002 on the European Arrest Warrant and the Surrender Procedures Between Member States, 2002/584/JHA, 2002 O.J. (L 190) 1

Directive 2004/35/CE of the European Parliament and of the Council of 21 April 2004 on Environmental Liability with Regard to the Prevention and Remedying of Environmental Damage, 2004 O.J. (L 143) 56

Communication from the Commission to the European Parliament and the Council Concerning Terrorist Recruitment: Addressing the Factors Contributing to Violent Radicalisation, COM(05)313 final

INDEX

MIX
Papier aus verantwortungsvollen Quellen
Paper from responsible sources
FSC® C105338
www.fsc.org

If you have any concerns about our products,
you can contact us on
ProductSafety@springernature.com

In case Publisher is established outside the EU,
the EU authorized representative is:
Springer Nature Customer Service Center GmbH
Europaplatz 3, 69115 Heidelberg, Germany

Printed by Libri Plureos GmbH
in Hamburg, Germany